D1195769

Rose

Rose

A BIOGRAPHY OF

Rose Fitzgerald Kennedy

Gail Cameron

London
MICHAEL JOSEPH

First published in Great Britain by
MICHAEL JOSEPH LTD
52 Bedford Square
London WC1
1972

7181 0989 9

Printed in Great Britain by Northumber-
land Press Limited, Gateshead, and bound
by Dorstel Press, Harlow

For Bob

with love and lasting thanks

Acknowledgments

This has been a longer and far more complicated task than I ever anticipated, and I have had the help and support of many good people along the way. I am deeply indebted to all of them, most especially to my agent and friend, Carol Brandt, whose professional wisdom and admirable calm, in the face of unprecedented challenges, managed to guide the project to its conclusion. I am grateful to her for many favours, past and present, but I will never be more grateful to her than I am for her role in this book.

Ten years ago, when I first began covering the Kennedys as a reporter for *Life* magazine in the late spring of 1960, there were only two books available on the family in Manhattan's largest and best-stocked bookstores. In retrospect, this seems astonishing, if not fantastic, in view of the tidal wave of Kennedy books, articles, and news stories we have experienced in the intervening decade. While few of them dealt in more than a passing manner with Rose Kennedy, a good many of them were invaluable in providing background information and historical detail, most particularly the following:

Laura Bergquist, "Rose Kennedy", *Look* magazine, November 26, 1968; Mary Colum, *Life and the Dream*; John Henry Cutler, *"Honey Fitz": Three Steps to the White House*; Leo Damore, *The Cape Cod Years of John Fitzgerald Kennedy*; Joseph Dinneen, *The Kennedy Family*; Paul B. Fay, Jr., *The Pleasure of His Company*; *Four Days* (The Historical Record of the Death of President Kennedy compiled by United Press International); Mary Barelli Gallagher, *My Life with Jacqueline Kennedy*; Marguerite Higgins, "Rose Fitzgerald Kennedy", *McCall's* magazine, May, 1961; John F. Kennedy, ed., *As We Remember Joe*; Joe McCarthy, *The Remarkable Kennedys*; William Manchester, *The Death of a President*; Jack Newfield, *Robert Kennedy*; Francis Russell, "Honey Fitz", *American Heritage*, 19, 5, 1968; Pierre Salinger, *With Kennedy*; Pierre Salinger and Sander Vanocur, eds., *A Tribute to John F. Kennedy*; Arthur M. Schlesinger, Jr., *A Thousand Days*;

Hank Searls, *The Lost Prince*; William V. Shannon, *The American Irish*; Theodore C. Sorenson, *Kennedy*; Nick Thimmesch and William Johnson, *Robert Kennedy at 40*; and Richard J. Whalen, *The Founding Father*.

In the end, however, my research was heavily dependent on interviews with Mrs. Kennedy's relatives, friends, and contemporaries who not only generously gave me the benefit of their excellent memories, but provided needed insights and, at times, documents and pictures unavailable to the public. Of the countless people I talked to—and I extend my thanks to them all—I am especially grateful to Barbara Fitzgerald Value, Thomas A. Fitzgerald, Jr., and their father, the late Thomas A. Fitzgerald. I am equally grateful, beyond any words, to Mrs. Vincent Greene, an old and dear friend of Mrs. Kennedy's whom my husband and I now consider an old and dear friend of our own; she not only provided invaluable perception and information, but shared her enviable sense of humour and healthy sense of logic. My thanks, in addition, to Mary Jo Clasby, Mrs. Tillie Gavin, Mrs. Howard Murphy, Mr. and Mrs. John Galvin, Pierre Salinger, Mrs. Polly Fitzgerald, Dave Powers, and Truman Capote.

In addition to Mrs. Kennedy's friends and relatives, I called on many of my own for assistance in gathering the research—ranging from a Smith College classmate, Anne Backus Wanzer, who did a superb job of interviewing Mrs. Kennedy's childhood friends in Concord, Massachusetts, up to and including my own mother, Mrs. James K. Cameron, who spent countless hours on the telephone ferreting out needed facts. My deepest possible thanks go to Martha Reker Durham, my longtime friend, for extraordinary research she did in my behalf in Paris. For their encouragement and generosity in many forms, I also extend my sincere gratitude to: Paul Kinloch, Mr. and Mrs. John E. Kenney, Iva Dee Hiatt, Jack McDermott, Sarah A. Cameron, Jane Lundy, Mr. and Mrs. Robert Zuckert, and my parents-in-law, Mr. and Mrs. Gustave Wescott.

Lastly, I am indebted to my next-door neighbour and friend, Nick Lyons, whose help and support at a crucial time could never be adequately acknowledged and to whom I can only say thank you.

To my husband, Robert Wise Wescott, who proved to be not only a skilful and perceptive interviewer, but a continuous and stalwart support in the best of times and the worst of times, my deepest thanks of all.

London   GAIL CAMERON WESCOTT
January 4, 1971

Contents

List of Illustrations

The Mother*

by Padraic Pearse

I do not grudge them; Lord I do not grudge
My two strong sons that I have seen go out
To break their strength and die, they and a few
In bloody protest for a glorious thing.
They shall be spoken of among their people
The generations shall remember them,
And call them blessed;
But I will speak their names to my own heart
In the long nights;
The little names that were familiar once
Round my dead hearth.
Lord, thou art hard on mothers:
We suffer in their coming and their going;
And tho' I grudge them not, I weary, weary
Of the long sorrow. And yet I have my joy:
My sons were faithful and they fought.

*Written in 1916 at the request of Padraic Pearse's mother.
Pearse and his brother were later executed. The poem stands
in a gold frame next to photographs of John F. Kennedy and
Robert F. Kennedy in Hyannis Port.

Prologue

It was an odd and strangely disorienting experience to be attending a Kennedy press conference in the troubled American spring of 1970. The room was as airless and oatmeal-coloured as endless other rooms in airports and hotels across the country that we had crowded into over the previous decade, but we were no longer there for campaign speeches or sudden catastrophes. We were there for Mother's Day. The mother was Rose Kennedy, and that of course, is what unnerved us.

In six shattering years two of her sons had been assassinated by senseless shots; her youngest child and only surviving son had barely emerged from the wreckage of a plane to make a miraculous physical recovery, only to jeopardize his whole political future in the murky waters under Dyke Bridge at Chappaquiddick. Then, in the closing days of the decade, she had lost her husband of fifty-five years, who had endured a long and cruel illness that had left him speechless and paralysed for eight years. We were about to face her.

On a damp and unseasonably bleak afternoon in early May, six months after becoming a widow, Rose Kennedy was holding a press conference at B. Altman & Company, a Fifth Avenue department store in Manhattan, after which she was scheduled to appear, improbable as it seemed, in the main-floor cosmetics department. She was there to promote a collection of perfumes made by mentally retarded men and women; the collection was called Flame of Hope.

The name itself was unsettling. The sixties had begun with the amplified hi-fi sound of "High Hopes" blaring out from sound trucks and improvised storefront headquarters in the frozen hills of Wisconsin as John F. Kennedy launched his campaign to become the thirty-fifth President of the United States. He had succeeded. He had ignited a nation's hopes for new frontiers and new generations of leadership, and we had become caught up in all his contagious charisma. The torch had been passed, and we had seen it end in a small eternal flame on a lonely hillside in Arlington, Virginia. Twice.

At twenty minutes after three Rose Kennedy entered the room, and we rose from our seats with the instinctive co-ordination of a well-rehearsed church choir and applauded. Then we sat down on our crumpled raincoats and quietly stared.

She was dazzling: purple and white silk midi from Givenchy, wide-brimmed white straw hat, crisp white gloves, large pearls and diamond earrings, and dark hair discreetly streaked with grey. Her face was buoyant and from a short distance looked astonishingly unlined; she looked, as Truman Capote once observed, "like she had just had a dozen B_{12} shots". Only her voice betrayed the fact that she was less than three months away from her eightieth birthday; it was a little hoarse, a little fluttering, but distinctly Kennedy both in inflection and mood. She spoke of her mentally retarded daughter—"just a year and a half younger than Jack, the President" —and of all the progress that had been made over the past half century. "We can view the present and future with great optimism," she said; and then, echoing the words of a brilliant winter day in 1960, she concluded: "We have begun, and that is the important thing."

It was awesome and slightly incomprehensible.

For many long months, day and night it seemed, I had been talking to a galaxy of people who had known Rose Kennedy at different stages of her long and extraordinary life: family and friends who had known her intimately and fleeting acquaintances such as a couple in West Concord, Massachusetts, who learned to master the schottische and the two-step with her at Saturday-afternoon dancing classes at the turn of the century. The portrait had grown increasingly complex. "No one really knows her," one of her nieces remarked. "Believe me, she's not going to tell her priest or her hairdresser what's really inside."

Her public image offered little clarity. She seems, at times, like a fleeting shadow on the incredible Kennedy landscape of the sixties, darting in and out of the public vision in a blurry montage of campaign smiles and newsprint glimpses, familiar, yet never quite understood: the confident Kennedy smile; the thick dark hair and trim shape in glittering Molyneux at the Inaugural Ball; the head held erect and dignified in its sombre funeral veil; the restless figure pacing endlessly back and forth, in solitary sorrow, bouncing a tennis ball in her Hyannis Port driveway after the death of Bobby, her third son.

Rose Fitzgerald Kennedy has remained elusive and enigmatic, just slightly out of range of the spotlight that has turned her children into mythical folk figures. In the midst of the Kennedys' massive and legendary togetherness, she has remained a solitary figure, part of, yet slightly removed from, the events swirling around her. She is, despite her extraordinary round of social activities, very much a lone figure.

She has lived her entire life in the public eye. "It began at the age of five," she often remarks, "when my father was a Congressman"; by the time she was fifteen, he was mayor of Boston, and even her high school graduation became first-page news. As the daughter of one of Boston's most colourful and romantic political figures, John F. "Honey Fitz" Fitzgerald—a man who profoundly influenced the course of her life—as wife of the Ambassador to the Court of St. James's and as mother of one of the most extraordinary families in the nation's history, she could not have avoided a public life, a life of service and commitment and all the accompanying pandemonium. There is no evidence that she wanted to.

She gave birth to nine children and became the first mother in history to see three of her sons elected to the Senate and one become President of the United States. This was scarcely a genetic accident. Her husband, Ambassador Joseph P. Kennedy, has traditionally received the major credit for the children's upbringing—urging them to win in competitive sports, encouraging their participation in politics—but he was, in fact, away from home a good deal of the time. Rose was there. She faced all the day-to-day trials of growing up, and her own way of life and even the inflection of her voice have been reflected in all of her children. "Joe provided the fire in the family, but Rose provided the steel, and she still does," observed Helene Arpels, one of her closest friends. Her son Jack constantly called her "the glue that has always held the family together".

This is what she still is. "I just made up my mind that I wasn't going to be vanquished by anything," she says. "If I collapsed, then it would have a very bad effect on the other members of the family, naturally.... And I think I owe them a certain calmness and encouragement, and that's what I try to do. I have children and grandchildren, and I refuse to be daunted." She recalls a motto that Jack loved and that she adopted as her own: "I know not age nor weariness nor defeat."

She is a woman of startling paradoxes. "She's not just that mother they always talk about with all those damned index cards on measles and mumps, you know," comments an old friend. "Rosie has a damned good intellect." She is referred to as both "the ageless colleen" and "the first Irish Brahmin" and is simultaneously credited with having "the sharpest and keenest political mind in Massachusetts". She is "Pope Rose" to her fellow communicants at St. Francis Xavier in Hyannis, while to her oldest friends she remains "Rosie Fitz". Her husband founded one of the great fortunes of the century, but to this day she will pop an uneaten banana into her handbag on a plane returning from a lavish ball in Venice rather than waste it; "I like bananas," she explained to a fellow first-class passenger. She is a linguist who still studies French on home records, a pianist, an art lover; she dresses almost entirely in Coutourier clothes and wears Galitzine pants suits at eighty—yet she loves to sport such dowdy combinations as socks and high heels, with slacks and babushka, in Hyannis Port, and doesn't much care who sees her. She has enormous strength of character and self-discipline, and though she has been called "selfish", her concern for others and their well-being is amazing. She communicates to her grandchildren by newsletter and sends Ethel Kennedy short notes advising her that next week is the Feast of the Ascension or that some other Catholic observance is near. She can be dazzling on a public platform, but a close friend of the Kennedy family says: "I always thought Rose was a little bit out of this world." Behind the public image known to millions, she is a lone woman who loves to walk by herself through Paris in semi-disguise, who needs and covets privacy, who goes her own way, who has always protected a part of herself from the tumult of the political arena in which she so strikingly shines.

She likes to say that her life has held agony and ecstasy. She has had more and lost more than most women who ever lived.

She saw her sons achieve meteoric triumphs and lived to see four of her children lose their lives in sudden tragedy or senseless violence; another child, her eldest daughter, was lost to her much earlier through mental retardation. On her eightieth birthday she was left with only four of her original nine children. "It's wrong for parents to bury their children," she told Emperor Haile Selassie at the President's funeral. "It should be the other way round."

She has lost what no woman can ever bear to lose and more than any human being will ever fully fathom. She has, in a very real sense, managed to bear the unbearable in a way that awes her closest friends. "One wonders how it's possible," says Marie Greene, a prominent Boston civic leader and a wise and humorous woman who has know Rose intimately since they were teenagers. "And yet there she was, not too many weeks after Bobby had been assassinated, calling me from the Cape to ask me about my problems— *my* problems—and insisting that I bring the children—I'm raising my three grand-children—down for two weeks. I don't know how she does it. I suppose it's because she's one of the few people in the world who really believes in God."

At the Altman's press conference she seemed only slightly worn. She reached for a glass of water a bit too often; her voice grew a trifle listless; she looked vaguely tired and she quietly asked for a cup of tea when it was over.

Later, downstairs, there was a chaotic mob scene of the kind we had seen a hundred times. It was wild, antic, chaotic. Shoppers— young and old—and salesgirls and nuns crowded thickly towards her, pressed against her booth, eager to get one of her perfume samples, eager simply to touch her. Well-dressed, middle-aged women abandoned all dignity and climbed on top of glass showcases to get a glimpse of her; klieg lights and flashbulbs shot up and down at her. But now she was unrattled and calm, poised behind her Flame of Hope booth, dispensing her perfumes, shaking hands, smiling, always smiling, fielding the crowds and the photographers easily, saying: "Don't take a close lens of me, please. Take me from a distance. I'm much better-looking." She had become again the consummate politician.

"She may look as fragile as a violet," Marie Greene remarks, "but don't be deceived for a minute: If Rose had been a boy, she

—not Jack—would have been the first Catholic President of the United States."

She is probably right.

Chapter One

"*Work Harder Than Anyone Else*"

What I undertake, I do. What I want, I get.
—JOHN F. FITZGERALD

Unlike most men, who harbour a deep and instinctive hope that their firstborn will be a son, John F. Fitzgerald was unabashedly euphoric when his wife, Josie, gave birth to a baby girl just two months before their first wedding anniversary. He was by nature a bubbling and extravagantly high-spirited man, but on that steaming summer night of July 22, 1890, when his daughter Rose Elizabeth was born in the kitchen of the Fitzgeralds' flat at 4 Garden Court Street in the North End of Boston, his exuberance knew no bounds.

The birth of a healthy child was cause enough for celebration, especially in 1890, but for Johnny Fitz, who had grown up with nine brothers, the birth of a female Fitzgerald was not only a novelty but something akin to a miracle. In all his twenty-seven years, he had never known anything but a household of males. The fourth of ten sons born to Thomas and Rosanna Fitzgerald, he had only the cloudiest memory of his two younger sisters: the first, Ellen Rosanna, had died at the age of eight months, when he was only seven years old; the other, Mary Ellen, the last of his parents' twelve children, lived only four days. When his mother died three months later, the last vestige of female influence had abruptly disappeared from his family life. Of all his own children—three sons and three daughters—none would ever matter more to Johnny Fitz than the tiny, dark-haired infant girl who was born on that summer night and whose eyes, even at birth, were as piercingly aqua-marine blue as his own. And none would be more like him. She caught his infectious enthusiasm and kept it all her life; she had, from earliest childhood, his will for hard work, his ambition, self-discipline, and instinctive ability to dazzle a crowd with consummate Irish charm. Rose, from the very beginning, was her father's daughter.

Beneath all the flamboyant fame of being a Kennedy, Rose has remained a Fitzgerald, and she has transmitted her pride in being a Fitzgerald to her own children despite her husband's indifference and occasional contempt for his in-laws—whom he frequently failed even to recognize. At a lavish family luncheon at the Mayflower Hotel following his son's swearing-in ceremony in 1960, Ambassador Joseph P. Kennedy, who was paying for the affair, summoned Tish Baldridge, the incoming White House social secretary who had arranged it, and inquired somewhat testily: "Just who are all these freeloaders?" When she replied that they were all "family", he became furious and started approaching his guests and asking them outright who they were. A goodly proportion, it turned out, were Fitzgeralds. One of them, Rose's younger brother Tom, had brought the Fitzgerald family Bible with him to Washington from his Dorchester home in a Supreme Supermarket shopping bag, and it was that Bible on which John Fitzgerald Kennedy, only an hour earlier, had placed his left hand as he raised his right in the blinding sunlight on the East Front of the Capitol, and said, in flat Bostonian tones: "I do solemnly swear that I will faithfully execute the Office of the President of the United States...."

Fitzgerald was a political name to contend with in Boston long before Kennedy. "Even after Jack became President," Tom Fitzgerald recalled shortly before his death in the summer of 1968, "I was never known as Jack Kennedy's uncle; I was still Tommy Fitz, Honey Fitz's son, the mayor's boy." And by then more than a half century had passed since Honey Fitz had last been mayor of Boston.

John F. Fitzgerald, the President's namesake, was not yet "Honey" Fitz when his daughter Rose was born—he was still Johnny Fitz or Fitzie or Little Johnny Fitz—but he had come a long way, through difficulties and hardships that his daughter would come to understand but never experience.

Rose's grandfather, Thomas Fitzgerald, had left County Wexford in Ireland during the potato famine of 1845. The odours of death and putrefying vegetation were everywhere over that blighted land, and a half million people had already perished in their humble cottages or along the roadsides. Fleeing from panic, hunger, and despair, Thomas Fitzgerald joined the hordes of his countrymen who walked the rutted dirt roads to the seaport town of New Ross. There he boarded one of the "coffin ships" of the Cunard Line—ships that killed one out of every four passengers who crammed the steering coops—and sailed westward in search of hope and a better life.

The Irish found little of either when they arrived in Boston— then the western terminus point for the Cunard Line—after a brutal six- to eight-week crossing. Puritan and Yankee Boston had only one native Irishman in every fifty people when Thomas Fitzgerald arrived, and it had never been hospitable to the Irish: in 1688 a Goody Glover was hanged on Boston Common as a witch for saying the rosary in Gaelic while kneeling before a statue of the Blessed Virgin; the Puritans claimed she was in league with Satan and that all Irishmen were devils—a New England legend that lasted 200 years.

When they arrived, the Irish lived in shantytowns, ghettos, "paddy-villes"—the first mass urban slums. The more they increased in number, the more they were scorned by the Yankees. "The scum of creation," they were called, "beaten men from beaten races, representing the worst failures in the struggle for existence." The elder Senator Henry Cabot Lodge announced that "the latter-day immigrants were inferior peoples whose prolific issue threatened the very foundations of Anglo-American civilization". More than a half century later, in the first months of his Presidency, John F. Kennedy remarked to his old friend Paul Fay: "Do you know it is impossible for an Irish Catholic to get into the Somerset Club in Boston? If I moved back to Boston after being President, it would make no difference."

For decades before Rose was born, the Irish received abrasively harsh treatment in New England; they were barred from many jobs and districts, and signs such as NO IRISH NEED APPLY and AMERICAN, SCOTCH, SWISS, OR AFRICAN—NO *Irish* were common in Boston. Irish settlements, rimming three miles of waterfront, were slums comparable to the worst of Harlem today. Shut off from the rest of the community, the people shared a clannish and, if often squalid, certainly proud and vigorous life. They shunned charity and would usually find real friendliness and help only from "people of their own kind"—and from their priests. Rose herself and Joe Kennedy had a determined sense of family loyalty—and Rose's loyalty to the church and to church causes is exceptional.

The Irish became blacksmiths, stevedores, coal heavers; they dug ditches for sewers and canals and levelled the hills of Boston; they were railroad workers and bartenders; they worked in sweatshops and lived in squalor. And they were called muckers and blacklegs and greenhorns and clodhoppers and micks. More than 2,000 Irish girls worked as domestics in Boston, and they were called biddies and kitchen canaries and bridgets. Johnny Fitz's ambition was as much away from this world, for himself and his family, as it was towards parity with the Yankees. The epithets were nearly gone when Rose and Joe Kennedy married, but not what lay behind them. The Kennedys left Boston when Joe was blackballed at the Cohasset Country Club for being Irish and Catholic.

A mere ten years after Rose's grandfather arrived, to begin working long hours as a farm labourer in South Acton at $6 a month, the ratio of Irishmen to the rest of the Boston population had dropped to one out of five. In 1877 Mayor Frederick O. Prince was defeated because he had been tolerant enough to appoint a few Irishmen to the police force; but in 1885, five years before Rose was born, Hugh O'Brien was elected the first Irish mayor of Boston, and since then there have been only three Yankees to hold that office: Boston politics has been dominated by Irish Catholics.

Rose's father, John F. Fitzgerald, was born on February 11, 1863, in a red-brick tenement at 30 Ferry Street—a four-storey, eight-family house near the Old North Church. His father ran a grocery and liquor store by this time, and his playgrounds, he liked to say, "were the streets and wharves, busy with ships from every part of the world". The thought of travel excited him—as it would excite Rose, who often accompanied him on his travels through Europe and South America; one day he would fondly refer to his daughter as his "rambling Rose".

With bare feet and patched pants, Johnny Fitz soon began to make his mark in the tight, bustling little Irish community, with its fish peddlers and tipcarts, its clattering horse-drawn wagons with ice and coal, fruit and vegetables—and its tough ward politics. He was neither the eldest nor the biggest of his brothers, but he was an instinctive leader—and his ambition was boundless. He joined and later led the most prominent social and athletic organizations in

the North End and showed himself to be a natural politi·
frequent picnics, outings, minstrel shows, suppers, d.
fairs. He played polo, football, and baseball; boys fro
Boston came to compete against him in footraces. He alw.,.
to "work harder than anyone else". And he did. Little Johnny Fitz,
contemporaries said, was the swiftest sprinter, fastest swimmer, best
dancer, most tuneful singer, and the most eloquent speaker in the
North End. Even as an adult he would boast that he had never
been beaten in a potato race. Later he would publicly adopt the
slogan: "What I undertake, I do. What I want, I get."

He went to Boston Latin School, where he managed and played
right field on the baseball team and captained the football squad
for two years, and was in his first year at Harvard Medical School
when his father died. The parish priest strongly urged the boys to
split up and go to live with friends, since there were no sisters or
aunts to look after them. Johnny Fitz, always fiercely clannish and
loyal, stubbornly refused, as later his daughter would refuse to
allow splits to threaten family unity. "We will never break up,"
he said. "I'll keep the family together." By his own account, he
usually "washed dishes, made beds, scrubbed floors, sifted ashes,
and brought up scuttles of coal and firewood, climbing three flights
of creaky stairs. . . . I even washed the faces of the older boys every
day, and often-times dressed them.

"My father left us a few thousand dollars," he later admitted.
"It was not enough to educate me, and I thought my life belonged
to my brothers, and that I could do better outside medical school,
so I gave it up and took the examination for the Custom House."
He passed and became a clerk under Leverett Saltonstall, grandfather of the man who would one day serve side by side in the
United States Senate with Johnny Fitz's grandsons.

When he was fifteen years old, Fitz met Mary Josephine Hannon,
a distant cousin, on one of the Fitzgerald family's frequent outings
to South Acton. She was as slender and petite as her daughter Rose
would become, with soft brown hair and an erect bearing she kept
all her life (she lived to the age of ninety-eight). "There was plenty
of competition and one or two quite serious country boys," recalls
their son Tom in a small, pencil-written family history, but Johnny
Fitz was determined to have her. On September 18, 1889, Johnny

and Josie—as they called each other for the next sixty-two years—
were married.

They took up residence first with John's brothers and then alone
at 4 Garden Court Street, in the shadow of the Old North Church
used to signal Paul Revere. Once it had been the site of Governor
Hutchinson's mansion; now the whole area was Irish Catholic.

Rose was born in an optimistic year. "If one couldn't make
money in the past year," the Boston *Herald* announced in 1890,
"his case was hopeless." Johnny's wasn't. He knew everyone and
was ideally suited to the real estate and insurance business he now
ran, with flourishing success. The American dream was coming
true, and Johnny Fitz, restless and ambitious, wanted his share
along with those other "shanty Irish" who were rising, with
ferocious determination, to higher social, economic, and political
spheres. They were all eager to speak without an accent and escape
the slums, eager to acquire lace curtains and cut glass. The lace
curtains were already there when Rose was a baby, but the energy
that had rocketed her father out of the slums kept driving him
throughout his entire life.

Many Boston Irish saw politics as the key to their climb, and
the wards and precincts were the key to Boston politics. Martin
Lomasney, the prototypical ward boss, would meet immigrants as
they disembarked and the politicking began at once. There were
scattered precincts of power, each ruled by a petty boss who in turn
was controlled by a bigger ward boss. Strong-arm tactics were often
employed, and it was not uncommon to see a solid phalanx of men
formed in front of a voting booth, bricks thrown at riotous rallies,
or a man hit with a lead pipe. It was sometimes called "blackjack
democracy". James M. Curley, who knew whereof he spoke, said:
"Politics and holiness are not always synonymous."

Holy or not, politics were much more exciting than insurance,
and within the North End Johnny Fitz was beginning to rise.
His athletic ability had given him contacts with people from all
over the city—and he used them. Short, stocky, handsome, and
vivacious, with ruddy complexion and piercing blue eyes, he was a
natural showman: full of drive, vigour, inexhaustible energy, and
capable either of easy informality or true graciousness—whichever
was needed. He learned and could teach Rose the "nuts and bolts"
of ward and precinct politics, the endless lists and visits and street

work; she would be better equipped than the most seasoned politicians when her son Jack ran for Congress in 1946. And she would also learn from him the political necessity of never showing your true feelings in public—unless, of course, they could bring in votes. "Never drop your guard"—this was the cardinal rule. Rose learned it well.

Fitz was already something of a minor legend in the North End when Rose was born, with his ability to talk at a dazzling machine-gun speed of 200 words a minute on any subject whatsoever, producing instant tears or sudden laughter in even the coolest campaign crowd with all the dexterity of a one-man soap opera. His prowess was celebrated in a popular ballad after he became mayor.

> Honey Fitz can talk you blind
> On any subject you can find.
> Fish or fishing, motor boats,
> Railroads, streetcars, getting votes,
> Proper way to open clams,
> How to cure existing shams.
> State Street, Goo-Goos, aeroplanes,
> Malefactors, thieving gains.
> Local transportation rate,
> How to run the nearby states.
> On all these things and many more
> Honey Fitz is crammed with lore.

He was always immaculately dressed—dapper, debonair, and bubbling with good cheer. He was an indefatigable member of committees and organizations of all kinds—a trait his daughter would inherit. Organizations were spheres of influence, training grounds for larger spheres; they could even become pockets of political power. Fitz could throw out compliments with abandon, speak of his "dear mother born in County Mayo", practise the "Irish switch" (talking with one person—or two, or three—while pumping the hand of another), burst into song, and snipe at the "scions of the blue-blooded aristocracy". His "Fitz-blarney" became a household word.

But the Fitzblarney always stopped, in later years, when he recalled the hot summer night his Rosie was born. He would fall into a mellow and totally uncharacteristic silence; his unending stream of family anecdotes would cease; he was never somehow able to articulate the special joy felt when he first viewed his daughter. "It just meant too much to him to talk about it," said an old family friend. "He just couldn't get over the fact that he had managed to produce a female Fitzgerald." They christened her Rose Elizabeth, but she was always Rosie to her family, and to her oldest friends, to this day, Rosie Fitz.

From the moment she was born she became the delight of his life, and he, in turn, the dominating and significant figure in her own. She even viewed herself at times not as Rose Elizabeth but as the mayor's daughter—and lived to meet this role. In many ways they were also incredibly alike—vivacious, gregarious, sharing a mutual flair for politics and for fashionable clothes, ambitious, athletic, severely self-disciplined. She even grew to share a good number of his idiosyncrasies—like taking catnaps in cars and later in planes and pinning notes to herself everywhere. Like him, she always wanted to be first—herself and her family. She would learn, in her own ways, to "work harder than anyone else".

Chapter Two

The Daughter of Shawn a Boo

*It began at five, when my father was
a Congressman.*
        —Rose Fitzgerald Kennedy

On the campaign trail for her sons in the fifties and sixties, Rose
Kennedy was always fond of pointing out to her audiences that her
children had all been rocked to sleep by political lullabys; few
people have ever been better equipped to sing such lullabys. Her
father, in everything he was, in everything he said and did, was
such a superb instructor in the political arts that in later years Rose's
only apolitical trait would be the vaguely un-American dislike of
dogs—a characteristic she has gone to great lengths to conceal. As
early as five, she says, "My father told me ... to stand up straight
and co-operate with photographers. They have a job to do, too."
She still does so at eighty.

As the balance of political power shifted decisively in Boston
from the Yankees to the Irish in the early nineties, Johnny Fitz's
political future began to rise rapidly. In 1892 he was elected to the
Boston Common Council, and in 1894, at thirty-one, after two years
in the State Senate, local cartoonists, to his absolute delight, were
depicting him as the "Napoleon of Ward Six". The physical re-
semblances between the two men were indeed startling—the short
and stocky shape, the animated and dramatic gestures—and it took
only a few manipulations on the face and a tricorn hat to turn a
drawing of Johnny Fitz into a cartoon that needed no caption. The
"Little General" always got what he wanted in those days, and in
1894, when his daughter Rose was four, what he wanted was the
United States Congress.

Backed by Martin Lomasney, the "Mahatma" of Ward Eight,
and P. J. Kennedy of East Boston (Joe's father, who was never a
personal admirer of Honey Fitz but respected his voter appeal), he

won the election against Congressman Joseph O'Neil and went to Washington representing the Eleventh District, the district from which fifty years later his grandson would launch a political career that would eventually make him the first Catholic President of the United States. Rose remembers with pride that her father was the only Democrat from New England and the only Catholic in Congress that session.

Fitz's career in Congress was, if ultimately unexceptional, often flamboyant. He was intensely interested in immigration problems, and his chief accomplishment was persuading President Grover Cleveland to veto a highly restrictive immigration bill. (Rose herself later won a high school debate in which she argued strenuously for easing the immigration laws, and her sons, Jack, Bobby, and Teddy, were always particularly concerned with this issue.) In an encounter with Henry Cabot Lodge, Fitz was told: "You are an impudent young man. Do you think the Jews and Italians have any right to this country?"

"As much right," he snapped back, "as your father or mine. It was only a difference of a few ships."

During the Spanish-American War, Fitz once barged into President McKinley's office, placed a piece of odd-looking meat on the Chief Executive's desk, and announced: "We are serving our boys embalmed beef!" He was always making and interrupting speeches in the House, particularly when Boston reporters or Associated Press photographers were in the gallery. "You are like a monkey on an organ-grinder's rope," Representative Charles Henry Grosvenor of Ohio told him brusquely, "always jumping around and chattering."

As Johnny Fitz's political ambitions expanded, so did his family. While still living at 4 Garden Court Street, Agnes, Rose's blonde-haired sister, and her first brother, Thomas, were born. All the children were baptized in St. Stephen's Church on Hanover Street, and Rose began school at St. John's Parochial. Fitz had initiated Patriot's Day as a legal holiday, and on April 19, 1895, he was invited to be the guest speaker for that occasion in Acton. What a patriotic daughter the town had, he told the crowd, for Josie had just given birth to their first son, that very day. He told them he was going to name the boy Thomas after his father and Acton after his wife's hometown. There were cheers and wild hurrahs, and later the town gave him a silver mug inscribed "Acton"; Tom, many years later, said he was extremely grateful that his mother wasn't from Marblehead.

By 1897, when Rose was seven, the apartment on Garden Court Street was becoming too small for the growing family, and Fitz decided to leave the North End and try a more rural life. He moved the family to Concord Junction, the railway stop that was, and still is, the industrial and less affluent part of Concord that is now called West Concord. South Acton was the next stop on the Fitchburg Line of the Boston & Maine Railroad.

He bought a large wooden house, the "William Simpson Place", with a broad veranda, a glassed-in conservatory, a barn, a hen house, and a sizeable tract of land. The house, larger than most in Concord Junction, was set back from Main Street behind a good number of trees; it sat up on a little hill or knoll and was considered a successful important man's house—which was how Fitz wanted it. On the Fourth of July the Fitzgeralds had fireworks on the broad front lawn sloping down to the sidewalk, and all the townspeople would gather to watch; through the flashing colours and the spritzing lights, Rose could see that her father was a prominent man, a man to whom the whole town looked up. He had acquired stature for his family at a young age and would continue to keep them all, particularly Rose—who often accompanied him on trips to Washington and New York—in the public eye for generations.

Fitz and Josie both had a great love of horses (which Rose never shared), and the Fitzgeralds owned or rented three: a pair of saddle horses named Maud and Black Hawk, and a huge animal, named fittingly, Napoleon. They also owned two carriages—a small one-seater with a folding top, similar to the baby carriages of today, and a two-seater like a surrey—and they borrowed one from the superintendent of the reformatory, a large, impressive vehicle known as a wagonette or "carryall", which had room for two persons up front and a large oval-shaped "basket" compartment in the back with cushions and a back rest; it was usually filled with eight to ten children, and Rose loved the thrill of riding in it, with Napoleon hauling and Johnny Fitz proudly holding the reins and talking constantly about everything at once.

On Sundays, the family, which was considered "very religious" by the neighbours, always went to St. Bernard's Church in Concord proper for mass, since there was no Roman Catholic church at the junction; the trip, about three miles, was always made in the wagonette, with Napoleon doing the hard work. West Concord's Our Lady Help of Christians Church was not built until 1907 when the Fitzgeralds had already moved to Dorchester.

Two more children—John F., Jr., and Eunice—were born in West Concord and then christened at St. Bernard's. Their father was earning about $5,000 as a Congressman, but with suits $9.50, silk petticoats $5, chicken 7 cents a pound and eggs 12 cents a dozen, the money went a long way. They are still remembered by contemporaries as a strikingly handsome family, with "a certain amount of glamour" and always "beautifully dressed". Johnny was a meticulous dresser, and Rose of course still appears regularly on the Best Dressed list.

Congressman Fitzgerald was particularly popular in the town, taking an interest in civic affairs, "always speaking at things", and taking the local children riding; he even thought to bring bags of candy to the children on Easter Sunday, after Lent.

Life was secure and ordered at 391 Main Street, though Fitz was away a good deal of the time. The household was Victorian and structured. The father was God and the mother was silent manager. The meatman arrived in his small wagon, and Josie went down the hill to the street to pick out what was needed for the family, giving the children each a small piece of beef to chew. She was a quiet, practical woman, whom Rose frequently credits with providing her with "common sense"; she was also unemotional, a person "who saw no use in getting excited over things. For her it wasn't a right way to act; partly, it's a New England quality," Rose says, and some of that indomitable stoicism which Rose displays no doubt comes from her mother.

Rose helped with the younger children, tended the family parrots, and was extremely conscientious about her schoolwork. Though she was rarely mischievous, in the fourth grade she enjoyed starting fires with a friend in the grass fields and then putting them out quickly. One fire got out of hand, began to spread, and the Concord Fire Department had to be called out.

At the Edward Everett Grammar School, Rose and her friends liked to gather at the girls' entrance to decide what colour hair ribbons they'd wear the next day. Several grades would occupy the same room, and though the curriculum was becoming more complex, Webster Spellers and McGuffy Readers were still standard fare. Rose was acknowledged the "prettiest girl in the class" and was always a superior student who got all A's. She was Johnny Fitz's daughter—and she did not take her responsibilities lightly.

Rose also attended dancing classes on Saturday afternoons, given by a Mr. Green at Association Hall on Commonwealth Avenue in West Concord. While a fiddler fiddled away, the young boys and girls learned ballroom etiquette, the waltz, the schottishe (a Scottish dance somewhat like the polka), the gallop, the caprice, the old-fashioned quadrille, and a new dance just then coming into fashion —the two-step. Like her father, who was a master, Rose loved to dance and even at eighty, at an April in Paris Ball will dance for hours.

Fitz became very fond of President McKinley and once brought Rose and Agnes, then seven and five, to see him in Washington. The President was immediately struck by Agnes' beauty and told her, so one version of the story goes: "You are the prettiest girl who has entered the White House." The anecdote is told several ways, as reported by Fitz and Rose, and it has been repeated over and over again to reporters and relatives and late-night television hosts. Rose herself continues to mention it with some frequency, adding that her son Jack once asked her why the President hadn't said it to her. Perhaps the repetition is the most interesting aspect of the whole little event—and makes it slightly less jocular and charming than it seems. It may well be that Agnes' golden brown-eyed beauty threatened Rose as a small child and that despite her own very obvious physical assets, she felt she had to prove herself in other ways. Rose admits this herself, saying that when McKinley called Agnes the most beautiful girl he had ever seen, "I knew right then that I would have to work hard to do something about myself." And Mary Jo Clasby, Agnes' daughter, speaks of Rose having "this one phrase that she always says, that my mother was so pretty, that she was so much prettier than she was, and she says that she had to develop a personality, and that she had to work on it all the time to develop this personality. She has always said that."

Clearly the two girls were different. Rose was favoured by her father, Agnes by her mother. Rose had blue eyes, lovely coal-black hair, and attractive pink cheeks; Agnes was a charming blonde with brown eyes. Both girls wore their hair in ringlets. While Rose was serious and dedicated, Agnes was gay and carefree. A classmate at Edward Everett found Rose, even then, somewhat "distant" and proper; she remembers Agnes coming out of the Fitzgerald house eating and Rose calling her sharply to account. "What's a Congressman's daughter doing eating bread and molasses?" she said, very much aware of her expected role.

Marie Greene, who was first Agnes' friend, says there was "never any sibling rivalry or anything like that, which is amazing when you think of it. Rose always felt this terrific need to excel, and she did; to this day, everything Rosie does, she does well. Agnes was not nearly so smart and she never tried to be; they still talk about the time Agnes was forced to sing in a school concert and opened her mouth and not one sound came out—and here was Rosie at the same time playing the piano beautifully. Agnes was much more shy than Rose. John F., of course, would give a speech at the drop of a hat, and Rose can do that too. But none of these differences between the girls seemed to matter. The younger brothers were often jealous of the girls, but the girls always got along beautifully with each other."

There is a fine old photograph of Rose, Agnes, and Tom, taken while they lived in West Concord, that shows the two girls dressed in high-lace patent-leather shoes, fur-trimmed coats, leather gloves, and frill and ostrich feather hats; their curls, as they always wore them, are caught at the nape of the neck. There is in Rose's face a picture of self-possession and pride. A neighbour, more than seventy years later, still vividly remembers the girls and their hats. "I can still see Rose and Agnes," she says. "Oh, my sister May and I were so envious of them, because they were so beautiful, and they always had these beautiful velvet hats with ostrich feathers. Oh, my—there's so much I forget about that whole time, but I can still see those hats as clear as day." A velvet hat with plumed ostrich feathers—in many ways it is a symbol of Rose's childhood. Not a silver spoon, not Kennedy wealth, but a proud and conspicuous hat, which awed neighbours and made them envious.

In the well-established Irish-Victorian home, Rose was already organized, methodical, and precisely scheduled. Her father's far-flung activities and interests had led to the habit of his writing little notes to himself and pinning them on curtains and on himself so he wouldn't forget; he was also an indefatigable collector of clippings on every possible subject. Rose's responsibilities and interests were increasing too. She became a dogged and persistent teacher of the younger children, but though Agnes could take her conscientiousness with benign indulgence, the boys could not, and a serious jealousy began to develop. "What I remember most about Rosie when we were growing up," said her late brother Tom, "was that she was always nagging me about studying Latin and playing the violin." He and the other boys became "extremely jealous" of Rose, a jealousy that persisted, through many "absurd incidents" into adulthood. It is no wonder, for Honey Fitz doted on his eldest daughter.

The boys never became good students. They disappointed Johnny and "nearly broke their mother's heart". One eventually "drank himself to death"; another served as a toll collector on the Mystic River Bridge as his nephew prepared to run for the Presidency. Johnny Fitz was such an overwhelming figure in his own household, such a colourful and very public figure, and doted so much on his beautiful daughters that the boys were never allowed to develop their own styles. Even when they were adults, they remained "Honey Fitz's boys", and their domineering father would call one of them on a Sunday afternoon, say he wanted to go for a drive, and the son would leave his own family at the dinner table and pick up Fitz at the Bellevue Hotel. John never learned to drive a car himself; he preferred to be chauffeured. Though fiercely competitive, with tremendous drive and strength, he never encouraged this in his own sons; the boys remained subservient to him all their lives, and Fitzgerald grandchildren still remember the "static and hostility" present at such traditional gatherings as Thanksgiving, when they all met at the Bellevue for dinner and to watch the Thanksgiving Day Parade.

His attitude towards Rose was different—and she was different. He poured all his magnificent hopes and enthusiasm into his daughter, took her on trips, talked to her constantly, and she, though she admired him immensely, learned from him but never lost something that was her own. Perhaps she saw the possible threat, perhaps she copied the model of her father as a man who himself was not subservient; she later kept her own character throughout her long marriage with Joe Kennedy—and he might have been an even greater threat.

Rose "took a real responsibility that none of the Fitzgerald kids did", says Marie Greene, "like doing well in her studies. She always wanted to do well for her father; it meant everything to her". Rose herself says: "I found the role my father played in my life a decisive one. He talked to me incessantly, all the time I was growing up. He told me a lot about the history of the Irish people, about their culture; we discussed politics and government constantly." Rose did this with her own children; politics and current events were an inevitable part of the Kennedy household, usurping small talk and gabble, becoming the very fabric of the young Kennedys' lives.

Honey Fitz was also insatiably curious about everything, about how a trolley worked or a German municipal council; he always took pains to explain things to Rose, and gradually she developed his capacity for wide-reaching interest, for collecting unexpected bits of information on every possible subject from—for her—the Abyssinian Church to bikinis. She imparted this infectious curiosity to her own children and to those, like Mary Jo Clasby, who lived and travelled with her. "We had to see *everything*—every sight-seeing tour that was available," says Mary Jo in reference to a trip to Japan, Hong Kong, and Thailand that she took with her aunt.

"Rose was like her father for all the world," says a childhood friend; "she was always quoting her father—in fact, we used to call her 'Father says'. He was on a pedestal for Rose. I remember how Agnes used to laugh about it; she'd say to me, 'Rose just got on the train with Daddy to go to New York, and honestly you'd think it was the Pope she was going with.'" But for all this, she remained herself—and when she met the man she loved, she refused to accept her father's disapproval.

Rose always says that she got her faith and common sense from her mother, who was much the opposite of Honey Fitz. A retiring person, she was forever in the background and disliked public appearances. When her husband became mayor for the second time, a reporter interviewing her found Josie "youthful in appearance as her own daughters, charming and gracious to meet, and necessarily a prominent figure wherever she goes.... Simplicity and common sense she insists upon in [her children's] clothes. Jewels she positively disapproves of for young girls".

She did not disapprove of them for herself. Her granddaughter Barbara remembers that "she was mad for beads and jewels . . . well into her nineties. I think that picture of her with the very straight back said a lot about her. I always remember her carrying herself so erectly".

An old neighbour remembers: "She was a Hannon, and had grown up under circumstances that some of us would have thought were less than comfortable," and a relative reports: "Josie was really a pill. She brought gloom into the house the minute she entered it. She was very proud and old-fashioned, but there wasn't anything warm about her."

"Josie, of course, was a bitch," quips an old friend of the family. "She was a shy woman, I suppose, but very cold and ungracious. She was a good-looking woman with a very trim figure; she had a beautiful figure, in fact, until the day she died. But she had grown up in Concord or Acton or somewhere and didn't really like politics, and she was badly suited for it; she made a very bad first impression. A very dull woman." Much later, when Fitz ran for the governorship, Josie stood with him in the receiving line at the Copley Plaza; someone came over to Rose and told her how terrible an impression her mother was making, and daughter successfully took the place of wife—as, by that time, she had done many times before. Rose always thrived on public appearances; her mother simply could not bear them.

Josie was clearly the very opposite of the dynamic "little general" and took as her chief role the establishment of a stable home life. "I am a home woman in every way," she said, "and my one ambition is to make the home a most happy and attractive place for my husband and children." She was economical and cautious, and from her Rose learned that "nothing is to be wasted".

Fitz, who was away from home at least as much as Joseph P. Kennedy for a great part of his life, proclaimed, at least publicly: "Whatever my public duties have been, no matter how much they have taken me away from my fireside, she has never complained, realizing that when I accepted a career in public life I had to fulfil my obligations. . . ." The statement would be echoed by Joe Kennedy, that Rose never once complained.

In 1901 Honey Fitz was defeated in his bid for a fourth term in

Congress. He returned to Concord Junction, apparently without regrets, still the leader of Ward Six and boss of the North End. One of the first of a series of brilliant political manoeuvres was his purchase of *The Republic*, a faltering Democratic newspaper, for $500. He soon turned it, with customary verve, into a thriving commercial success—and also into the mouthpiece for his own local ambitions, plastering billboards all over the city with large pictures of himself above the caption: PUBLISHER OF THE REPUBLIC. What Honey Fitz wanted next, it became increasingly clear, was City Hall.

In 1903, in accordance with their increased income and a desire to be nearer Boston, the Fitzgeralds moved to Dorchester, a sprawling, heavily Catholic suburb. Rose was thirteen at the time and had finished her freshman year at Concord High School with another round of straight A's. Their huge new house, described by a contemporary as a "refitted mansion of the towered grandeur of the architecture of the seventies", was at 39 Welles Avenue, again perched prominently on the top of a hill. It became the family seat and later was the setting for lavish entertaining during the mayoralty years. Rose's extravagant début, and her modest wedding reception. It had a porch decorated with scrollwork and a prominent mansard turret. At the top of the stairs, Honey Fitz installed a large stained-glass window bearing the coats of arms of the many ancestors of the Fitzgeralds. For the centre shield he picked the Gaelic motto SHAWN A BOO—which meant John the Bold.

Rose loved the high-ceilinged and spacious rooms, in the style of the time. There were big parlours with large overstuffed furniture, a music room with a baby grand piano that she played frequently, a billiard room, a solarium for the children in the rear, a large library filled with *Congressional Records*, big brass beds, a big barn in the backyard, and a curving driveway in the front; the house was filled with impressive statuary. One of the Fitzgerald grandchildren, recalling a first visit to the house as a small child, says: "I can remember walking into that huge hall and saying, 'But it's even bigger than a church.' And it had a solarium and I had never heard of such a thing before." John the Bold did not live small.

Everyone, without even being asked, remembers the superb food that was always served. A cook named Catherine Coffee claimed that "corned beef and cabbage was good enough" for Honey Fitz "when he didn't have Prince So-and-so or Duke Such-and-such to dinner. For visiting royalty he had canvasback duck and *pâté de foie gras*". Sir Thomas Lipton, the lovable tea tycoon, became one of Fitz's closest friends; after a particularly succulent dinner one night he said he would exchange a couple of billion pounds of teas for 130 pounds of Coffee.

The house never had the turmoil and athletic pandemonium that characterized the Kennedy households. Rose's friends remember that the atmosphere was generally quiet and serene inside—as Josie insisted—and that the athletic activity was confined to the boys tearing about outside in the neighbourhood and on the property, caring little, as usual, for studious pursuits. The house at 39 Welles Avenue has been torn down now, and five tract-type houses stand on the original property, but from the time the family moved in, Rose loved the prestige and prominence it brought the family.

On weekends, the Fitzgeralds often drove back to West Concord. They arrived in great big cars—usually two of them—with chauffeurs. Johnny always wanted to go on to Acton, but Josie would always get right out of the car at the house of their Hannon cousins and stubbornly refuse to go farther. She did not want to return to Acton, not ever. Sometimes, when her parents allowed her to, Rose would go to dances at the private O.K. Club in Concord; they were held at Town Hall, and her escort was often Roger Sherman Hoar, the only Democrat in the famous Republican family of judges and senators. He remained interested in Rose for a number of years and came to see her in Dorchester and Boston.

The Republic was soon earning John the then munificent sum of $25,000 a year, and the family was able to buy a house in Hull, overlooking Boston Harbour. They also began periodic trips to Palm Beach in the winter—often with Honey Fitz taking only Agnes and Rose with him. It was at Palm Beach in 1905, when he was forty and Rose fourteen, that Honey Fitz declared himself a candidate for mayor of Boston. He had been planning this moment for twenty years.

For years Johnny had gone to every dance and social event in the North End and elsewhere in Boston where he was received. He had meticulously kept a card index of all those in his precinct who needed a job or some other form of aid. At such prominent holidays as Thanksgiving and Christmas, he often came by with turkey baskets and other treats, with Rose at his side. Rarely did he miss a wedding in the North End, and since he religiously read the obituaries and death notices every morning in the Boston *Globe*, he knew of every wake: A wake without Johnny Fitz present and weeping was unheard of.

Unlike her mother and sisters, Rose loved politics from the beginning, really enjoyed it, found it fun and exciting and not a burden. She watched a master at work and learned every technique. But she was capable of translating what seems clearly a political ploy—concern for others—into a genuine character trait. Part of her greatness as a woman and as a mother, says an astute nephew, is that she is "extremely sensitive to people's needs". She was concerned even with the affairs of relatives that seemed small and trivial and showed this concern in a way that "gave the impression that she really meant it"! Endlessly thoughtful, she managed to find time on that summer night in 1960 when her son was acclaimed the Democratic nominee for President to write her nephew Tom Fitzgerald a note congratulating him on his forthcoming marriage. She learned how to make prospective voters feel important, by dressing carefully for them and addressing them on intimate terms, but she never forgot that true concern comes from the heart, not the political head.

Her father's contacts had multiplied; his "Dearos", supporters who took their name from the number of times he spoke of his "dear old North End", were everywhere. Boston now held more Irishmen than Dublin; 60 per cent of the total vote was Irish and 75 per cent Catholic. He spoke nostalgically of Ireland and the "dingy brick tenement" in which he had been born. He appealed to the city's sense of civic pride, to the people's love of spectacle. He claimed he was making his contest "single-handed against the machine, the bosses, and the corporations". He carried his campaign into the department stores so often it was called the "soda water campaign"; as usual, he flattered all the women.

Fitz beat City Clerk Edward Donovan, the choice of Lomasney and P. J. Kennedy, in the primaries and took on Republicans Henry Dewey and Louis Frothingham for the mayoralty.

It was a marvellously theatrical campaign, and Rose saw it all, delighting in her father's extravagance—and his success. She heard the crowds and watched the way he moved them. She saw his impeccable preparations and his ceaseless energy, his unfailing interest in meeting each of the thousands of small demands that bring in the votes, one by one. His ringing motto—"Bigger, Better, Busier Boston"—was everywhere, but then so was he. His men pasted up posters of him on vacant walls faster than opponents could tear them down. He organized the first political motorcade and swept through the precincts in a large red car, followed by hordes of what were called Napoleon's Lancers. In every precinct, crowds of devoted Dearos met him and helped him and whooped up the crowd. He and his men worked harder and more imaginatively than anyone else.

On December 12, the final count was made; little Johnny Fitz had won by 8,000 votes. He proudly said that he would be the "mayor of the whole people".

In January, 1906, he was inaugurated, and six months later the Boston *Sunday Post* ran a photograph of Mayor Fitzgerald presenting a graduation diploma from Dorchester High School to his daughter Rose Elizabeth. At fifteen, she was the youngest student ever to graduate from the school and the only person to receive "his or her diploma from the hand of a father who reigned as the chief executive of the city at the time". Early success as a family tradition had begun with her father; she continued it, and her own children were remarkable for their early achievements. Whenever she had to defend Jack, Bobby, or Ted against charges of being too young, she would trot out an impressive family history of which she was a part. Not only youth but also youthfulness became part of the Kennedy-Fitzgerald legend; just as her mother was often mistaken for one of her own daughters, so would Rose be on countless occasions. Even the man she married was scarcely a late bloomer.

A tumult of applause filled the hall when Rose, in a simple dress of white India muslin, advanced to receive her diploma for "honourable and meritorious study"; she was, characteristically, one of the three highest in the class of 285. When she met her father on the platform, cluttered with a bountiful supply of ferns, palms, and potted plants, the "applause was deafening".

It was an exhilarating day for Rose, full of grand romantic aura and prominence that filled her head. It was all very real—her scholastic success, the magnificent silver jewellery set her father gave her, with coiffure ornaments of solid silver, her father's prestige, the extensive coverage by the press, the deafening applause. But there was a touch of fantasy about it all, too. It was difficult to believe it all could last, but she did. At fifteen nearly everything seemed possible. The graduation programme included "Build Me Straight", a duet called "Beautiful They Were, in Sooth", "Sail On, nor Fear", "To Thee, O Country", and also Kinross' "The Fairy Revel".

Chapter Three

Very Public, Very Devout

*It's just not Rose Fitzgerald Kennedy to do any-
thing that would be out of line or not the right thing
to do. I can't imagine her doing anything wrong.*
—MARY JO CLASBY

On her sixteenth birthday, in July, 1906, following her graduation
from Dorchester High School, Rose already seemed to have the
world in her hand—as she would for most of her life. If she had suffered the customary agonies of adolescence, they were not visible
to her contemporaries. Her dark Irish beauty was in full bloom, she
was popular with young men of promise, like Roger Sherman Hoar,
and she was smart: she had passed the entrance examinations for
Wellesley College and fully expected to go there in the fall.

Then, at almost the last minute, everything changed. Her father
decided she was too young for Wellesley and entered her instead in
the Sacred Heart Convent on Commonwealth Avenue in Boston.
She later attended Sacred Heart convents in New York and in
Europe, and their teachings formed the firm foundation of her
whole philosophy of life; she was one day to send her own daughters
to Sacred Heart schools in America and England and disputed a
niece's decision to attend Middlebury College, a nonsectarian, co-
educational school in Vermont. "If you're worried about getting a
husband," she pointed out with a straight face, "just look how well
Ethel made out at Manhattanville." (Ethel was Jean's room-mate
and met Bobby through Jean, and Joan met Teddy when he went
to Manhattanville to dedicate a gymnasium.)

But in the summer of 1906 Rose wanted Wellesley very badly,
and a vague undercurrent of disappointment that she never got to
go would emerge on and off for the rest of her life. As late as 1969
she brought the subject up again with a stranger at a Fourth of
July reception at the Paris Embassy when her son-in-law Sargent

Shriver was serving as United States Ambassador and the times were rife with campus turmoil and generation gaps. "I was accepted at Wellesley, and I wanted to go," she said, and then added matter-of-factly, "but in those days you didn't argue with your father."

Other than Wellesley, there was little to argue about in those days, for Rose, even as she commuted daily from the big house on Welles Avenue in Dorchester to her classes on Commonwealth Avenue that fall, began to bask fully in the consistent glow of her father's spotlight: she was sixteen and often went with him on his endless round of parties, banquets, rallies, and meetings; it made her special, and she thrived on it. She took piano and dancing lessons and was socially accomplished. That year, in the first of a lifetime of ship launchings, she smashed a bottle of champagne across the hull of the *Bunker Hill*, and that year she made a speech that brought her a headline of her own. Demonstrating the same linguistic agility and natural charm that her daughter-in-law Jacqueline was one day to display in the White House, Rose welcomed a visiting delegation of German students to Boston, and spoke to them in their native tongue. ROSE FITZGERALD'S SPEECH A BIG HIT, a local paper declared the next day.

The Fitzgerald household, as always, revolved around her hyper-active father, who was rarely there but whose presence was felt like a continuing hurricane, as he whirled in and out en route to every corner of Boston. "Nimble as a chipmunk", as one newspaper described him, his bouncy form was seen everywhere. In the first two years of his first term, a contemporary news account read, "he averaged two dinners and three dances a night, to say nothing of six speeches. In all, he attended 1,200 dinners, 1,500 dances, 200 picnics, and 1,000 meetings. He made 3,000 speeches and gave some 5,000 girls the proud recollection of a dance apiece with Fitzy"— but not the tango or the turkey trot, which, along with a perform-ance of *Salome*, he puritanically banned. (He had other puritanical traits and neither drank nor smoked—nor did Rose; the Kennedy children were encouraged to do likewise.) He went to ball games and auctions, ship christenings and wakes. He was always available when celebrities came to town and during his two terms in office welcomed or fêted or honoured, often with Rose at his side, such diverse people as Governor Woodrow Wilson, Tom Longboat (a Canadian Indian who had won the Boston Marathon), Admiral

Heihachiro Togo of Japan, Babe Ruth, Teddy Roosevelt, William
Jennings Bryan, Houdini, Prince Wilhelm of Sweden, and scores
of others. His good friend the robust and genial and idiosyncratic
Sir Thomas Lipton was a frequent guest—full of jokes and put-ons
and flattery that beggared even Fitz's.

Lipton once toasted Agnes as "the most beautiful girl in the
world" and often complimented her profusely. One night after a
banquet at the Copley Plaza Hotel, about thirty close friends of
Fitz's, including wives and daughters, sat down together. The
women began to tease Sir Thomas, who was then in his sixties,
about rumours of his attachment to a woman in Denver and possible
other romantic liaisons.

"If you want to know who Lady Lipton is going to be," he said
in reply, "she is right in this room. Stand up, Rose."

Rose Fitzgerald stood, smiled, and quickly quipped: "I won't
accept you, Sir Thomas. I think you are altogether too fickle."

While the whole group laughed wildly, Lipton said with a touch
of sadness: "Now I know how it feels to be jilted."

The reaction of the voters to too much circus and too many
rumours of patronage and graft caused Honey Fitz to lose to George
A. Hibbard in the election of 1907. John A. Coulthurst, the third
candidate, called Fitz "scandalously incompetent and hopelessly dis-
honest"; Fitz's brother Joseph was termed the "human postage
stamp" in this campaign because he was paid $1,400 a year by the
city for carrying daily reports from the Warren Bridge to City Hall
—a route customarily managed with the aid of a two-cent stamp.
Hibbard's simple campaign promise to "clean up the mess" was
devastating.

But Fitz came back to beat James Jackson Storrow in a back-
breaking campaign in 1909, stumping day and night, attending up
to thirty-five rallies in one good evening's work. He launched a
vigorous attack on Harvard (which was to figure prominently in
the lives of the Kennedys) for not paying taxes on "nearly $400,000
worth of vacant land, a large part of which is used for pasturage
and meadow and not in accordance with the purpose for which
Harvard was incorporated". And he fought wealth (which was to
figure even more prominently in the lives of the Kennedys); a
Boston Herald headline proclaimed: "FITZGERALD SAYS HE FIGHTS
WEALTH—Declares It May Come to Pass That a Rockefeller Can

with His Money Become President of the United States." He could not possibly have foreseen that all his grandsons would face such charges—of buying elections—or that Rose would one day blurt in the midst of her son Bobby's Presidential primary in Indiana: "It's our money, and we can do with it what we choose"—the only public blunder she ever made.

In the Storrow campaign, a particularly historic event took place: one night at a rally, with words recently taught him by Rose, Fitz sang "Sweet Adeline". The effect was spectacular, and the song became his hallmark. He is reputed to have sung it thereafter at every conceivable occasion other than a wake. He sang it for Kaiser Wilhelm in Berlin and for President Taft at the summer White House and for the King and Queen of Spain. Once, after he had been run down by a truck, he sang "Sweet Adeline" to cheer up the onlookers who felt sorry for him. When Franklin Roosevelt made a state visit to South America in the wake of a Honey Fitz trip, a local band broke spontaneously into "Sweet Adeline", thinking it was the American national anthem, and FDR thereafter greeted Fitz as "La Adelina Dulce". And he would sing it and dance a jig on a table, in his seventies, when his grandson John was elected to the House of Representatives.

Sharply dressed in his black cutaway coat and vest, his grey checkered trousers, white shirt, green tie, and straw hat, he was a one-man vaudeville show. If he could astonish the Germans by referring to "other great German cities, Vienna and Budapest", and talk his Fitzblarney in snappy sentences with a measured touch of the brogue from morning until late at night, people always seemed more interested in the "event" of the nimble little man with the laughing blue eyes than in what he was actually saying. "I learned," he said, "that everywhere a mayor went, no one wanted to hear a speech—so I sang." And he sang. And he sang. Rose often accompanied him on the piano. Later, though she never sang herself, she did avoid the issues when she campaigned for her boys, substituting entertaining anecdotes that she told with impeccable skill; she learned from her father how much more an audience preferred an "image" to a lecture.

Fitz's round-the-clock politicking left little time that year for life in the big Victorian mansion on Welles Avenue. But with instinctive moxie, he thought nothing of having a campaign photograph of the entire Fitzgerald family blown up to poster size and boldly proclaiming a new motto in banner type beneath it: MAN-HOOD AGAINST MONEY. And he liked to refer, at the proper moment, to "the six at home". But in fact, he was rarely even home for dinner except on Sundays and holidays or when he was entertaining a visiting dignitary or hosting a band concert on the Fitzgerald lawn for 3,000 Dorchester neighbours, followed by fireworks in the street. In later years, when her husband, Joe, stayed away from home for long periods on business and other affairs, Rose was already prepared; to her there had always been a distinct difference between a man's and woman's worlds, and her own role was clear: the man was supreme, and her duty was to accept without complaint.

When a reporter from the Boston *Post* visited the family one night, Josie smiled in sweet understatement at her husband and observed: "John, it does seem refreshing to have you here. I am not sorry you are to have photographs taken to mark the evening. I am going to frame one and place a card over it on which I will write: 'Taken on his one evening at home'."

The mayor, whose image awareness would never have required the aid of Madison Avenue, jumped quickly into the conversation. "Now you will make Miss Burt think that I neglect my family. I spend every Sunday with them, Miss Burt, and I have them in town at least once a week," he said. "I am a family man. And the reason I am such is because I was one of many children. I took care of my brothers, did all the buying for the family, and was father and mother in one. This early training enabled me to shop wisely. Why, I think nothing of buying hats and coats for my girls. Just a little while ago I happened to see two coats I thought were quite attractive, so I bought them."

"And they were perfect fits," said Agnes.

"I'm never surprised when he brings me home a suit," Josie said. "I will admit that although he doesn't spend many evenings at home with us during the week, he seems to have us on his mind a great deal."

When he was at home, he and Rose often teamed up for some family entertainment. "Turn on the phonograph, Rose," he'd say when the family was gathered in the large library, "and we will liven things up a bit." And sometimes Rose sat down at the piano while her father and either Eunice or Agnes danced an old-fashioned waltz.

Rose was not only on his mind but actually accompanying him more and more frequently on the political and ceremonial rounds that her mother found so distasteful. Politics was still very much a man's business in those years—women did not even have the vote—and there was no necessity for a wifely presence on every public platform, so no one thought anything of it as Rose increasingly filled in for her mother at what Josie considered "ribbon-cutting folderol". Rose mixed well and showed remarkable tact and poise for her age; "brimming with animation and charm and girlish spirits", a reporter said, "she displays depth and strength of mind rarely found in so young a woman. Undoubtedly her father's influence upon her life has broadened her outlook, so that she lives much more vividly than most girls of her age."

Most important, Rose genuinely *liked* politics—not only the outward, centre-stage frills of blaring brass bands and red, white, and blue tornadoes of confetti and signs, but all the musty backroom strategy and behind-the-scenes manoeuvring that brought things about. "She damn well knows all the nuts and bolts of politics," Pierre Salinger, John Kennedy's press secretary, remarked with some awe after watching her in two campaigns. "She knows how to get the votes out, how you make the phone calls, raise money, and all that; and as a speaker, she's an absolute spellbinder. I mean, people are just riveted by her and"—he added with some surprise—"she never talks about the issues; the issues are a total void with her, I think. She always talks about family." But for Rose, family and politics had always been synonymous, and when she reared her own children, she did so with politics in mind, just as she used carefully fashioned family stories as her primary stumping device.

"If you really analyse all her publicity," observes her niece Barbara Fitzgerald Value, "it's never in terms of herself but always in terms of the men in her family: the Mayor's daughter, the Ambassador's wife, the President's mother. She's always been tremendously interested in certain causes, of course, like the mentally retarded and the Alliance Française, and will make public appearances because she knows it helps. But she really hates publicity centred on her alone; basically, it's all been for the men in her family. I think she thinks of herself as a tributary of a great river." And Rose herself, when once contemplating writing an autobiography, announced that it would be divided into the same three sections: "The Mayor's Daughter", "The Ambassador's Wife", "The President's Mother". Spurred by her relationship to a father whom she idolized, she always saw part of herself in terms of duty and devotion to the men in her life, but there was also another part, that had always been there, a part that was concerned with self-discipline and self-accomplishment.

By the time she was seventeen a second man had entered her life, and while she kept it a secret from her parents, Rose was beginning to fall in love. She had first met the ambitious, brash, and redheaded Joe Kennedy at Old Orchard Beach in Maine; Joe was the son of P. J. Kennedy, the powerful political leader of East Boston who wore a magnificent handlebar moustache and rimless glasses. Kennedy, a saloon-keeper and then banker, had a reputation for being intelligent, shrewd, and impeccably fair and honest; he was one of five kingmakers who handpicked Massachusetts mayors and Congressmen. P. J. and Honey Fitz went to Maine either for vacations or for daylong Democratic Club outings, and the children met often after that, though Joe said he still thought girls were "less than human" at the time. There was little affection between the two fathers—and frequent fallings-out: P. J. found Honey Fitz a good candidate but personally somewhat frivolous and a little idiotic for his tastes, and Honey Fitz, in return, looked down on the Kennedys socially. By virtue of his position as mayor of Boston, he considered the Fitzgeralds to be a notch above his political colleague; they had come from the same backgrounds, but Fitz considered himself—as his later rival, James M. Curley, would mockingly put it—one of the FIF's, First Irish Families. Fitz had presented young Joe with the Mayor's Cup for the most outstanding batting average in Boston (an astounding .667) when he was attending his own alma mater, Boston Latin, and Honey Fitz loved excellence. But a baseball diamond and his daughter's hand were two very different things, and he clearly felt that Joe, with all his brash ambitions and red-headed good looks and sparkling damn-you eyes, was not good enough for his Rose. It's unlikely that anyone ever would have been.

Of Rose's many suitors, he favoured Hugh Nawn, the son of Harry Nawn, a wealthy building contractor and close friend and neighbour who frequently served Fitz peanut-butter sandwiches late at night after a round of rigorous campaigning and whose family often vacationed with the Fitzgeralds. After he began to suspect Rose's affection for Joe Kennedy, Honey Fitz, always a master strategist, began to arrange trips to avoid one and meet the other. But in July, 1908, when the Fitzgerald family sailed for Europe aboard the *Cymric*, Rose, who would do almost anything not to displease her father, had Joe's picture hidden in her suitcase. She was going to be away for a long time.

It was not just a summer tour: Rose and Agnes were going abroad to study for a year at the Convent of the Sacred Heart in Blumenthal, Prussia, on the border of Germany and Holland. Rose had wanted to attend a French convent, but they had recently been closed after a severe quarrel between church and state over the question of government aid to the Catholic schools; the French nuns had even been expatriated, and there were a good number of them at Blumenthal. Margaret Finnegan and Ruth Evans, good friends from Boston, were also there. It would be one of the single most important years in Rose's life.

Religion had always played a central role in Rose's development, but the year at the convent strengthened, channelled, and gave permanent form to her devotion and faith. Her total and unquestioning belief in the Catholic Church and her strict and regular adherence to its sacraments and rituals have been the anchor of her life. In a letter to her husband in London, just before the war, she advised: "I am praying that I shall see you soon. Do pray, too, as it is very important in my life that you do just that." She has always steadfastly believed that faith is the single most important source of strength for children. "I don't know about it as a national or political issue," she said in the Presidential election, "but I think it is wonderful for children. Most children seek this stability and purpose." Wherever in the world she might be at the time, daily throughout her life, Rose has attended early-morning mass, and she participates regularly in religious retreats (at Portsmouth Priory she met another prominent Catholic who goes on retreat annually, the elder Mrs. Aloise Buckley—who was distressed that Rose got the only room with a private bathroom).

In 1951 she had the rare title of Papal Countess conferred upon her by the Vatican, in recognition of her "exemplary motherhood and many charitable works"; she was only the sixth American woman to have this title bestowed on her by the Holy See—it is granted to Catholic women who by good works have furthered the church, the Holy See, and society. In outward charity, good works, and inward strength she shows a religion that lives deeply and fully in her. "I can't imagine her doing anything wrong," says Mary Jo Clasby, "and not because she's a goody good or pious—but just because it's not Rose Fitzgerald Kennedy to do anything that would be out of line or not the right thing to do. She has tremendous faith in God and tremendous faith in her own religion and believes in it wholeheartedly. And this most likely is the background for why she is the way she is. And *positively* completely charitable."

Of the Fitzgeralds, a grandchild says: "Grandpa and Grandma were really not all that devout—I hope lightning doesn't come right through the ceiling and strike me for saying that, but it's really true. Grandpa probably sent his daughters to the convent in Blumenthal for a particular kind of finishing-school education—not spiritual values." But in the process, Rose found something: she became truly devout in a way that Agnes and the others who went there never did.

She also has a puritanical streak, similar to that in her father. Marie Greene once showed her a book called *When the Saints Go Marching Out*, and she didn't find it a bit funny. "Whenever I begin to tell a joke," says Marie Greene, "she invariably says, 'Marie, is this going to be one of those dirty stories, because if so, I don't want to hear it.' And I'm not talking about filth, but just stories that are slightly off-colour and wouldn't offend anyone. But they offend Rose." But such puritanism is not the measure of her faith. That is more evident in the simple image of a bereaved mother in a little clapboard church in Hyannis, staunchly remaining after early-morning mass to study the fourteen stations of the cross— doing so morning after morning, seeking guidance and solace for deep grief.

Rose's previous year at the Boston convent and her subsequent year at the Convent of the Sacred Heart in Manhattanville, New York, were no doubt fundamental in framing and reinforcing her religious discipline, but more than any other religious instruction she received, her nine months in Prussia built her faith. She earned more than a gold medal for piano accomplishment there; she earned discipline and order and a total philosophy for Christian living, in a

Continental convent where there were few of the distractions common to her in America.

The Society of the Sacred Heart, originated by Mother Madeleine Sophie Barat in France in 1800 was probably the ideal instrument for her religious training. Its goal was the preparation of young girls—in mind, will, heart, and hand—for complete Christian living. The schools were designed for training girls from the upper level of society, women whose character might well prove influential in the destinies of important people. "Incalculable good," stressed Mother Barat, "can be done by a truly Christian wife and mother. The order and regularity of everyday life, the peace and good behaviour of servants, and above all the earliest education of children depend principally upon the mother of the family, and it is through that knowledge that knowledge, love, and practise of religion are transmitted to the next generation."

These goals, in every particular, became Rose Fitzgerald Kennedy's.

Though the Blumenthal convent was a small, strict, self-contained world, where life was lived according to a rigid schedule with penalties for those who could not keep to it, life there was happy. Standards of unselfishness, duty, and devotion to others were encouraged—and in Rose's case became standards that she scrupulously tried to keep throughout her life. The nuns were thoughtful and often gifted teachers, and plays such as Schiller's *Joan of Arc*, staged after elaborate preparations, gave animation to the school year. Rose's friend Ruth Evans has described the difference in the quality of the religious experience: "At home, we had heard the worst music, and had attended the ugliest churches.... We had to learn the catechism by heart but had no religious feeling. Then we were transported to a world physically austere, but so beautiful we both experienced a spiritual transformation, living in a world where the chief concern was to know, to love, and to serve God."

The class hours were long, and the ritual was demanding. Young women from Germany, Ireland, England, America, and France learned the classics, music, home economics, cooking, and French and German. Only on Sundays and Thursdays and during recreation were the girls permitted to talk freely; they spoke German and French on walks and said prayers in these languages also. A soft, resolute voice was encouraged, with clear but unaffected diction.

The nuns constantly encouraged duty as a standard of conduct—
and her sense of duty has always been one of Rose's dominant
characteristics; it is a hard doctrine, but she has lived it along with
the Sacred Heart goals of service, sacrifice, responsibility, and church
loyalty.

The first images of her extraordinary devotion begin to appear
at Blumenthal. "I used to be behind her in confession," says Margaret Finnegan. "My God, I used to have to wait an hour, waiting
for her to come out of the confessional box." And later, back on
Welles Avenue, she once moved up to the attic "to mortify herself";
she felt she'd had too much of the "world's goods". Agnes and some
of their friends thought it was all hilarious, but Rose was intensely
serious. Her retreats, her trips to places like the fourth-century Île
St.-Honorat monastery (where, employing her papal title, she signed
the guest register "Countess Rose Kennedy"), and her scrupulous
attention to the Catholic calendar show that she has been serious
ever since then.

She was also one of the few really pretty and chic girls at the
school and as an American went frequently to town with a
chaperone to shop and have her hair attended; at such times she
could wear her fancy American clothes rather than the traditional
drab uniform. But if there was something of the finishing school,
with all its social trappings, about some aspects of life at the convent, these were the least part of her experience there, for she was
allying herself with its larger religious goals.

Eventually Rose requested and was finally accepted in the sodality
the Children of Mary of the Sacred Heart, the highest lifelong
commitment a Sacred Heart student can make. It is not just a club
but a guide for life devoted to following the example of the Im-
maculate Mother; it carries with it both a distinction and also a deep
personal commitment to build one's own character and that of others
and to progress constantly in piety. Along with such rituals as an
annual retreat, regular attendance at daily mass, and going to a
special mass for Children of Mary on the first Friday of every
month, the sodality stresses the imperative to renew one's religion
each day, so that it becomes inseparable from one's life. Of the
promises she made when she became a Child of Mary, these were
most important to Rose:

—holding my soul free in the face of changes of fortune ...

—forming my will to courage and patience in privations ...

—showing myself truly Christian everywhere by living my convictions ...

—making the effort necessary to practise those family virtues suited to my position of daughter, wife, mother, such as kindness, gift of self, abnegation, evenness

—guarding myself by prayer, watchfulness, a certain habit of mortification

—in difficult moments obtaining from "Our Lady of Sorrows" courage to suffer as she did, standing at the foot of the Cross.

"Hell itself," said Mother Barat in one of her letters, "can do nothing against Children of Mary." According to her close friends, Rose has always believed that.

The sodality is deeply meaningful to Rose; she lives the promises she made, and it has been a strength to her in all her suffering. To this day she will add the initials E.D.M. (Enfant de Marie, "Child of Mary") to some of her letters. If anything, she may have learned her lessons too well, for friends often complain that Rose is such a giver that she really doesn't know how to take. Her discipline extends even to being happy, and one relative remarked: "It's like you can't be depressed; it's your solemn duty to find something to be happy about."

But there were other calls besides those of duty and severe self-discipline; over her nightstand all that long, seminal year in Europe stood a photograph of a striking young man named Joseph P. Kennedy. The day Rose returned to Boston she called Margaret Finnegan in Cambridge and told her: "Now I am not going to marry that Hugh Nawn."

Chapter Four

The Ace of Clubs and Prince of Hearts

*I hope that you will pick out a man who
is the equal of your father.*
— SIR THOMAS LIPTON

When Rose returned to Boston from her year abroad and a subsequent year at Manhattanville, Boston society was still solidly
divided into Yankee Brahmins and Irish Catholics, but the second-
and third-generation Irish, characteristically, were more interested
in forming their own society—often repeating the same patterns as
those of Yankee Boston—than in crashing the George Apley world
of the Adamses, the Lowells, and the Cabots. The "high Irish"
stuck together. They went away during the summer and winter
vacations in family groups of thirty and forty, including the children
—to Hull (where the Fitzgeralds owned the old Douglas estate on
the South Shore) and Palm Beach and Old Orchard Beach in Maine,
and they held their gay and elaborate social events with a pride
that bespoke their growing sense of security and self-confidence as
a group. Rose's spectacular début, paralleling a long-established
Yankee tradition, was such an event (throughout all of 1910, Rose
thought and dreamed of it); so were the Irish Catholic clubs.

Boston clubs were the core of the Boston social system. Here the
young debutantes launched their social careers under the guise of
doing charitable work; to be *anyone* you had to belong. But Rose
never sought to penetrate the reigning Protestant world. "She had
a much better time where she was," says an intimate of those days.
"It was always more fun in the Irish group, much more fun—you
see this one thing is true of all inbred society like Protestant Boston
—they're great, and you like them, but not for a good time." Under
any circumstances, Rose and her young lady friends were ineligible
for such Brahmin bulwarks as the Junior League and the Vincent
Club, which demanded that one not only be rich, well-bred, and

well-born, but also Protestant. They joined the Irish Catholic Cecil-ian Guild, the counterpart to the Junior League, and Rose founded their own club—an idea suggested by Honey Fitz, who got them a room downstairs at the Somerset Hotel, where they met every Tuesday.

Rose was finished with all her formal schooling now and was free to use most of her day as she chose. She was a serious young woman, with an extraordinary group of projects, and she seemed always to be looking for more. A friend speaks of her as already being "undemonstrative" and adds, "You could get a laugh out of her, but you had to go looking for it." She already had that control of her emotions for which a nation later held her in awe. But often, during those years of founding clubs and scurrying from one commitment to another, she would be—uncharacteristically—late, and she would appear with her clothes in some disorder, her dress creased, her heels run-down. Friends report a dramatic change in her appearance and punctuality when she became engaged to Joe Kennedy, but in those early years he himself was driving himself at breakneck speed. He was older than Rose, but she had finished her schooling early; Joe had remained at Boston Latin an extra year to take over courses that he had not passed, and he was still at Harvard. He served as assistant freshman football coach at Harvard and ran as part owner a sight-seeing bus to all the historic land-marks in Boston; he even played some semipro baseball.

Travelling throughout Boston, Rose often did not carry money with her, a habit begun in high school, maintained to this day, and inherited by her children. Friends remember her getting on the electric trolley car that took them to Dorchester High School and, without being able to produce a cent for fare, saying: "I'm Rose Fitzgerald, and I don't have any money with me, and could you take me to my high school?" There is a touch of arrogance in the gesture and a touch of indifference to money; her son Jack rarely carried money either, and reporters remember being stuck with the tab for a quick lunch when he was campaigning.

Marie Greene, whose maiden name had been Paterson and who, in her own description, "didn't look Irish", remembers the social scene from a unique vantage point. As a woman active in Boston civic groups of all kinds, even as a young woman she would frequently serve on committees that permitted only one Jew and one Catholic; a Patricia Whitman, she remembers, was always the Jew and she, invariably, the Catholic, and they would, with amusement, look for each other at meetings. The others would "go all around Robin Hood's barn" to find out if she was Catholic, and she'd just let them hedge—"because, you see, they were afraid to come right out and ask me if I was Catholic for fear that if I wasn't, I'd be insulted, but I'd just make them come out finally and say it—'Are you a Catholic?'—and I'd say, 'Yes, and what are you?' It was simply a fact that they didn't know us." Some of the Irish, like Joe Kennedy, desperately wanted to crack that Boston Brahmin society and felt like outsiders to it, but the Fitzgeralds had made their peace with it and could confidently go their own way. Rose herself was too proud to risk the embarrassment of those innuendos and whispers and felt little qualm about standing apart from Brahmin society. An extremely good Irish Catholic society was developing, and she was very much a part of the founding force behind it.

Characteristically, the exclusive sewing circle kind of social club bored her. More than one person, including her daughters, has observed that everything Rose does has a purpose. When she founded a club, its purposes were more educational than social. The Ace of Clubs (the name had been suggested by Honey Fitz) began with eight charter members and Rose as its first president. It has, over the years, grown into a social club of great importance, with more than 250 active and provisional members today and long waiting lists. In 1960 it celebrated its fiftieth anniversary, and its programmes include monthly talks on such enticing topics as "Scandinavia", "Extrasensory Perception", "The Plight of the Poor Consumer", and "The Mysteries of the Unidentified Flying Objects"; museum tours, a "Gentleman's Night", and the annual Spring Dance at the Ritz Carlton are other highlights of the year. Though it now engages in a host of charitable activities too, when Rose founded the club, its objects were purely educational.

The group was small, quite exclusive, and cultural. All the girls were single, and all had been to Europe, so they had a common background. They were girls who, in Catholic circles, "belonged". "They were all from substantial homes," recalls Marie Greene, "and so they didn't really need the whole New England thing." The young women came together in the Rose Room that Honey Fitz had arranged for them at the Somerset, served tea, and discussed current events. They would invite prominent figures to address them on political and social matters of the moment and maintained regular Tuesday study and discussion sessions. Honey Fitz actively promoted the club and often buttonholed visiting dignitaries to address the young women. He brought Jimmy Walker once, and the flamboyant New York mayor began: "Well, so this is the Ace of Clubs. Many a night I've longed for the Ace of Clubs."

The club served as a superb training ground for Rose in public speaking. At first the pressure of speaking before a small intimate group was difficult. She had made public speeches for her father, but this was different: the group was more select; they all knew her well; there was a more personal involvement. "I remember the first time she spoke at the Ace of Clubs," recalls a charter member. "She was so nervous before she began—she kept asking me how she looked and I told her to take off her pearls; I said she was loaded down with them. So she took them off, and the next thing I knew she was on her way to New York or somewhere, and I was still holding them in my hand." Often after she spoke, she'd ask one of her friends, "Did I sound all right? What I said, was it the right thing to say?" But the nervousness did not last long, for Rose soon became, by repeated efforts and determination, a skilled speaker on a variety of social and political issues, and she continued to develop her ability through the years in such private groups until it emerged full-blossomed and tremendously effective in the teas she held during Jack's Senatorial campaign.

There were also periodic dances, called Assemblies and organized by Mrs. James W. Morrison; these gave Honey Fitz still another chance to sing "Sweet Adeline"—though one friend of Rose's, who by then had heard it enough, turned the lights out on him so the song had to be cancelled. Joe Kennedy often escorted her to the Assemblies, which were held three times a year, and she loved the way he always complimented her, telling her that she was the "belle of the ball" and had on the prettiest dress. Hugh Nawn, now working as a contractor with his father, several times led the cotillion with Rose at the Somerset Hotel. Often the same girls would meet the boys from Harvard at Bailey's Candy Store and Ice Cream Shop on West Street for ice-cream sodas.

Rose was also a member of the Abbotsford Club, founded by Mrs.

Morrison. This was a dramatics club that met at "Mrs. Morrison's Castle"—a huge stone mansion in Roxbury—and a poor rehearsal usually meant a summary loss of a part for one of the girls. They would rehearse intently during Lent and then hold all their performances for a week in Jordan Hall, at $2.50 a ticket. Broadway successes were their usual fare, and though they were advised that they would not make money, since they were such amateurs, after the first year their success was so great that they never had to open the box office. All profits were given to charity. A few of the girls "went professional", and one began a successful career in opera; but most simply married, and that broke up the Abbotsford Club. Interestingly, Rose's work with the group was considered "inhibited"; whatever skill she had in public speaking—where she developed an exceptionally intimate approach—she did not have the ability to enter freely into the life of another dramatic character.

Rose also organized the Travel Club, composed of girls who had been to Europe, and was president of the Lenox Club, and she engaged herself in a thorough round of regular civic activities, including work in settlement houses and social agencies. Like her father, she was becoming involved in an incredible number of clubs and other projects, and he kept encouraging her to do even more. She was the youngest member of the Public Library Investigating Committee, which developed lists of suitable books for children to read, and she and Agnes taught sewing to a class of Italian children in the North End and also a Sunday school class. Former pupils remember Rose as "a painstaking catechism instructor", who prodded and encouraged them to win one prize after another in the annual competitions. She had her father's will to win, and her training was not lost on her own children.

Rose also drove herself to further self-improvement, whether it was at the courses she took at the New England Conservatory in piano or her special classes in the history of grand opera every Saturday afternoon for three years. She regularly attended public current events lectures in Boston and swam and played tennis and continued to serve as official hostess for her father, who showed not the slightest sign of slowing down his manic pace of life. She and Agnes were his interpreters for French and German delegates who came to Boston for an international congress, and in 1911, on the way to Palm Beach, she went with her father to the White House and was proudly introduced to President William Howard Taft. Rose still quoted Honey Fitz so often that the young men at the dances, as well as her girl-friends, called her "Father Says".

With all of Honey Fitz's busyness, he had developed one habit that served to keep him fresh: catnapping in cars. On a trip to Springfield, he quickly shut his eyes and then slept the whole way, and he often did so between speaking engagements when time permitted. Rose does the same thing, especially when she is off on a whirl of campaigning. She loves sleep and can "turn off" whenever she chooses, no matter who is with her. "Call it a good conscience or anything you want," remarked a friend some years back, "but they can get off to sleep ... even Jack." More than conscience, this ability to sleep on planes, in cars, anywhere, no matter what reporters or friends may be with her, suggests a complete social confidence that only a handful of public figures possess.

Monday, January 2, 1911, was the culminating point in Rose's early social life. It was a triumph for the Fitzgeralds and an emblem of how far they had come; it was also a triumph for Irish Catholic society. The City Council of Boston voted to postpone its scheduled meeting on that day, for all its members were invited guests to one of the most gala events of the season: the coming-out party for Rose Elizabeth Fitzgerald.

The night before was a "riot of confusion", exuded the papers in a riot of prose. Rose was "delightfully excited", and Honey Fitz, for once, was relegated to the background, fussing chiefly over whether the piazza conservatory would be fittingly decorated. Josie was in a flurry over the arrangement of the reception and dining rooms, the decorations for the parlours, and her daughter's gown. The bewildered reporter for the Boston *Post*, who was not the regular society columnist, saw only "a bunch of silk and ribbons and lace and things" and had to accept Rose's own description of her gown: "The dress itself is of white satin with crepe meteor over it, and on the skirt is a border of Italian embroidery over yellow silk ribbon, and there is Italian embroidery over the bodice." There was also a demitrain, and this particularly delighted her since it was the first train of any kind that she had ever worn.

The rain the next day could not dampen her excitement. The more than 450 guests began to arrive shortly after four o'clock, and both the Welles Avenue and Harley Street entrances to the big

Victorian house were soon congested with polished limousines and handsome covered carriages. Honey Fitz had until four o'clock remained on the first floor, fussing frenetically and putting his inimitable finishing touches on everything; then he had dressed hurriedly and was soon back and everywhere: clasping hands; assisting ushers; pouring chocolate; directing carriages.

Every corner of the Fitzgerald home, from the music room on the first floor to the children's room upstairs, was alive with jovial talk and bright decoration and bustling activity. So many roses were strung, hung, potted, banked, basketed, and piled throughout the house that their aroma filtered out into the cold, wet street, and when guests arrived under the awnings, walked between the spruce and fir trees lining the two approaches, and entered the house, they had the distinct impression that they were entering an exquisite greenhouse ablaze with lights, a "palace of fair blossoms".

Rose, in her white gown and carrying violets for modesty and lilies of the valley for beauty, and Josie, dressed in black Chantilly lace, received all the guests in the drawing room as they entered. Mountain laurel was twined and crisscrossed about the upper portions of the wall, around the staircases, light fixtures, and paintings, and roses, rare orchids, pinks, lilies of the valley, slender Bavarian palms, Japanese dwarf trees, and other flowers and plants were set with "artistic taste" all over the room. Rose was beautiful and gracious—and inwardly thrilled. Her face was frank and smiling; her handshake firm and genuinely friendly. The *Globe* reporter observed that "witchery danced in eyes that matched her raven hair, but it was not the witchery of Circe on a pedestal behind her to the right, but rather that of Petrarch's immortal Laura, a marble bust of whom was at the debutante's left". He found her "revealed as the antithesis of affectation"—without a jewel, with only a simple silver ribbon twisted in her hair and white gloves to the elbow. She had "pleasant words for all and a laugh that was musical". As person after person trooped in out of the rain, she greeted them without the slightest indication of boredom or fatigue—a trait she has kept to this day, when she can stand and shake endless hands in a reception line and only—as in a recent party for Teddy—become upset when certain people come through twice.

By six the party was at its height. Carriages and motor cars continued to arrive in a steady stream, and the guests, many of them already known to one another and representing the highest echelons of Boston society, were enjoying themselves immensely. Governor-elect Eugene N. Foss was there, and so were men prominent in business as well as politics—Congressmen William F. Murray and James Curley, bankers, and judges. Coffee and chocolate and tea were served to the women "in queenly fashion" by a charming group of eight of Rose's closest friends.

When the reception was over, Rose and the girls, along with a group of young men, began a spirited little party of their own in the children's room upstairs, whose rafters were strung with roses. First there was a delicious banquet and then a dance. Hugh Nawn was there, and Roger Sherman Hoar from Concord (who was still "sweet on Rose"), and also Joe Kennedy.

Among the hundreds of telegrams that poured in from all over the world was a cable from Fitz's close friend Sir Thomas Lipton:

> I extend my heartiest congratulations to you on the occa-
> sion of your coming-out. I suppose that in a short time I will
> be sending congratulations for another occasion of great
> joy, that of your marriage. Before that occurs I hope that
> you will pick out a man who is the equal of your father.

Honey Fitz continued to think that Joe Kennedy was neither his own nor his daughter's equal. Often Rose and Joe met at dances or social events, and Joe was always terribly solicitous and compli-mented her on her dress and how her hair was done; Joe Kennedy wanted the best, and there was no one comparable to the beautiful daughter of Honey Fitz. And Rose, even when she did not come with Joe to a dance, often covered her dance card with fake initials so that no one else would know that she was taking all her dances with Joe. He was always on her mind now; his energy and ambition and attentions were compelling. Their relationship was becoming intense, and when they quarrelled or he said something sharp to her, her sisters and girlfriends would laugh at the way she turned his picture on her dressing table to the wall. But he would come looking for her in Cambridge and Dorchester, asking the other girls, "Rosie, where's Rosie, my Rosie?"

Honey Fitz, still convinced that his daughter could do better, con-tinued to put impediments between the two, and they were forced

John F. and Josephine Fitzgerald in a rare photograph
from a family locket.

Agnes, Tom and Rose — about 1898.

One of many
contemporary cartoons
depicting Honey Fitz as
Napoleon.

Mayor Fitzgerald on Mac,
after winning a blue ribbon
for jumping at the
Metropolitan Driving Club
in May, 1912.

Even in his later years, the
repressible Honey Fitz
needed little urging to sing
"Sweet Adeline".

MAYOR PRESENTS DIPLOMA TO HIS OWN DAUGHTER AT DORCHESTER HIGH

MAYOR FITZGERALD PRESENTING DIPLOMA OF GRADUATION AT DORCHESTER HIGH SCHOOL TO HIS DAUGHTER, ROSE ELIZABETH.

Youngest Student Who Ever Graduated From the School

An event said to be without parallel in the history of the public schools of Boston occurred last night, when Mayor John F. Fitzgerald presented to his daughter, Rose Elizabeth, her diploma of graduating exercises at the Dorchester High School. It is said in the history never before.

father who reigned as the chief executive of the city at the time.

At the moment that Miss Fitzgerald advanced to receive the coveted diploma for honorable and meritorious study from the hands of her father, a tumult of applause rang through the hall. The very oddity of the situation appealed to every auditor, and when father and daughter met the roar of applause coming from the audience was almost deafening.

Miss Fitzgerald, gowned in white in muslin, and devoid of a particle of ornamentation or jewelry, looked charmingly simple in her graduating dress. She is a very pretty girl of the petite type. When father and daughter parted to make way for the others in the order of graduation, both were smiling joyously.

Among the entire group of girl gradu-

It is said that Mrs. Fitzgerald and the Mayor decided that their daughter should, on the occasion of her graduation, set a standard of simplicity, which she as the chief executive of the city hoped might be followed by parents of other graduates in the future.

Following an old custom that obtains wherever young women are graduated from the public schools, the usual graduation gift was made to Miss Fitzgerald on her return home.

The Mayor and Mrs. Fitzgerald gave to their eldest daughter a magnificent silver set, including toilet accessories and ornaments of solid silver.

A year from the present time the Mayor will have the pleasure of presenting to another daughter, her diploma of graduation. This will be at the time of the graduation of his second eldest daughter, Miss Mary Fitzgerald, who is about to enter the graduating class of the High

Rose's graduation from Dorchester High
School made front-page news in the Boston *Post*.

MISS FITZGERALD'S DEBUT
IS ATTENDED BY NOTABLES

FIGHT ON
FOR EVA
MILLI

Relatives, Some
Distant, Open
test for Sha

STATE A LOSER OF
THOUSANDS IN

Concluding Clai
Will Starts Clai
to $20,000,0

**ayor's Home Rose-
Garlanded for
Occasion**

DISPLAY ADVERTISING

Front-page coverage of Rose's début in the Boston *Post* and Boston *Globe*.

Miss Rose E. Fitzgerald, Gowned in White, Rec
More Than 500 Friends at Mayor's Hom

Rose with Sir Thomas
Lipton and her sisters,
Eunice and Agnes,
aboard the lovable tea
tycoon's yacht
Shamrock.

Below: Rose with
her mother and father
in Palm Beach.

MISS ROSE FITZGERALD IS BRIDE OF JOSEPH P. KENNEDY

ESCORTING THE BRIDE FROM THE HOME OF CARDINAL O'CONNELL.

Rose, Honey Fitz, and Agnes in a wedding photo appearing in the Boston *Post*.

Rose and Joe on the steps of William Cardinal O'Connell's home following their marriage ceremony.

Rose in an early
photograph.

Rose with her mother.

Joe Kennedy, newly appointed Ambassador to the Court of St. James's, and Rose with five of their children in London, spring, 1938. (*Left to right*): Kathleen, Teddy, Patricia, Jean and Bobby. Radio Times Hulton Picture Library.

Teddy and Bobby Kennedy opening the children's zoo in Regent's Park. Radio Times Hulton Picture Library.

Rosemary and Eunice
Kennedy being greeted by
their father and Teddy at
Paddington Station upon
arriving in England. Radio
Times Hulton Picture Library.

Rose and Joe strolling in the
garden of the Embassy
residence, 14 Prince's Gate.
Radio Times Hulton
Picture Library.

Kathleen, Rose and Rosemary just before leaving for Buckingham
Palace to be presented at the first Court of the season, May, 1938.
Radio Times Hulton Picture Library.

Rose and Joe with
Kathleen after attending
a wedding at the
Caxton Hall Register
Office in London. Radio
Times Hulton Picture
Library.

Rose and Joe greeting
guests at the Embassy
in the summer of 1939.
Radio Times Hulton
Picture Library.

Hartington and Kick after their marriage; with them
are the Duke and Duchess of Devonshire and Joe
Kennedy, Jr.

A slim and hesitant Jack Kennedy (*lower left*) marches the streets of Honey Fitz's
Eleventh District in his bid for a Congressional seat in 1946.

The proud parents of the newly elected President of the United States pose with Jack and Jackie in Hyannis Port immediately following the news of his victory over Richard Nixon, November, 1960. Associated Press Ltd.

With his mother and wife looking on, John F. Kennedy speaks to the people of the United States over television for the first time as President-elect. Associated Press Ltd.

...se at a private audience with ...pe John XXIII at the Vatican in ... autumn of 1961. ...sociated Press Ltd.

Rose leaves early mass in Hyannis Port after learning that her son, Bobby, had been shot in Los Angeles the previous night; he died later the same day. Associated Press Ltd.

Rose, Jean, and Pat walk the beach at Hyannis Port
— as they had done after Jack's and Bobby's deaths
— following the death of Joseph P. Kennedy in
November, 1969. Associated Press Ltd.

Rose with her only surviving son, Senator Edward Kennedy, and her
partially paralysed husband, expressing thanks to the American people
for the strength and hope they received from the nation's response to
Bobby's death. Associated Press Ltd.

Rose, holding Caroline Kennedy's hand, walks behind Jackie and John F. Kennedy, Jr. following the wedding of Jackie's secretary, Pamela Tunure in New York City. Associated Press Ltd.

One month before her eighty-first birthday, Rose chats to David Frost on television in New York. Associated Press Ltd.

to meet secretly at the house of Margaret Finnegan in Cambridge, across the street from the Holy Ghost Hospital near Harvard, or, amusingly, in the Christian Science Church in Boston. Fifty years later, passing that church, they were reminded of their surreptitious meetings and decided to give it a donation. Agnes, whose beau Joe Gargan was also unable to win Fitz's approval, held secret meetings at Tillie Gavin's house. Once at Scarboro Pond near Franklin Park, Rose wore a dark veil while she and Joe were skating—though all their friends knew who they were. Friends of both girls still remember how Agnes showed little hesitation about discussing her feelings for Joe Gargan, but how Rose, even to her closest friends, kept her relationship to herself. It was characteristic; to this day she will say, "Why should I disclose my emotions? I don't need the publicity."

Throughout this period, Rose continued to accompany her father almost everywhere. She went with him to the International Municipal Congress and Exposition in Chicago and attended the 1912 Democratic National Convention. She was even present when he won blue ribbons in horse-jumping exhibitions; after one such victory, the Boston *Post* ran a three-column cartoon of Fitz titled "No Hurdle Too High", picturing him on a horse clearing the highest hurdle, labelled "U.S. Senator" (below it were hurdles marked "Governor" and "Vice President").

In February after her début, Rose and the mayor, together with a group of his political cronies and relatives, took one of their increasingly frequent winter trips to Palm Beach; Josie and the younger children did not go. It was a marvellous vacation and a quiet rest for the mayor, "dodging dukes, duchesses, and millionaires, etc." He wrote to his city via the Boston *Post*: "I was on my feet seventeen hours a day for six months, and it is now the rest cure for me, with a little baseball, golf, swimming and dancing thrown in." The irrepressible Fitzy found a few dozen occasions on which it seemed appropriate to sing "Sweet Adeline". Rose was charmed by Palm Beach and found it "a veritable fairyland".

Several days after they arrived, the headlines in the Boston *Post* ran: BUSY DAY FOR MAYOR IN FLORIDA—BREASTS TIDE WITH MISS ROSE AND WINS APPLAUSE. They had gone down to the beach together in a "big double-wheel chair", and though it was a rough day, "Father and daughter breasted the tide that so many were afraid of." Then they went up to the casino and gave a diving exhibition that attracted considerable attention, and finally, the resting mayor raced his daughter in the pool while 200 to 300 wildly cheering spectators looked on. The mayor, always fiercely competitive, won —but only after a "decided spurt at the end of the race", for Rose too was an excellent swimmer.

When, several days later, the city had not heard a word from their mayor in more than forty-eight hours, there were whimsical speculations that he had been eaten by an alligator. But these led to counterspeculations that if there indeed had been such a confrontation, "it was the gator that got stung" or, perhaps, the mayor had put "the Indian sign on his amphibious highness by warbling 'Sweet Adeline' into what he used for ears until someone could hand the gator an administration lemon".

By Sunday there were clear reports that the mayor and his beautiful daughter were indeed well. At breakfast Honey Fitz sang a few bars of "My Hero", along with "Sweet Adeline", and later broke "the Palm Beach long-distance record for simultaneous swimming and spouting. He delivered an oration ten nautical miles long, and at one time was out of sight of the thousands on the beach, but as clear as crystal his liquid words floated over the water to the shore. In the afternoon he entertained the ladies in their long white dresses by turning handsprings on the hotel lawn." Palm Beach went Fitz-frenzied. "There are Fitzgerald canes, Fitzgerald fans, Fitzgerald oranges, and Fitzgerald lemons," a Boston paper twitted. "One shop has sold more than fifty Fitzgerald bathing suits." The "lemons" were being "shipped north for use in Boston".

Rose, of course, was dazzled and delighted by all the energy her father displayed, all the publicity he received. His vitality was contagious, and life with him was constantly charged with excitement. He could dedicate a half-mile track at Franklin Field in Philadelphia and then compete in and win the first footrace; on vacation at Old Orchard Beach, Maine, he could replace a baseball pitcher and then strike out sixteen batters in seven innings. He created a romantic aura of the improbable hero capable of matching her dreams and gave her, along with all else she was to possess, a lifelong love of excelling and standing out in any social situation.

In June, Rose and the mayor were off again, this time with Agnes, on the *Franconia*, bound for Europe. Standing between his girls and facing the thousands of friends and political associates who crowded the decks of tugs and other small craft as the liner rounded Boston Light, giving him the most "wildly enthusiastic good-bye which has ever signalled the departure of any Bostonian", Fitz sang, over the quickly hushed seas:

> Sweet Adeline, my Adeline
> At night, dear heart,
> For you I pine.
> In all my dreams,
> Your fair face beams,
> You're the flower of my heart,
> Sweet Adeline.

While prominent officials speculated publicly on whether the city paid "the mayor's bills on joy rides", he and the girls were having a wonderful and instructive trip. They went to Munich and Vienna, to Hamburg, Paris, Brussels, Dresden, and Berlin. He compared every city with his beloved Boston—his unimpeachable love—and studied the burgeoning industrial works throughout Europe, predicting that Germany would before long begin a war.

On one such European trip, he had gone to Cowes, England, to watch a regatta. From the docks Rose had spotted the *Erin*, Sir Thomas Lipton's yacht, and Honey Fitz immediately decided to find a motor launch to take them to it. There were no commercial boats available, but the King of England's was nearby; Fitz, without hesitation, addressed the skipper with such "swaggering assurance" that royal permission was taken for granted. "Lipton, *Erin*," Fitz said briskly as he came aboard with Rose and Agnes. The crew saluted, and the launch was soon cutting its way out to the *Erin*. Lipton saw them through his glass and promptly announced to his guests, who were set into a flurry of excitement, that the King and Queen were on their way out. The ladies at once began to practise their curtsying, and Lipton lined up his crew at attention. But a few moments later he took another look and exclaimed: "My heavens, it's my friend John Fitzgerald of Boston, with Rose and Agnes." When the party came aboard, he said, "My word, Fitz, but you have arrived in great style," to which Honey Fitz nonchalantly replied: "What do you mean? I took the best boat I could see available...."

Rose and Agnes were deeply moved by the inferior position of women on their 1911 trip abroad and in an interview spoke feelingly of seeing them cut hay and wheat and rye in the fields, clean the streets of Vienna and the parks of Budapest. Women even worked on the railroads in Budapest, and they saw them driving spikes with heavy sledgehammers, lifting heavy ties, and carrying the bricks. It was a world they had never known. When Fitz and the girls returned in mid-August on the *Franconia*, they occupied rooms 44 to 48; in room 50 during that long crossing was a young man named Hugh Nawn.

Joe Kennedy could manipulate, too, and though he was devoted to Rose, he once expressly invited Ruth Rea, whose father was president of the Pennsylvania Railroad, to a Harvard-Princeton football game. He knew Fitz would be there and made a huge show of his intimacy with the prominent Rea family for the benefit of Rose's father. "We went steady for seven years before we were married," Joe said in later years. "But going steady in those days was a different proposition from the way kids go steady today." During that time Rose had gone to the convent in Europe and to the Sacred Heart Academy in Manhattanville, and he had been at Harvard, had played baseball for the Bethlehem ball team in the White Mountains semipro league for a few summers, and had run his successful sight-seeing bus with Joe Donovan, a friend from Harvard. "But I was never seriously interested in anyone else," he said. Neither was Rose.

Fitz finally lost his little battle to keep Rose and Joe Kennedy apart. Joe's eighteen months as a low-paid state bank examiner had taught him the clockworks of every important bank in Massachusetts. Soon, through a series of manoeuvres that would become typical of his style, he was president of the Columbia Trust Company. At twenty-five he was the youngest bank president in America —and Honey Fitz had to be impressed.

By twenty-four Rose had travelled widely throughout South America, Europe, and the United States; she had been a leader among the young Socialites of Irish Catholic Boston; and she had been the official hostess and frequent companion of the most flamboyant mayor Boston had ever known. If she was, as some acquaintances say, somewhat "spoiled" by it all, she was also self-disciplined, poised, and cultured. She had developed a puritanically purposeful style of life, and a mind very much her own—a practical mind that organized clubs, chose proper books for children, and constantly sought to improve itself.

At twenty-four she was ready for adventure of another sort, marriage and motherhood—and her father's repeated opposition to the prince of her heart could not stop her. One day on a grey Boston street, since he was still not allowed in her house, Joe Kennedy slipped an engagement ring on Rose's finger. The simple nuptial announcement read:

Mr. and Mrs. John Francis Fitzgerald
announce the marriage of their daughter
Rose Elizabeth
to
Mr. Joseph Patrick Kennedy
on Wednesday the seventh of October
one thousand nine hundred and fourteen
Boston Massachusetts

And on that day, the modest wedding took place at nine o'clock in the morning in the private chapel of His Eminence William Cardinal O'Connell, Archbishop of Boston; the chapel adjoined his house at 25 Granby Street in Back Bay. It was attended by less than a fourth the number of people that attended Rose's début and received only minimal coverage in the Boston papers, much less than her début; there was only a short notice and one photograph.

Agnes, in rose-pink velvet and a black hat, was maid of honour for her sister, and Joe Donovan was best man. Rose wore a gown of white duchesse satin, trimmed with rose point lace and decorated with silver and pearls; her tulle veil was attached to a delicate lace Normandie cap, and she carried a bridal bouquet the size of a small rhododendron bush.

Following the hour-long nuptial mass, solemnized by the cardinal himself, the small wedding party left in a motorcade for the Fitzgerald home on Welles Avenue, where seventy-five guests gathered for a wedding breakfast. Just as they left the cardinal's residence, pausing briefly for photographs on the steps, the morning sun broke through the overcast sky. To everyone there it seemed an omen of everything to come for Joe and Rose Kennedy.

Chapter Five

The Brookline Years

You've always got to remember that they started
on Beals Street with diapers on the back of the
stove—even if it seems ridiculous ... which it does.
—Marie Greene

It was almost November when Rose and Joe Kennedy returned
from their wedding trip to the Greenbrier Hotel in White Sulphur
Springs, West Virginia, and moved into their first home—the only
modest one they would ever live in—at 83 Beals Street in Brookline.
Their three-storey grey frame house, with its white front porch
and small square patches of grass in front and back, was not much
different from all the other houses on the block, which stood side
by side along the maple-shaded streets in insular Yankee proximity
—and a probable Yankee awareness of the value of land only two
or three miles from the Boston Common.

Joe Kennedy, who had read Horatio Alger as a boy and who was
soon to launch a personal blitz on the financial world, was still in
debt at the time from his manipulations at Columbia Trust; he
had to borrow the $2,000 down payment on the $6,000 house. A
half century later, the Kennedys would pay $55,000 to repurchase
the old place, refurnish it with everything from the original Victorian furniture to Jack's bassinet, and then turn the deed over to
the government, to maintain as a national historic shrine: the
birthplace of the thirty-fifth President, who, even before he was
nominated, was fond of pointing out his Beals Street origins to
friends as being "just like Abe Lincoln and his log cabin". At the
official dedication in 1969, Rose stood on the front porch she had
crossed as a bride and spoke briefly to a crowd of 700 people
gathered in the street. "We were very happy here," she said, "and
though we did not know about the days ahead, we were optimistic
about the future."

As Rose and Joe settled into their new lives, the world beyond Beals Street was changing dramatically. Several months before their marriage, a Serbian patriot had fired the shot that exploded the powder keg of Europe into the largest war the world had yet known. By the time their second son, John F. Kennedy was born in 1917, it would also be America's war, and the momentous Russian Revolution would be challenging the destiny of the country he would one day face as a world power in a perilous nuclear age. But the war still seemed very far away to Americans in the autumn of 1914, and life in Brookline was tranquil and unhurried as Rose set about decorating the nine rooms of her new home. The halls were narrow and the rooms small, and in the kitchen there was a huge black-iron coal and gas stove. In keeping with the setting and their income, Rose bought simple, unpretentious furniture—comfortable, over-stuffed chairs and sofa, a dining-room set they would later give away, an Oriental rug for the living room on which her children would eventually learn to crawl, and green-lace curtains for the windows. Joe's sister, Mrs. Charles Burke, painted the gold trim on the family's dining-room china, and Rose frequently sat alone in the sewing room on the second floor, knitting or sewing. She had once made layettes at the Cecilian Guild.

If it all bore little resemblance to Abe Lincoln's log cabin, it was still a great distance from the piazza-conservatory opulence of Welles Avenue. For the first time since she had left the North End as a little girl, Rose no longer lived in a big house on a hill above her neighbours, and her neighbours, for the first time, were all Protestant—a fact of some significance to Joe but which mattered little to Rose. What mattered to Rose as Christmas approached was that she was already pregnant with her first child.

As she awaited the birth during the winter and spring of 1915, Rose continued to attend luncheons and teas and club meetings with her old friends. Joe was working sixteen hours a day at the bank, but she was determined not to be lonely, not to brood, while he was away. She did not complain then, and she never complained even when his absences grew to weeks and months, when he later entered the movie business. "Everyone was always giving luncheons and teas in those days," says a close friend. "Don't ask me why, but they were. They were usually at home, everything was held at home then, although come to think of it, the first time I ever remember seeing Rosie at a luncheon was on a destroyer in the Boston harbour. It makes no sense, but there we were, and I can't remember why." Rose also played golf regularly, and her friends were delighted that she now appeared on time at the green; it was Joe's influence, they insisted, and also noted that she now regularly carried a little black appointment and note book.

Rose also made frequent visits back to Welles Avenue to see her parents and her brothers and sisters. She was the first to marry, and Agnes was still seeing Joe Gargan regularly. Some of the old romantic lustre was gone on Welles Street. She had tried her hardest, perhaps too hard, to teach her brothers, and now they showed little of that vigour or direction she valued; they were "ciphers", dependent on their father, a relative claims. Rose remembered the days when she'd exchanged visits with girlfriends, often so that she could meet Joe at another house. When the girls returned the visit, they'd push the great big brass beds in Rose's room together, and then her father and mother could come in, and Josie's hair would be let down to the ground, and she'd brush and brush, for hours, while Honey Fitz talked on and on until two or three in the morning. It was quieter now on Welles Avenue, and it was quieter on Beals Street.

Honey Fitz was still a magic name in Boston, but although he didn't realize it at the time, he was heading towards his "last hurrah". Near the end of his four-year term as mayor, he had reneged on an earlier promise to vacate his seat quietly and had decided to run for re-election. But James M. Curley, then a Congressman, had begun to make a decisive move towards the mayoralty. "You are an old man," he told Fitz. "Get your slippers and pipe and stretch out in your hammock and read the *Ladies' Home Journal*." Fitz could not, at only forty-nine, resist the chance for another campaign, but as the primary fight approached, the shrewd and wolfish Curley struck out savagely at his longtime rival. And he took flesh. He announced a brief series of lectures contrasting the mayor and his regime with other personalities and periods in history. The first, "Graft in Ancient times versus Graft in Modern Times", was duly delivered at Rose's alma mater, Dorchester High School. The second was to be called "Great Lovers: From Cleopatra to Toodles". The reference was to Toodles Ryan, a blonde cigarette girl at the Ferncroft Inn, and Fitz indeed knew her—

though quite how well has never been disclosed. His puritanical streak could not allow the lecture to take place, and knowing that even "Sweet Adeline" could not win for him this time, he withdrew from the race before Curley could disclose precisely what he knew about the "Great Lovers" of history. Rose took the rumours of her father's affair as she took those that later trailed her husband and even her sons: she said nothing.

Though Honey Fitz was to be a candidate several more times and remain intensely interested in politics all his life, he never again held an elective public office. He constantly added his inimitable richness to Rose's life and the lives of her children, but his effective influence on her life—and it was deep—by now was virtually complete. More and more now her fortunes were inextricably linked with those of her lanky redheaded husband, so much so that Tillie Gavin, one of the same friends who called her "Father Says", was to say, in Joe Kennedy's last years, "I dread the day he goes out, because it's going to be the first time Rose is going to break." (Rose did not break; she never has.) People were already predicting the day when Honey Fitz would be known as Joe Kennedy's father-in-law, and as for Joe, he had already begun to look upon his jaunty father-in-law as an indulgence he could now afford.

Rose made no effort to persuade her husband to try a political career; she saw that the marketplace, not the stumping platform, was the arena in which his future would be won. The incisive manoeuvres that led to his gaining control of Columbia Trust at a precocious age were emblematic of a career that would exploit to the utmost his capacities for clockwork timing, bold action, long-term planning, and the severest competitive spirit. He could move with decision and with icy and deliberate care, and like his father-in-law in at least this, he could "work harder than anyone else". Rose understood such restless energy, and she admired it. When the banking business proved too slow a route to Joe's goal of becoming a millionaire by thirty-five, he accepted a challenging managerial position at Bethlehem's Fore River shipbuilding yard at Quincy, which became wildly busy just before and then during the years of World War I. He was rarely home now, but he did his job and did it well. He also noticed the need for eating facilities, opened the

Victory Lunchroom, and turned a solid profit by feeding 22,000 workers a day.

Before the end of the war and the inevitable slackening of ship-building activity, he quit Bethlehem and went to work, at half his previous salary, for the brilliant financier Galen Stone, as manager of the Boston branch of Hayden, Stone & Company. Like Franklin Roosevelt and, later, his own son Jack, he had a genius for picking brilliant men to advise and to instruct him, and he learned so much from his mentor that when Stone split with Hayden, Joe struck out on his own and vigorously, quietly, often ruthlessly carved out an immensely successful career—even an empire—as an independent "lone wolf" capitalist, bound to no desk or office, but free and ever acquisitive. Perhaps remembering Honey Fitz's coolness to his prospects and the goading presence of a cool Yankee Boston, he advanced his family with uncanny skill and speed. "He wanted Rose to have everything," says a friend. "He was very determined, and he was going to have her a queen, which she is. And in a way he got what he wanted. He put her above everybody"—just as her father had done.

In 1917 Joe's salary was $10,000 a year; nine years later, when he left Brookline in "grandly defiant style" for Riverdale, New York, he was many times a millionaire and had established trust funds for his children that would perpetuate the Kennedy millions in-definitely. It was all always for Rose and for his children, he insisted. "There is no other success for a father and mother," he was fond of saying, than to feel that they have made "some contribution to the development of their children." Money made it possible.

The first summer of their marriage, Rose and Joe rented a big house on Beach Avenue at Hull, where they entertained their family and friends as Rose's time drew near. Rose would play the piano in the evening, and everyone would join in with such current popular hits as "I Didn't Raise My Boy to Be a Soldier" and "By the Light of the Silvery Moon". It was simple, it was relaxed, and it was gay, and they were extremely happy that summer. But they were never happier than the night of July 25, 1915, when their first son, Joseph Patrick Kennedy Jr., was born in an upstairs bedroom of the big house in Hull. Their delight over their first son was as excessive as Honey Fitz's had been over his first daughter; Joe, Jr., became a virtual Prince of Wales, and from that moment on, motherhood became the most important role in Rose's life.

Along with all the wholesale praise of Rose's role as a mother, there has always been an undercurrent of often unspoken hostility towards her. It surfaced a number of times after Ted's Chappaquiddick incident. She had stressed in a magazine interview that the important thing was to "cope"; *she* had, but many readers doubted that this was what Ted had done. "We've all heard of the iron-willed theatrical mother," one reader wrote in, "who pushes and pushes her kids to the top. Those mothers could all take lessons from Mrs. Rose Kennedy. She never takes 'No' for an answer. No wonder tragedy has stalked the lives of this blighted family." And there were others. *Did* she drive the children too hard? Was she heartless and cold and over-ambitious for them? There were stories filed by leading reporters, which never got printed, that also took a less than rosy view. Yet keen minds and painfully honest men like Arthur Krock, who knew the family well, thought otherwise. "She was a marvellous mother," he said, "calm, serene, reserved, extremely well educated but nothing stuffy about her." Clearly her influence on her children was potent. A friend has said that "when Jack spoke, I would hear his mother's voice." But the influence went even deeper.

Joe was soon rocketing ahead at breakneck speed, but Rose claims she was never aware, specifically, of what he was doing. "My husband," she recalls, "changed jobs so fast that I simply never knew what business he was in." Like her father, he would also be away from home for long periods of time—travelling more and more frequently to New York and, later, Hollywood. He rarely consulted Rose on business decisions of any kind, but when he did, he usually took her advice. When he became involved with the Film Booking Office, he said to her: "I feel sure I can take this thing and make a go of it."

"Why not?" she asked him.

"I don't like the business. Motion pictures are not my idea of a sound and progressive career."

But Rose had been trained by a father who took chances. "All the more reason that you should get into them," she said. And he did.

Though she had ample help, it was not entirely easy for her after Joe, Jr., was born; the Kennedy children began to arrive every year or so with such regularity that, as a friend says, "she had the doctors crazy, she had her babies so fast." In future campaigns, Rose was to remark: "I don't drink, I don't smoke, but I have lots of children." Four of them were born while they lived on Beals Street—all but Joe, Jr., in a second-floor bedroom, in a bed near the window, "to give the doctor plenty of light": John on May 29, 1917; Rosemary in 1919; and Kathleen—whom the family called Kick—a year later. Eunice, Patricia, and Robert were born after they moved to a more elegant twelve-room house on the corner of Naples Road and Abbotsford, a short walk from Beals Street; Jean and then Edward, her last child, were born in New York.

Several years after they married, Joe came home with the family's first car. It was a small shiny-black Model T Ford, and both Joe and Rose were extraordinarily elated by the event. Joe, impetuous as always, insisted on taking Rose for a ride immediately, and they both got in and lurched off to near disaster. The car careered through a red light and crashed through a road repair area into the next street. Rose was injured—and the Ford was ruined.

Joe hired a nurse named Kikoo Convoy (who spoke with an Irish brogue and still believed in leprechauns and elves) and an all-purpose live-in maid; they cost him $12 and $7 a week, respectively. He came home whenever he could, and when he did, he spent as much time playing with the children as possible; he liked to sit in the living room reading the Boston *Transcript* in the evenings or singing with the children while Rose played the piano. She loved to sit down at the piano, play popular songs, and have children or friends join in with the words.

Though Rose continued her social engagements in Boston, at the Ace of Clubs and other civic and social groups, she made no engagements after five in the evening—"that's the time that coughs start and the time the maids are apt to be tired"—and she would help the children with their homework, prod them like a catechism instructor to do better, and listen to all they had done that day. She was extremely organized and began to incorporate into their lives that order for which she would be noted all her life. "You have to work hard at everything in this life," she later said, "do you not —whether it is your marriage, your cooking, your children, or your face." She viewed her role as mother in subtle but decisive terms, no doubt remembering Mother Barat's thoughts on the rearing of children. "You have to tend to the roots," Rose later said, "as well as the stems, and slowly and carefully plant ideas and concepts of right and wrong, religion and social implications and applications." Every morning she would attend early-morning mass at St. Aidan's Roman Catholic Church, where the children were baptized and where young Joe and Jack served as altar boys. Every evening she would tell or read the children stories, from Biblical parables and tales to *King Arthur and His Knights*. James Fenimore Cooper was a great favourite, and Jack read Thornton Burgess' nature stories religiously in a Boston newspaper; he especially liked Burgess' *The Adventures of Reddy Fox* and later invited the author to the White House. One day Josie brought over a book called *Billy Whiskers*, which Rose calls "just an adventure book of a goat ... very, very poorly illustrated. The colours were very brash and very flamboyant." But Jack adored it. One day he asked his mother where the Sandwich Islands were. She didn't know but she said she would look—and then did. After some difficulty she learned that they were now called Hawaii, told Jack, and asked if he was studying about them in school. He said no; that was where Billy Whiskers had stopped on his way across the Pacific.

It was not always easy for a woman who had lived so social and lively a life, but she puritanically took it to be her duty. Jack had trouble eating when he was an infant; then he contracted scarlet fever; he was always ill, and the children were always bruised or battered. The daily routine she had established in the home could have been lethal to Rose, even with help. "It was monotonous for me to tell bedtime stories for twenty years, but I did so." When the weather was pleasant, she wheeled the smallest child in a carriage while two or three others "toddled along" with her. For Saturday dinner there were usually baked beans served from the big bean pot, and then the beans were warmed over and served again for Sunday breakfast. Even when he was spending much of his time in New York, Joe would return on weekends. Marie and Vin Greene or another close couple would come over and then walk with the Kennedys around the Chestnut Hill Reservoir, or play bridge on Friday night, or perhaps have dinner together on Sunday. "Rose and I played with great seriousness," says Marie Greene of the bridge games, "showing our hand and bidding up." The men were more cautious. They would wait patiently, then double and usually set the women. Afterwards Joe ordered ice cream from

Murray's on Boylston Street, and after it had been delivered in a cab, they'd all sit around eating it with great delight. "It was simple living," said Marie, "but full of happiness."

On Saturday nights Joe and Rose would attend the symphony in Boston; music was one of Joe Kennedy's little-publicized loves, a deep love he had acquired at Harvard, and he and Rose were devoted patrons during the Brookline years. Often on Sundays the family would pile into the Model T and drive ten miles to Winthrop to visit the Kennedy in-laws.

Rose's precepts of motherhood were simple, direct, and sometimes eloquent. "Whenever I held my newborn baby in my arms," she says, "I used to think that what I said and did to him could have influence not only on him but on all whom he met, not only for a day or a month or a year, but for all eternity—a very, very challenging and exciting thought for a mother." She was a natural and determined teacher, who led the children by discovery, by story, by inspiration, by example, and by hard work; she had been a superior catechism instructor in the North End.

"Children," in her view, "should be stimulated by their parents to see, and touch, and know, and understand, and appreciate." She never preached or lectured to them about politics or art or religion but engaged them in conversation about these subjects, told them vivid stories, took them to Bunker Hill and Concord and Plymouth Rock. She did not let them merely listen, but drew them out. "When she would teach you something," says Mary Jo Clasby, who spent her summers with the Kennedys and was virtually reared by them after the deaths of Agnes and Joe Gargan, "you would have to do it by yourself. She wouldn't do it for you and then have this pleasant, pretty thing happen. She really would want you to do it yourself, to find out that you can do it."

Religion, of course, was a central part of their life—a living presence and an important aspect of the children's education. "This woman's family," said a friend much later, "has arrived at its present point of distinction on Rose Kennedy's spiritual coattails." None of the children developed what Eunice has called the "burning faith similar to that of the great martyrs," which Rose possesses, but religion was a rock for them all. Even when the children were infants, Rose tried to take them to church every day, for a visit, so that they would "form a habit of making God and religion part of their daily lives, not something to be reserved for Sundays." She knew the value of repetition, the value of what is dramatic and concrete, so she always tried to key the discussions to what was immediate and present. On Christmas she discussed Bethlehem, then and now; on Thanksgiving, what the Pilgrims ate in 1620 and what was set before them then. After Sunday mass, when they all were seated at the dinner table, she would ask the children what colour vestments the priest wore and what the true message of the sermon had been. At Easter she talked to them about "what a wonderful miracle the Resurrection was", and after they had talked about the early Christians who were martyred in the arenas of Rome, when they went to the zoo she would be sure to point out to the children the lions. (Is there something almost frighteningly purposeful and grim in Rose's comment that "nothing trivial was ever discussed at the table"?) One Easter story, concerning Christ's entrance into Jerusalem on a donkey, the Crucifixion, entombment, and Resurrection, prompted the query from quick-witted little Jack: "Mother, we know what happened to Jesus Christ, but what happened to the donkey?" Religion, said Rose, gave the children "a sense of responsibility and a sense of security. They knew exactly what they were expected to do and tried to do it for the most part, and the confidence, I think, of stability, which some children do not have and which older people do not always have, and I always told them that if they were given faith when they were young, they should try to nurture it and guard it because it's really a gift that older people valued so much when sorrow came or difficulty came."

She also encouraged them in the social graces and in athletics. When they were still quite young, all the children regularly attended dancing classes and took lessons in tennis and golf. Rose and Marie Greene would take the boys skating on a nearby flooded field, and all the children played lots of baseball and football, tennis and golf; they were taught to ski and to swim, and later all the Kennedys were to take a keen interest in sailing—except for Rose, who showed little interest even in the special jargon of sailing and in later years rarely even went out on the family yacht.

Competition was always encouraged, not only by Joe but also by Honey Fitz's daughter. "We would try to instill into them the idea that no matter what you did, you should try to be first," says

Rose. A sharp rivalry developed between the oldest boys, who vied with each other throughout their teens and into their early twenties; they once rammed into each other on bicycles, because neither would yield. Rose insists: "The competition between the two boys was very good, as it is good for any children. . . ." She believed in having a full programme planned for them, especially during holidays, and this usually included competitive activities: "They raced against one another and as a family team against others on foot, in swimming, and in boats during the summer."

Business was Joe's department; "hot water" was hers. But she knew that discipline would not work if she had not first gained her children's respect in her judgment. "You always take the time to explain why you take a certain action," she says. "You explain your attitude, and you make it clear. This applies to big things; it applies as well to small things." One morning Kathleen decided she needed a new book bag for school and announced this to the family. Her older brother Joe was not convinced. "She doesn't need a new schoolbag," he told his mother. Kathleen thought she did, and a lively argument took place for a few moments until Rose said sharply: "Joe, you go upstairs and—"

"Mind my own business?"

Yes, insisted Rose. That's what he should do. And she also insisted that he write it out: "A hundred times—'I must mind my own business'."

Rose also believes that "physical punishment is rather a good thing. I used to have a ruler around and paddle them occasionally because when they are young that's all they understand." But when they grew older, she and Joe rarely had to raise their voices to have discipline enforced, their instructions followed. They had a natural authority. Joe would "pull down his horn-rimmed glasses" and look down the table, says Mary Jo Clasby, and Rose would say, "Now dear, that is not to be done," in such a way that it was not done. Bicycles had to be brought in; obligations had to be met. Lunch was served promptly at one, dinner at seven fifteen; the late child had to start with the course then being served (though Jack, a frequent offender, would take the last spoonful of dessert that was left and could then usually charm a whole meal out of the cook later).

Rose instilled the idea that if you worked hard at something, you could do it—that everything involves hard work and that there is no easy way out. She gave the children the confidence to feel that they could do whatever they wanted to do or set out to do—by hard work. Even when they had a chauffeur, the boys had to fix their own bicycles, and they had to earn the money they received, which was always sparingly dispensed. They were brought up with the idea "that brains and talent and money should not be treated lightly", but that these "advantages" imposed obligations and responsibilities. She always preferred the word "advantages" to "money" or "wealth".

Slender, dark-haired, and perpetually so youthful in appearance that she was often taken to be her children's older sister, Rose yet maintained incisive control over her household, managing the increasingly difficult logistical problems of a large family with the skill of a trained executive. She is notorious for the careful records she began to keep of all the children, in the sewing room off the master bedroom on the second floor. One of her famous index cards —which were later trotted out with great frequency during her campaigning years—in part reads:

> JOHN FITZGERALD KENNEDY
> born Brookline, Mass. (83 Beals Street) May 29, 1917
> Has had whooping cough, measles—chicken pox
> Had scarlet fever—February 20—1920
> At City Hospital, Boston—with Dr. Hill—Dr. Rearden
>   took care of ear
> German measles 1928
> Schick test 1928
> Bronchitis occasionally

Other invaluable information on the cards—which she claims were not "American efficiency" but "Kennedy desperation"—included day-by-day and then month-by-month weight counts for the younger children, shoe sizes, dental treatment, eye examinations, even which side for the mumps—in fact, everything but the state of their souls, which Rose Kennedy was tending herself with the greatest care and which required no index cards as records. She was extremely careful of their health, right down to keeping a hot-water bottle in the children's carriages to keep the babies' feet warm;

she recommends this to her daughters and daughters-in-law and also sends on warm underwear regularly. All the Kennedy children had their teeth straightened ... and straightened; it seemed to go on for years. And Rose was extremely careful about what food the children ate, which goes a long way towards explaining her own excellent health and unbelievable figure. To this day she will go into the kitchen to check the food her grandchildren and grand-nieces and nephews eat, she will weigh and measure her own food, and she will even bring her own food to certain events—including a roast beef sandwich to at least one wake.

Her own principle of being an example for all the children was handed down to the older Kennedys. She tried to bring them up "older children so they do things in a good way, and give them a lot of attention", since the younger ones are "great imitators and will follow the older ones' example". When one of the girls was wearing too much lipstick, she spoke to Jack about it, telling him to suggest to her that he thought it was too much. Coming from him, it would mean more. Did he do so? "Well, he had a few words to say, too," says Rose, "about all of them."

The Kennedys never became replicas of one another, though. In fact, one of the most interesting paradoxes in the family has been their famous sense of togetherness, their image of being a "self-contained unit", coupled with an independence of spirit. Mary Jo Clasby speaks of how Joe and Rose were able to create a "magic" in the family—"the whole range in ages could find a lot of pleasure together"—but they were also competitive with each other and went their separate ways: in their teens and twenties, all might go from Washington to New York on different trains, go their separate ways in the city, stay at different hotels, and then contact one another for a dinner or party.

When they were little, Rose divided the front porch on Naples Road into cubicles with accordion barriers so that the children would have room to play but would not "knock each other down and gouge each other in the eyes with blunt toys". She strove to give each a sense of independence and privateness by, whenever possible, letting them have their own rooms, their own toys, their own belongings. Though she could put the same colour bathing caps on them all (so a nurse could easily spot a Kennedy child in the sea) and dress them in similar clothes (so there wouldn't be jealousy and quarrels), she did not want the children to be the same and encouraged each according to his special talents. "If one child excelled in athletics, we would try to encourage another to excel in some form of literature, or music, or other activity."

The young children, up to six, would eat an hour early, with Rose in attendance; the older ones would sit down to dinner with their parents. Everyone who ever sat at a Kennedy family dinner marvels at the degree to which the children, from the earliest age, were brought vigorously into the discussions. Interesting people, like Irving Berlin and Harold Laski, were brought home so that the children could meet, hear, and talk to them. And each child, as he grew old enough, was encouraged to keep a private diary, in which he recorded interesting impressions and thoughts.

Was it all too mechanical, too planned and programmed? Was there no heart or irreverence or stillness in it all? Eunice says: "We were computerized at an early age, but fortunately by a very compassionate computer."

The boys were developing strong and defined personalities. From the time Joe, Jr., had been inadvertently dropped out of a home-made box sled one morning at Poland Springs, while his father was intently talking to Eddie Moore (his private secretary and close friend) and was later found content in a snow-bank, their oldest son showed every sign of vigour and good cheer. He "threw his heart and soul and every ounce of energy" into any job at hand, say the Moores, and often helped his mother push a younger child in the carriage. When he was five, he entered the local public school, Edward Devotion, which Jack also attended, and then in 1924 they both were registered in the small and exclusive Noble and Greenough School on St. Paul Street, where "Kennedy was the only Irish name on the rolls". When they weren't fighting each other, they made a tough athletic combination. Joe became a fastball pitcher of some skill, and Jack, despite his size, had to hang in with all his courage to catch him—but he usually did. The boys were also disarmingly frank. When Margaret Ambrose came to work as their cook, Joe, Jr., and Jack looked her over carefully and then asked bluntly: "Can you make fudge?"

"Sure I can," she said, smiling. "I love to make fudge."

"Okay," said Joe, and Jack nodded his approval. They were satisfied.

Rosemary was one of the best-looking in a family of extremely handsome children. But she had less of the Kennedy will to excel. A sweet and gentle girl, she was slower learning to crawl and then had difficulty learning to walk. She could not write or read as easily as her brothers. She also entered Edward Devotion School, but at the end of the first year her parents were told that she would not be promoted into the first grade. She repeated kindergarten and this time earned a C, but Rose knew that something was wrong; for a woman who had herself been so skilled and so successful all her life, her first daughter's problems were extremely difficult to accept. Though the other children kept her as close a part of the family group as they could, treating her only more carefully and gently, it was soon obvious that she was different. She couldn't stay on a sled like the others; she couldn't balance herself on a bicycle or throw a ball with ease. During the summer the other children went out in boats alone; she couldn't. Rosemary could not understand why she had to be left behind or why, at dancing school, she was neglected. "Mother," she said, "the boys danced with Eunice and Mary and Jean, but not with me." Frequently she had unexplained tantrums. But they trained her in good behaviour, and Rose taught her not to complain—a trait more suited to her own strong tempera-ment. Once at a summer camp Rosemary is reported to have worn shoes that did not fit so long without complaining that her feet bled before the problem was discovered. Rose and Joe very much wanted to keep Rosemary as part of the family, but they also wanted her to appear normal to outsiders—and trained her to do so. Not until 1960—after Jack had won the Democratic Presidential nomination —did Joe speak publicly and honestly about his daughter.

"I went first to the family physician," Rose recalled recently, more than fifty years later but still with pain, "then to two psychologists at Harvard, and then to a Catholic priest who was in Washington— and to every source they suggested." But it was too early: there was inadequate knowledge then, and too much social stigma, especially for the Kennedys. They had a nurse and a tutor for Rosemary, but this didn't help. Even after she *knew*, Rose had difficulty talking about her oldest daughter and did not fully acknowledge the facts for decades: her firstborn daughter was retarded. In speaking of it in recent years, Rose often points out that she had six healthy children afterwards. She still thinks it important to stress that the problem was not in her genes.

Sadly, Rose watched Honey Fitz's political woes continue with losses to Senator Henry Cabot Lodge in 1916—in a family rivalry that would continue for nearly forty years; a win against Peter Tague in 1918—as Congressman for the Tenth District—for which he was disqualified for ballot stuffing, fraud, and illegal registration in some precincts; and then a humiliating defeat for the governorship in 1922. But he grew increasingly popular with his grandchildren: they enjoyed campaigning with him in 1922, going to the zoo and ball parks with him, and listening to his endless stories about the dear old North End, his days as Congressman and mayor, and the tough road of ward politics. They enjoyed visiting him at the Bellevue Hotel and must have noticed the curious similarity of all their mother's notes to herself and to them—pinned on her clothes and on pillows and everywhere—and the incredible number of notes and political clippings that Honey Fitz had all over his room, pinned up and down the curtains. They remembered all their lives how, in his last campaign, he got up proudly and sang "Sweet Adeline". Joe, Jr., was always deeply devoted to "The Greatest Mayor Boston Ever Had", and much later, while at Harvard, he once ordered a close friend from his room after a mild gibe at corruption in Boston politics. Another grandchild named his Presidential powerboat *Honey Fitz*.

By the time they moved to Naples Road the Kennedys were a wealthy family, with governesses and cooks and an air of sweet success and independence that they wore with increasing ease. A chauffeur became a regular member of their entourage, and they would always thereafter employ one or more. For a time they had a very British chauffeur named Paris, and Marie Greene tells the story of Rose's concern that her canaries weren't singing. Marie told her: "You know, Rose, I read that they have a seed, you know, that you give canaries to make them sing." Rose, who more and more had become an administrator who delegated domestic chores to her employees, sent Paris to the drugstore to buy some of that special seed. The druggist greeted him with the abrupt question "Would you like them to dance, too?"—and Paris almost quit.

"Rose would try anything like that," says Marie. "She wasn't gullible. Anything she asked you, if she asked you a question—and I had a habit if I was sure she didn't know the answer, of making it up—she'd go right home and check it with Joe. Then I'd either be right or wrong, and she'd be glad to tell me which I was, I must tell you"—a human characterization, somewhat at odds with the popular concept of Rose as a pious figure, "running to church all the time".

It is from a few close friends like Marie Greene that the more intimate and frank portrait of Rose Kennedy and her family emerges, for there is an unavoidably preplanned quality about the public Rose Kennedy, and she is chiefly seen in that public role or in the carefully honed images of her family life that she used in campaign speeches.

As the family grew larger, Rose often had trouble keeping the children entertained in Brookline, and a number of times she relied on Marie Greene to help out. "Would you mind if I send a couple of the girls up for supper?" she'd say. Apparently life was not the same at the Greenes' as the Kennedys'. One night Marie didn't have any vegetables in the house, so she ran down to the corner to pick up some asparagus. "Well, it was the last bunch of asparagus," she says, "and I tell you, it was thin asparagus. So Kathleen and Eunice came up ... and they were very interested in the fact that I did not have a bedroom to myself, that I slept in the room with my husband, you know; they thought that was very odd." They sat down for dinner, and Kick said: "Oh, my goodness, I've never seen asparagus as thin as this." And then Eunice said: "Well, it isn't *too* bad, of course; it isn't too good, but it isn't too bad."

Once Marie was asked to take Rosemary home for dinner. She did so, sitting with Paris in the front of the Kennedys' new Rolls-Royce, suddenly she noticed that everybody was turning around giving her "the dirtiest looks". She wondered whether they didn't like the Rolls-Royce, but when she turned around, she saw that it was Rosemary, "kneeling up in the back seat and sticking out her tongue at everybody."

Marie says: "Rosie knows I shoot from the hip. I've never taken Rosie seriously, and I think this is probably the reason we've always been so close." (To this day Marie is ebullient and frank, and uninhibited; she will answer her phone at eleven in the evening with "Poolroom Kelly's", and she is one of the few friends with whom Rose can truly have fun.) "It's also, come to think of it," she continues, "the reason her mother never liked me."

Another friend, whom Josie did like, says, "I scribble a little bit. I have since high school days, and I have yet to find words to describe that girl [Rose]. It is utterly impossible to describe her. ... Only God can make a tree, and only God can make a woman like Rose Kennedy."*

Despite Joe's far-flung business dealings, Rose had for many years resisted the temptation to follow him with the family and relocate their home. She loved Boston and her roots, and she wanted more than anything for the children to have a regular and ordered home; she wanted them to keep their friends and the familiar neighbour-hood and remain at their schools. This was not to be. Before they finished their education, Bobby attended twelve schools, Ted ten; and the others at least a half dozen each.

But Joe's life was becoming more and more centred on Wall Street. The family had spent their last few summers at Cohasset, and then the tug of New York was coupled by a nasty blackball when Joe tried to join the exclusive Cohasset Country Club; he had not made the best Protestant clubs at Harvard, and social rejection still dogged him. He decided it was finally time to leave Boston and take his family elsewhere. He had fought the Boston Brahmin, and in many ways he had won. But in the spring of 1926 he put his entire family on an extravagant private railroad car and headed for a newer and freer world—Riverdale.

As Rose looked out of the window on the trip she'd often taken with her father when she was a girl, she realized that Boston had been her whole life—its people, its politics, its Irish Catholic clubs. Though she loved to travel, she also loved roots—and hers were deep in New England soil. This was the first time she was leaving Boston when she did not know precisely when she would return.

---

* On hearing this, Marie Greene told the author: "If you use that, I will not only throw up, but you will shatter my confidence in judging people forever!"

Chapter Six

Hyannis Port

Our family would rather be in Hyannis Port in
the summer than any place else in the world. After
a "get-acquainted" period of twenty-six years, Cape
Cod is very close to the Kennedy family's heart.
— ROSE KENNEDY, 1952

The white three-gabled house in Hyannis Port is large and rambling, with wide porches and broad vistas. It is a kind of flagship
perched on a large green bluff at the end of Scudder Avenue,
dominating a tennis court, surrounded by well-tended lawns that
slope gently off into wild dune grass, a lonely stretch of beach
that Rose has always walked in times of tragedy, and icy salt water
that even in August can turn limbs blue. Today it stands with the
permanence of a monument, and all summer long sight-seeing
launches crammed with tourists and their Instamatic cameras chug
by at intervals as irregular but never-ending as the New York City
subways, hoping to catch a glimpse of Rose, Jackie, Ethel, a
Kennedy child—anyone at all out water-skiing or swimming or
doing some legendary Kennedy feat they can remember all their
lives. More often than not, they point to the wrong house—the
elegant McElvey mansion, which is next door to the Kennedys.

Joe and Rose first took their family to Hyannis Port in the summer of 1926, shortly after their exodus from Boston to Riverdale,
when it was the "Malcolm Place". Two years later it became the
"Kennedy place", although it would never be known as that, but
always the "Big House"; for Rose and Joe and all their children,
it would simply be home. The salt air and crisp breeze refreshed
their minds and made them stronger; the ocean and sweeping
lawns gave them space to swim and sail and play touch football—
to develop their bodies and their capacities for rugged competition.
They went to Hyannis Port for fun and for renewal—and found

it there. Rose also found solitude, and was able to see her friends
and relatives from Boston more easily; she watched her children
grow strong and vigorous at Hyannis Port, and ironically, she was
there when they died. Hyannis Port was the place, wherever else
she might live, that retained for her her New England roots; it is
also a place curiously mingled with all her sorrows.

Rose knew that Joe would never go back to Brahmin Cohasset,
where he had been humiliated the year before, and by the mid-
twenties Cape Cod was already fashionable enough to satisfy her
social needs and ideally situated for the family to indulge its love
of water sports; if even here they were to be "Irish newcomers"
(twenty-five years later a seventy-year resident called Joe a "Johnny-
come-lately"), Hyannis Port was sufficiently mixed in its summer
and resident populations to accept Catholics without undue display.
But most of all, Rose wanted her children to have the sea—and
New England.

Promoters and developers were working overtime in the mid-
twenties to convert the once-isolated and idyllic Cape into a massive
resort, and their inveterate "boosterism" was already taking effect
when Rose and her family first arrived: thousands upon thousands
of cars swarmed out along the white-grey highways every day of
the summer, bringing hot vacationers to try the exquisite beaches
and fine sailing seas, as well as a host of special attractions—strawberry festivals, clambakes, quilting pageants, circuses, summer
theatres, and softball games. As puritanical about having fun as
about working, Rose saw to it that the family tried them all, adding
blueberry picking, picnics, and much else.

In 1926 land was already scarce, and most newcomers chose to
buy an older house and then renovate it to suit their personal needs.
Rose later observed that the Kennedys never built a home of their
own; for vacations they always preferred a place with direct access
to the sea, and these were always built up already. After renting the
"Malcolm Place" for several summers, Joe and Rose saw that they
could do no better on the booming Cape and purchased the place
for about $25,000. The house was already more than twenty-five
years old and not nearly large enough for their still-burgeoning
family, so they had it remodelled by its original architect, L. Frank
Paine, and with additions it was made into a comfortable fifteen-
room nine-bath home. Rose furnished it with early American furni-

ture and later added some eighteenth-century English pieces from the Riverdale home; she put Currier & Ives prints on the walls, some English prints by Morland, and, later, a Grandma Moses, and she had a large glass-panelled display case built for her permanent collection of more than 200 dolls, of every kind and variety, from all over the world. She furnished the large family dining room handsomely with a fruitwood table and an elegant antique sideboard. The house became comfortable, not stylish, durable and to-be-enjoyed, not cold and elegant; it remains a mixture of several styles, not quite unified. Rose always wanted it to be a house that could be *lived* in, and she gave the children ready access to every room in the place.

During the year Rose scattered her children throughout carefully selected New England schools, Joe Kennedy vigorously pursued still more movie millions, and the family, while living in Riverdale and then Bronxville, was often separated. At Hyannis Port, they were together. Here they built the selfcontained strength for which they are famous. They grew to know one another intimately, to compete with one another to the last breath, to depend on one another. Jack could even call the summer of 1929 the summer he "met" Bobby Kennedy—though his younger brother was by then nearly four. Far more than their Palm Beach home or their rented villa at Cap d'Antibes or any other home, Hyannis Port became the family seat.

Their sense of unity is seen in everything they did, from the way Rose made the older children godparents for the younger ones to the way the younger ones served as crew on their big brothers' boats. "We decided that our children were going to be our best friends and that we never could see too much of them," says Rose. "The Kennedys are a self-contained unit. If any of us wants to sail or play golf or go walking or just talk, there's always a Kennedy to join in." For years they had a family Wianno Class sailboat named *Tenovus*, but after Ted's birth in 1932, they bought another and promptly called it *Onemore*. Local people still remember the hilarious sight of Joe driving his 1928 Chevy to the beach, jammed full of the family, with arms and legs hanging out all over the place, and the sight of the big boisterous family squeezed into the big Rolls-Royce touring car on its way to Wequaquet Lake for freshwater swimming.

There were intimate and joyous birthday parties for Rose in July and for Joe in early September on the Cape, a gala fortieth wedding anniversary for Honey Fitz and Josie, and they established a family tradition of holding large dinners on the Cape as late in the year as Thanksgiving. Today Rose remembers the days when "the children filled the air with their laughter, their games of charades, their tennis and golf matches, and their debates". It is quieter now.

Life on the Cape was warm, vigorous, highly competitive, and informal, though Rose saw that certain rituals were maintained. She eventually had electric clocks put in every room—"I insist on this because then no one has an excuse for being late to meals." She says: "Promptness at lunch and dinner time is absolutely essential in a big family. We have always been very strict about this in our family. We lunch at one fifteen and dine at seven thirty." Rose planned the menus, and the food was sturdy New England fare, with clam chowder a favourite and ice cream the best dessert. Rich and fancy sauces were taboo, and Rose saw to it that the children drank enormous amounts of milk; with her own portion included and all the children home, twenty quarts a day was not uncommon. Picnic suppers were frequent.

The older boys usually rose about seven and did calisthenics with a batch of local friends on the broad front lawn or on the beach; for many years they had a full-time physical education instructor in residence to help the boys. The children, like their parents, rarely went to bed late and always woke early. There was a governess, Alice Cahill, for the older children and a nurse for the younger ones; the little ones were not allowed to ride their bikes off the property boundaries, and the older kids had to be home by dusk. Curfew was at nine or ten o'clock, depending on a child's age, and Mary Jo Clasby says: "If we weren't home, she'd be out in the car, a blue coupe in our day, and she could hardly see over the steering wheel because she was so short, but you would know that it was her coming, you knew when you saw this car coming up the road." Rose has said that "general tidiness" was never overemphasized, and in fact, the children often left their wet towels on the floors and had difficulty remembering to pick up their clothes. The family atmosphere was something like "organized confusion", says Rose, but "everybody was supposed to have something to contribute; otherwise you weren't in it, you were a bore."

To keep her control in the midst of all this "organized confusion", Rose resorted more and more to writing notes to herself like: "Tell cook to look up recipe on page 86", "tell gardener the petunias need water in the front of the house". A niece says: "You'd always see her with at least one piece of paper; they're never neat—they're torn-off corners." She pinned them to her clothes and to any convenient piece of cloth. People began to give her pens that pinned on to a suit or blouse, so she could pull it down and write at any time. She received scores of them over the years.

Sometimes a note wasn't enough; she'd need another servant, on a full-time basis or for some special occasion. Then Rose would drive to Boston herself to hire one. At the agency she'd say she had five girls. But then, while she was driving the new maid or waitress to Hyannis Port—when she was about halfway there—she'd casually mention that she also had four boys. She sometimes went even further to cushion the shock. Once when she had just hired a new waitress, she made sure that one boy came to the first meal alone, then another, and then, somewhat later, still another. She had no desire to frighten a servant off.

Rose's summer philosophy included continuing efforts to improve the children in mind and body and also to keep them busy. "If you are doing anything," said Rose, "you are just left in a corner." She made special lists of books for each of the children (and saw that reading lamps were placed all over the house to encourage reading); she saw to it that regular attention was paid to current events. Joe encouraged the children to swim and to play tennis and to sail, and there was usually a barefoot softball game every Fourth of July and a touch football game after Thanksgiving dinner. He demanded that his children "win, win, win"; as early as six or seven, the girls too were urged on, and Eunice remembers being told that "coming in second was just no good".

Rose was especially adept at finding fruitful chores and projects when the children got restless, or in poor weather. Busyness and activity held her father together and would always hold her together; she instilled these qualities in her family. Activity and prayer—these and her own solidity are what enabled her to keep her balance and to keep family balance and endurance in the often difficult coming years. There was something severely puritanical about her demands for activity, activity, but she also tried to keep vitality, even joy in the forefront.

One rainy day, young Joe, for want of something to do, was giving the whole family a good deal of trouble. Rose told him to go out and get enough scallops for the whole family; she promised to pay him for them. Joe went out to the low-lying sandy spit of a shore, and by the time he had dug enough scallops for ten to twelve people and got them out of their shells, the day was about up and he was tired and content. That's the problem with youth, Rose insists; "so many of them haven't got enough to do, and that's why they get into so much trouble."

Some projects were less successful. One summer she thought it would be instructive and fun for the children to learn just how long it took to pick a full quart of blueberries. They were plentiful on the Cape in those days, and when Rose started out with a group of children, they were full of confidence and high spirits. One by one the berries came off the low bushes and plinked into the tin pail they'd bought. But they had scarcely covered the bottom of the pail when the expedition collapsed. Eunice got stung by a bee, and Jack sat on an anthill. And before long, ants were crawling all over him. "Everyone became rather nervous even at the sight of a butterfly," remembers Rose, so, reluctantly, she packed them all back into the family station wagon and returned to the Big House—stopping to buy a couple of quarts of blueberries in the country store on the way back.

Her continued efforts to make the children tidier and more reliable were doomed to failure. Kick's job would be to cut flowers, but she'd forget to put water in the vase so that by mealtime the flowers would be dead. None of the children could learn to pick up their clothes regularly. There seemed too much hovering excitement about their lives to pay their mother's attention to detail.

Rose valued the large veranda that faced out over the blue-grey sea, where the children could play on rainy days, out of the house, and where they could "get used to damp and cold air". Usually the children had no difficulty entertaining themselves. They loved Monopoly and Twenty Questions and were popular with hosts of other children. On a rainy Saturday the children often went to the local Idlehours Theatre, an event followed by ice cream at the Cape Code Creamery on Sea Street. Joe had an elaborate motion-picture theatre built in the children's playroom in the basement—the first "talkie" privately installed in New England—and home movies in the twenty-seven-seat private theatre, with its wide screen and soft seats, helped enliven the evenings, along with family singing—with Rose at the piano. She would invite someone to choose any song he thought of and then play it by ear while the others sang. Often she went over to the club to watch the children dance, and then the next day she invariably had a comment: "Now, dear, really you'd look much better if you danced this way and not that way."

Sailing dominated the children's summers. From the beginning the boys loved to sail. Joe recalled that his two oldest boys "were out in sailboats alone here in Hyannis Port when they were so small you couldn't see their heads. It looked from shore as if the boats were empty". Their first boat was christened the *Rose Elizabeth*, and Joe, Jr., and Jack spent countless hours tinkering with it and learning to sail it with consummate skill and winning speed. In 1927, when they were only twelve and ten, they were already winning local races, and once, spotting an overturned boat from their veranda, they raced out and effected what the Boston *Post* called a "daring rescue"; Honey Fitz had filed the story.

They were all, except for Rose, avid sailors, and the ritual of sailing drew them closer. Though Rosemary could not captain a boat, they let her serve as crew; Jack, then Bobby, and then Ted were responsible for rigging an older brother's boat first thing every morning. When Ted was seven, he begged to race with his oldest brother. Joe let him, but when, in the first race, he told Teddy to pull the jib, Ted had no idea what he was talking about. Joe asked again; then he leaped up, grabbed the jib, and then seized Teddy by the seat of his pants and threw him into the sea. Teddy was scared to death, but Joe leaped in, rescued him, got his boat in second, and then whispered severely to Ted that he should tell no one, ever, what had happened.

Rose was never easily pacified after such horseplay. When the older boys left Kathleen stranded on a rock and didn't come back for more than two hours, she was furious. For years, she told each girl, "Now be careful, dear," before they took any trip with the boys.

The children entered every available swimming competition—which often saw a half dozen Kennedys in different age pairings

—at West Beach Club; for years they were leaders in the sailing events. They developed a reputation for being determined and daring competitors and even at moments brought a religious devotion to the task (Eunice once said before a race: "All right, now: everyone say a Hail Mary"). Once they were called to account for carrying too full a sail, and to the reputation of being "graceless losers" was added the constant innuendo that they would do anything to win; neither reputation ever quite left the Kennedy children at Hyannis Port. The races were always hotly contested, to be followed, when they were over, by frequent unbridled releases of tension. After the Edgartown Regatta in 1935, the boys hosted a rather wild party at a local hotel, got much too rowdy and boisterous, and later had to spend a long night in Edgartown's small, cramped jail.

Rose disliked all forms of boating and held to this idiosyncrasy, as she did her others—a dislike of dogs, an indifference to the horses her father and husband liked so much—all her life, despite the urgings of her family. She remained always her own woman. Joe, not long before his stroke, still had to ask her: "Why don't you just try it?" And Rose, reluctantly, went down to the pier with him, boarded a Kennedy powerboat, left the docks with it, and then, at the breakwater insisted that the captain let her out. Which he did.

Honey Fitz was a frequent—and popular—summer visitor at Hyannis Port. He often rented a house in nearby West Hyannis Port, and one of Rose's friends remembers staying with him, being awakened before seven o'clock, and standing groggy-eyed while the aging politician *cum* poet expostulated broadly on the beauties of the sunrise. In 1939, at seventy-six, Fitz was especially active on the Cape. And vocal. A flock of terns began to swoop down on him, and he and Rose began to wear wastepaper and peach baskets on their heads for protection; for Rose, they didn't look much worse than the babushkas she frequently wore while playing golf. But the terns remained pests, and Fitz appealed to Hyannis selectmen for aid. They could only refer him to the local conservation officer, who tried to frighten the birds off by firing blank cartridges in their direction. The birds would soar upward to twenty or thirty feet and then return as soon as the revolver stopped smoking. Stumped, the officer suggested to the state conservation commissioner that the birds be shot, but the commissioner said that his department had no authority to do this since there were firm federal statutes against it. Fitz, undaunted, told local officials that he would appeal directly to the federal government, but there is no evidence that he did so.

That same summer, while Barnstable was celebrating its three hundredth anniversary, Fitz gave a bold address to the Hyannis Rotary Club about the incredibly poor railroad service that had just recently kept him from getting to Fenway Park for the annual Old Timers game. He said sternly that he had already spoken with a representative of the Interstate Commerce Commission about the deplorable situation and then, with a rapid and irresistible switch, ended his speech by leading the local Rotarians in a rousing rendition of his favourite tune.

Rose's brothers and sisters came to the Cape on occasion also, though Joe was often cold to the men. One of her brothers, described by a contemporary as "a classic example of someone taking up space", was conspicuous in his efforts to "rub shoulders" with the Kennedys; he drank too much, and Rose hardly ever imbibed at all, and Joe never went beyond one daiquiri before dinner. Joe "always measured people by their worth", a relative says, which may explain his attitude to Rose's brothers; she, on the other hand, remained warm and not at all condescending to her brothers, who were living in an entirely different world. One, so far as anyone remembers, "died of dissipation in his late twenties", sometime after his wife left a note—and him—saying simply, "Don't be mad at me"; she waited for nearly forty years to remarry because she was so proud of being a Fitzgerald and didn't want her name changed. Another had asked a cousin to put a pint bottle in his coffin when he died, and the relative did.

Among the scores of storied and famous guests whom Rose and Joe invited down to the Cape, none made a greater impression on a Hyannis Port sceptical of the newcomers than the fabled Gloria Swanson. They still remember how that Sikorsky amphibious airplane swooped down and landed on the harbour not far from the Big House and how, when the propellers had stopped, they watched, gaping, as the delicate and elegantly dressed actress came out, waving. There was a tremendous amount of gossip—and still is—about Joe and Gloria Swanson. Joe was for a number of years her banker, intimate adviser, close friend, and frequent companion in New York and California; they became so close that Gloria, the dazzling Queen of Hollywood, named her adopted son Joseph. A close friend of the family confides that Rose and Gloria were actually friends and that their children often played together while the mothers sat nearby talking. Later, when Joe was directing the actress' career and affairs, the three often travelled together in Europe. There were other rumours, of girls in Palm Beach and one woman whom FDR eventually had to advise Joe against seeing further (to which he retorted: "Not until you get rid of Missy Lehand"). "I don't know whether Joe ever went to bed with Gloria or not," the friend observes discreetly, "but I don't think Rose thought so. If she had, I think she would have locked her door."

Over the years the Kennedys developed a regular routine for their life in Hyannis Port, and visitors—thrust abruptly into it—often came away astonished, bewildered, or exhausted. Or all three.

"I suppose," says Rose, "if you're not used to it, a weekend with us can be exhausting. Pooping, I believe, is the word."

In the early summers the whole family was there all week, but as the boys went off to school and Europe and then later into politics, the weekend regimen would begin with arrivals on Friday afternoon. The schedule was rugged. Golf, swimming, sailing— these all began immediately. Friday evening was home-movie night —and still is, for the grandchildren—and Saturday was another round of wildly vigorous athletic events and then, perhaps, another home movie. Though Sunday began peacefully enough with church in the morning, the afternoons were usually dominated by the notorious Kennedy touch football games. Much later, a friend of Jack's recalled that on a day he visited, Honey Fitz was "a-shouting and a-carrying on about the Port of Boston", the younger children were jabbering away about books they had just read, Jack was talking proudly of his recent success with *Why England Slept* and contemplating out loud about a possible future for himself in literature, and there were simultaneous discussions on such subjects as Ingrid Bergman's waistline and the gold standard.

If visitors survived, they were sometimes furious. "Kennedys always tossed the ball to Kennedys," one said. "They never, any one of them, tossed the ball to anyone else." Being cut out was the least of it—and perhaps a distinct advantage. Senator Joe McCarthy, a close friend in the late forties, suffered a cracked rib playing touch football à la Kennedy and once was summarily removed from the lineup during a family softball game after making a humiliating four errors at shortstop. At least they valued the cracked rib. Though Rose abstained, even pregnant daughters and daughters--in-law eventually played in the vigorous touch football games. Rose, for herself, always preferred her sports private—golf or swimming.

One exhausted weekend visitor wrote up a set of "Rules for Visiting the Kennedys":

"Prepare yourself by reading *The Congressional Record, US News & World Report, Time, Newsweek, Fortune, The Nation, How to Play Sneaky Tennis*, and *The Democratic Digest*. Memorize at least three good jokes. Anticipate that each Kennedy will ask you what you think of another Kennedy's (a) dress, (b) hairdo, (c) backhand, (d) latest public achievement. Be sure to answer 'Terrific'. This should get you through dinner. Now for the football field. It's 'touch', but it's murder. If you don't want to play, don't come. If you do come, play, or you'll be fed in the kitchen and nobody will speak to you. Don't let the girls fool you. Even pregnant, they can make you look silly. If Harvard played touch, they'd be on the varsity. Above all, don't suggest any plays, even if you played quarterback at school. The Kennedys have the signal-calling department sewed up, and all of them have A-pluses in leadership. If one of them makes a mistake, keep still. But don't stand still. Run madly on every play and make a lot of noise. Don't appear to be having too much fun, though. They'll accuse you of not taking the game seriously enough.... Don't criticize the other team, either. It's bound to be full of Kennedys too, and the Kennedys don't like that sort of thing. To become really popular, you must show raw guts. To show raw guts, fall on your face now and then. Smash into the house once in a while, going after a pass. Laugh off a twisted ankle or a big hole torn in your best suit. They like this. It shows you take the game as seriously as they do. But remember. Don't be too good." For indeed the Kennedys insisted upon winning; both Rose and Joe had brought them up to insist upon winning. Marie Greene is, of course, a delightful antidote to all this activity and furore over winning. "What's wrong with third or fourth?" she asks.

Was there too much competition? Too much urgency to be first? Did it push the children on to heights they did not really want to achieve? There are, of course, differing views on this. Most of the children thrived on it all. Joe, Jr., had an "astonishing vitality", and he had, in Jack's words, "a sense of motion forcibly restrained". But then there was Rosemary, who increasingly felt intimidated by all the Kennedy will to succeed—and all their very palpable successes. And there is a sadness in Ted's private remark not long ago, "What no one can seem to understand is that I don't *ever* want to be President." Rose, who always encouraged the competition, can be mildly ironic towards this Kennedy passion. After Bobby's tenth child was born, she said: "If I had known this was going to be a contest, I would not have stopped at nine." But there is something deeper in her musing: "Sometimes I wonder if there is something about my family which invites violence."

For herself, Rose grew to love the little clapboard church, St. Francis Xavier, in Hyannis and became a regular communicant, attending early mass every morning; when the children grew older and brought home friends on the weekends, she often met them at the bottom of the stairs and handed each a prayer book before Sunday mass. Bobby showed the most religious promise and knew the mass so well that he could step over the rail at St. Francis Xavier and serve flawlessly as a substitute altar boy when one was needed.

Rose had season tickets to the Cape Playhouse, swam regularly in the sea, and played golf almost every day at the difficult Hyannisport Club, beginning on the back nine and invariably carrying her own clubs. The course is often shrouded in fog and buffeted by stiff breezes; tough, wiry roughs, small greens, narrow fairways bounded by marshes, clumps of low-lying brush, and wiry weeds —all these make it one of the most difficult courses in the East. And the wet breezes coming in off Nantucket Sound shift constantly. But even on foggy or downright rainy days, Rose still, to this day, likes to fix a head scarf on securely, slip on a windbreaker, and shoot her daily short round, oblivious to the elements. She has done so in times of deepest tragedy, playing tautly against the tough course, hitting "not very hard but very straight", playing intently and with great care.

And at Hyannis Port, Rose could even gain a solitude not possible during the year—and which, throughout her life, she has periodically sought. When the children became self-generating and increasingly boisterous, she retreated to a small cottage on a far corner of the property for privacy. When the original and then a second cottage were blown away by hurricanes, she finally bought and had erected a small but firm prefabricated house on the same spot. "It's solitary confinement, not splendour, I need," she said when the little place was put up. It was like a spare little room in the back of the Ritz, where Rose also goes to seek solitude and privacy when in Paris. But the last cottage was also blown down.

Rose, always a great walker, also liked to take long strolls along the kelp-strewn shore; it was always one of the best ways she could find the proper solitude to think. Joe did his meditating while taking long horseback rides near Osterville, and said that this was, for him, like Moses going to the mountaintop to reflect; "the kids nicknamed his horse Mount Sinai", Rose recalls with amusement. But Rose also walked for exercise. "If you lose your figure at thirty-five," she said, "you'll never get it back." She didn't lose it; she never has.

As many of the family as possible always returned to Hyannis Port in the late fall for weekends and for their traditional Thanksgiving Dinner. On turkey Thursday, Rose saw that the big table was carefully set in the ivory-and-gold dining room, with Victorian sterling and Lenox china edged in gold. Joe sat at one end of the table, Rose at the other. There was usually a centrepiece of gourds, a small pumpkin, bright autumn leaves, bananas and apples, and four silver candlesticks. Outside, the weather already might be chill and sharp and overcast, as the benediction was said.

"Bless us, O Lord," Joe would say across the table of bowed heads, "and these Thy gifts we are about to receive from Thy bounty through Christ our Lord. Amen." And then the hot clam broth would be brought in, and the raucous political discussions would start, and perhaps Rose would ask one of the younger children, as she had all their brothers and sisters, what the meaning of Thanksgiving was, why it was celebrated, what the Pilgrims ate, and what was before them. And then the big twenty-six-pound turkey would appear, butter-browned and garnished with bright green parsley, on a silver platter. There was always homemade cranberry sauce, creamed onions, buttered string beans, and mashed orange sweet potatoes with melted marshmallow topping. Rose always planned the meal and saw to it that there were mugs of cider nearby, plenty of corn muffins, dishes of celery and olives, and then a delicious dessert of apple or pumpkin pie and ice cream.

And then after dinner, if the weather wasn't too grim, the children would play touch football on the sweeping lawn or stroll on the beach—and Rose would watch or sit inside beside the blazing fire and quietly read a book.

In later years, other houses (Bobby's and Jack's, on Irving Avenue) were acquired and added to what was to be known the world over as the Kennedy Compound, and by then the original white-gabled house, so fully lived in for so many years, would take on the title the Big House. The Compound would be the family's political base, the hub of their far-flung campaigns and conquests, overrun with news tickers and special long-distance telephone hookups and secret skull sessions with brain-trust advisers and constantly flickering television sets. Secret Service agents and special police and hovering helicopters would become commonplace. Sometimes there seemed to be a reporter behind every bush. Thousands of the curious would queue up at St. Francis Xavier to catch a glimpse of the legendary family going to church, and Rose would have to turn around, peeved, to shush reporters in the back pews; brash tourists, up to a few years ago, would even sneak up to the Big House and walk right on to the large porch and peer into the windows while the family was eating or watching television. To this day, floodlights are turned on Jack's house at dusk, and as the house grows bright, a guard begins his rounds of protecting the place from vandals or souvenir hunters.

For Rose, mingled into her many varied memories of Hyannis Port are a peculiar amalgamation of close and wildly active family days, political triumphs, and shattering tragedies. Over the coming years, so many explosive events—both happy and deeply wounding —were to occur while she was there that the place often seems the focal point of some towering Greek or endless Eugene O'Neill tragedy.

Chapter Seven

Riverdale and Bronxville

*She says she couldn't sleep at night if she couldn't
write down the things that she thought about.*
—MARY JO CLASBY

Rose Kennedy could never sleep at night without a note pad at her
bedside. She had to be able to write down all those innumerable
thoughts, about her children and her household, that constantly
cross her mind. She was always the first one up in the morning,
so she could get to mass and be back in time to have breakfast with
the children before they went to school, and she was always the last
one to bed, so she would be sure the household was in order and
all the lights were out. She wrote notes to herself and pinned notes
to her children's pillows, telling them to turn off the lights, telling
the girls to take off their lipstick before they went to bed so that
the pillows would not get stained; she left notes for neighbours,
advising them to be sure to bring in their bicycles, since it was going
to rain. She wrote notes on whatever paper was handy, even bits
of cash-register tape. She writes them all the time. She wrote one to
Robert Luddington, head of the interior design department at
Jordan Marsh and constant adviser to all the Kennedys on matters
of home decoration, that bounced all over the stationery; it was
obviously hurriedly scrawled and ended: "P.S. Written in a sway-
ing taxi. Sorry about that." When returning from Egypt on one of
her frequent and far-flung trips, she once wrote to Marie Greene:
"Have just had a cable from Joe that we are to represent the United
States at Pope Pius XII coronation." The note was on a piece of
common brown wrapping paper.

Her notes are not mere idiosyncrasy. In her eighties, she still
writes them to children and grandchildren, nieces and nephews
and friends and even people she has merely read about, who have
suffered greatly, as an act of *caritas*, charity. The notes are a sure

sign of her constant concern, her almost unbelievable conscientious-ness, for people whom she thinks she can aid. Rose cares—and cares deeply—about the life and welfare of her family and relatives and writes notes regarding everything from upcoming Catholic festivals to the need to wear long underwear "woollies" at upcoming foot-ball games.

"The joke," a teacher from a Riverdale school says, "was that every time Mrs. Kennedy had a baby, she hired another nurse and took another trip abroad." And the same teacher says that she was "never impressed by her depth of thinking—it was more society varnish". And it is true enough that when Rose came to live on the corner of 252nd Street and Independence Avenue in Riverdale in 1926, she was already wealthy, very wealthy; she had the trap-pings of wealth and, from all her years in Boston Irish society, both a delight and a lively interest in the social world of clubs and teas and parties. But—what the teacher apparently missed—she also had a very keen and well-disciplined mind, one that always worked in subtle but potent ways, and she used it during those years in River-dale and Bronxville to direct, manage, and control her household and the upbringing of her children. Her notes are the surest evi-dence of her intelligent concern.

Though Rose might not know precisely where her husband's money was coming from, there was plenty of it in the late twenties and thirties, and she found ways to use it fruitfully. Her large slate-roofed house, with its attractive circular driveway, was so well staffed that she was free from the drudgery of housework; wealth helped her retain her own serenity and character in the midst of a tumultuous life, and thus she always had more than words and instructions for her children; she maintained and continued to develop her own highly individualized and vital personality, and she gave them that. "She was a little removed, and still is," said Joe some years ago, "which I think is the only way to survive when you have nine children." Wealth enabled Rose to disengage herself when she needed to, to travel widely throughout the world, en-riching herself and bringing varied images and experiences back to her home.

Joe also used his wealth to protect his wife and his family. After the Lindbergh kidnapping and the first public disclosures of his wealth, he became cautious of publicity. From the time the family moved to Riverdale until Jack's Presidential campaign, he was capable of maintaining an uncanny protection of his family from unwanted press intrusion; his careful shielding of Rosemary's condition is the best example of this. Often it took extraordinary discipline on the part of members of the family. Numerous articles appeared, but they all were carefully phrased, filled with many of the same genial family anecdotes, and usually full of admiration. To this day Rose keeps the same kind of control when she can—right down to deleting passages in a magazine article, before publication, that could unflatteringly reveal that she dislikes dogs. Only Joe, after his ambassadorship, got a really adverse press; but his wife and children were on a pedestal, and he saw that they did not. Perhaps he already had political ambitions.

The children themselves were kept from knowing precisely how wealthy the family was, and Rose was strict with money. "We never gave them allowances," she recalls, "that were any bigger than those of the neighbourhood children. We never put value on anything just because it was expensive. Nobody talks about money in Boston, and we made it a rule never to speak about money in our house." Joe had set up trusts that would provide well over a million dollars for each of his children when they reached twenty-one. There were no strings attached. He wanted to fix it that any of his children could look him in the eye, "financially speaking", and tell him "to go to hell". He and Rose also wanted to impress upon them "advantages"—a word Rose uses frequently—bred responsibility and service, "the other side of the coin".

Riverdale in 1926 was not the cluster of sterile apartment dwellings it is today or the forced overflowing of an overcrowded metropolis. It was downright rural when the Kennedys moved there, with large sections still heavily wooded and even sheep grazing here and there on certain of the more affluent estates. From their house the children could see the Hudson River, and the older boys explored its shores, as well as the creeks and nearby woods whenever they could. They attended Riverdale Country Day School, which was one of the reasons Rose had chosen Riverdale: she was always eager to be near good schools.

Riverdale Country Day was a good traditional school with progressive ideas. There was firm discipline, but also freedom; the administration was considered "enlightened". The younger children attended the Neighbourhood School, the affiliated lower school.

Rose might indeed hire another nurse and take another trip when a new child was born, but no number of nurses and governesses and no number of trips could keep her from the children. She was strict—and she was "there". Joe Kennedy was home so little that Joe, Jr., was delegated a kind of surrogate father, whom the younger children idolized; he received his directions from Rose. Young Joe was supposed to help and advise his younger brothers and sisters, which he did, but he was not allowed to exert unwarranted power. Nor did Rose, ever, for all her strictness, ever want to dominate their lives. Discipline, yes; but she also tried to give them a chance to explore and test their potentialities. She was always deeply interested in how each of them did in school and checked their work regularly; she was also interested that they become widely concerned about public affairs, like her father, and as they grew older, "The News of the Week in Review" section of the Sunday New York *Times* became required reading, and they all discussed it at the table, even while Joe was away. She made them that "self-contained unit"—self-sustaining, intimate, with each able to go his own way but interested in the life of the others. But she also maintained her especially firm hand. She could be handy with a ruler and once summarily used it on Joe, Jr., Jack, and then Bobby—in turn—after they had been mischievous in church. "Mother would have been a great featherweight," says Ted; "she had a mean right hand."

Joe, using his genius for securing the best counsel—in this case Galen Stone and Matt Brush, who could not "both be wrong"—resisted the itch and pressure to invest heavily in the Florida land boom of the mid-twenties. He could not have acted with more foresight. The bubble burst in 1926, and thereafter, at his leisure, he was able to pick up excellent bargains—including, in 1933, the family's seven-bedroom white-stucco winter home in Palm Beach. The house on North Ocean Boulevard in Palm Beach became the winter home for the Kennedys. Built in 1923 by Addison Mizner for Rodman Wanamaker, it fronts the beach and has a swimming pool and tennis court; the vast lawn, surrounded by towering palms, stretches down to a lovely patch of roaring surf. More modest than many of the extravagant homes clustered around it, it has a characteristic Kennedy comfortableness and has served them well through the years. Inside, Italian and Spanish antique furniture predominate, and there are contemporary chintzes, Rose says, "to make the house gay and bright".

Rose had first been to Palm Beach with her father, and she never forgot the pleasure of those trips. Here Rose swam and expanded her social world still further and daily attended mass at St. Edward's Catholic Church. Here the family dined outdoors or ran in from the shore at the clanging sound of the dinner bell, "better known for its noisiness than its melodic sound". Here they invariably celebrated Christmas together, their brightly decked tree standing big and bold in the large red-tiled living room.

With his base office on Broadway in New York, Joe Kennedy launched boldly into the dramatic and highly competitive world of Hollywood moviemaking, matching wits with such early tycoons as Adolph Zukor, Marcus Loew, Louis B. Mayer, Samuel Goldwyn, Cecil B. DeMille, and the four Warner Brothers; "pants pressers", he snidely called them and was convinced that if they could make millions, he could do equally well in the fantasy factory on the West Coast. In thirty-two hectic months, his company produced more than fifty films—Westerns with Tom Mix and the enormously popular Fred Thompson and quick melodramas. They were low-budget bread-and-butter films, made at breakneck speed, but this was the way of operating Joe knew best—through speed and economy—and the pictures proved, if surely not classics, highly successful at the box office. Though he rarely mixed business with family, he sometimes sought their advice on special matters. He asked his children whether or not they thought Red Grange would make a successful actor and, on their enthusiastic Yes, hired the athlete. He went to Rose for a different kind of advice. Once he showed her a new film that had been given a solid "sex punch"; she vetoed it, and the film was never released. For their help, the boys were brought home Tom Mix "chaps", and their stock in the new neighbourhood rose sharply.

Always restless and striving, Joe constantly made new deals, new mergers and found new sources of income. He completed a $500,000 merger with David Sarnoff of RCA one afternoon on a street corner, with a handshake; he became chairman of the board of the new Keith-Albee-Orpheum amalgamate; he became a high-salaried adviser to Pathé. And at each turn he acquired new and substantial stock options. The market was soaring, and so were his fortunes. He was even clever and foresighted enough to anticipate the crash, buy short, and then pick up Depression bargains while the rest of the country stood on breadlines. "After all," Rose once said quietly, "somebody had to do the providing."

Joe was so busy doing the providing and acquiring the advantages that, when he grew tired of renting the Riverdale house, he gave Eddie Moore, his close friend and longtime secretary, the job of finding a new home for his family. The new Kennedy home, purchased for $250,000 in 1929, the year they permanently acquired the Hyannis Port property, was a huge Georgian mansion with red brick walls and large white columns in front; it was at 294 Pondfield Road, in the Republican stronghold of Bronxville, had twenty rooms and extra dwellings for the gardener and chauffeur, a winding approach, and a beautiful arched doorway. The more than five acres of superbly landscaped property on which the house stood included broad, carefully clipped lawns and dozens of handsome elms. In the spring, the property was radiant with its rich green foliage and picture-book gardens full of bright blue, yellow, red, and purple flowers. It was the most elegant house Rose had ever lived in—far more distinguished than the Fitzgerald mansion on Welles Avenue in Dorchester, which she had left only fifteen years earlier to marry an intense, ambitious young man and move into an undistinguished frame house in Brookline.

Rose would never allow even such a house as this to become a mere showplace. The Kennedy children played constantly on the lawns—baseball and the inevitable touch football—and would often gang up together against visiting opponents. Tom Schriber, a friend of young Joe's, remembers how there would be children hanging all over him in their games, how he'd always have to run looking out for the trees, as well as for the ball. "But Joe and Jack and Bobby never did, and WHANG!, that was that. They were always knocking themselves out. I can remember many occasions when one or the other of the boys would be picked up unconscious, and they were always bandaged and bruised all over."

Rose tended them when they came in wounded from their wars but continued to encourage the rough-and-tumble spirit; it reminded her of her father, it encouraged independence. Ethel Kennedy, Bobby's wife, followed her practice many years later. "I try to do what Mr. and Mrs. Kennedy did," she says, recounting the lists of broken bones her children have suffered. "Sure there are risks ... if they're going to develop independence, they have to do it while they're young. I want my children to grow up with as little fear as possible, because the less they fear, the more they can accomplish. This outweighs the risk." It always did for Rose, too. When Bobby set off to climb the 14,000-foot Mount Kennedy in the rugged Yukon some years ago, she offered him the mildest injunction, bred from years of experience: "Don't slip, dear." She had worried at first that Bobby, who grew up in the shadow of Joe and Jack, with his sisters and Ted, the baby, might become "puny and girlish"—he was always smallest and thinnest—but she soon realized that there was no fear of that.

When the last Kennedy was born in 1932, he was named after Edward Moore. "There were so many Kennedys even then," says Mrs. Moore, "that you sometimes forgot little Ted swaddled in his baby crib." Rose had to make a greater effort to tell still *more* bedtime stories, but she did, and if, as the other Kennedy children sometimes remark, "the discipline was breaking down" by the time Teddy arrived, Rose was still up to delivering a firm spanking when Ted walked home alone from kindergarten after he had been told to wait.

Kathleen, Eunice, Pat, Bobby, and eventually little Ted all attended the Bronxville School, though as their needs shifted, Rose saw to it that they transferred to private or parochial schools, sometimes for a year or two; all the Kennedys attended, before they were through, an enormous number of different schools. For the girls, when they were old enough, she chose religious schools. "Children respect their parents and their parents' opinions, but religious education helps buttress stability, reinforces their faith," she says. She wanted the boys to go to parochial schools also, but Joe overrode her on this; he wanted a broader base for the boys, more variety in the young men they met, a better chance to go on to Harvard, his own alma mater.

Joe, Jr., went to Choate in Wallingford, Connecticut, where, after a short period of adjustment, he did brilliantly, winning the coveted Harvard Trophy for "the student who best combined

scholarship and sportsmanship". His early maturity and his pronounced success made him his father's favourite, and his mother, to
whom he wrote constantly about his religious activities, also insisted that young Joe was most like her—"he liked to travel alone".
Rose sent him, and eventually the other children, the New York
Times regularly.

Jack went for most of a year to Canterbury, a Catholic prepara-
tory school, but after a sharp attack of appendicitis during Easter he
had to be withdrawn. He *always* seemed to be ill or incapacitated
in some way. Rose had been terrified when he'd had scarlet fever
as a young child, and then he'd contracted diphtheria; he always
seemed to have some sort of back injury. Bobby once said: "When
we were growing up together, we used to laugh about the great risk
a mosquito took in biting Jack Kennedy—with some of his blood
the mosquito was almost sure to die." Rose wrote to Choate before
Jack took his entrance examinations and named the books he was
currently reading. Would they help prepare him? she asked. Was
there any further preparation with which she could provide him?

Jack entered Choate the next year, two years behind his older
brother and always in his shadow. English and history fired his
imagination, but not much else; Rose has noted that his spelling
was always "imaginative". When he had difficulty in Latin, Rose,
always deeply concerned about her children's progress, saw to it
that he was given private tutoring that summer. But she could not,
long distance, get him to straighten out the rest of his school life;
though he loved *Ivanhoe* or some other novel and did well when
tested on it, he studied for most subjects at the last possible moment,
was incorrigibly careless with his room and property, and was often
late to appointments. When Rose sent him oranges from Palm
Beach one winter, he promptly got into trouble for throwing them
out the window. She tried to stress religious values and requested
periodic "accounts"; "I received Communion this morning," Jack
once wrote to her, "and am going to church on Tuesday. I received
the prayer book and would you please send me a puff because it
is cold."

Though Jack's IQ was high, his academic work during the
Choate years never matched his potential; his mind was unconven-
tional, and he clearly resented the model of his brother, to whom he
was constantly compared by schoolmates and teachers alike—and

by himself. During his Presidential campaign, Rose was fond of stressing how good he had been in school, but afterwards she admitted he was "generally a nuisance at school and was wasting his time and the time of a lot of the masters". In his senior year he was a prime mover in a group of young rebels that included his roommate Lem Billings—to this day considered the most difficult group of young men ever to attend Choate—who called themselves the Muckers. Finally, Joe Kennedy had to be called up to the school —he was then in Washington, as chairman of the Securities and Exchange Commission—and though Roosevelt advised him to stay put ("We have a financial crisis here in Washington"), he went. Kennedy, his second son, and George St. John, the headmaster, sat down together and "rehearsed the chapter and verse of things that had happened". Never one to shield his children if they were wrong, Joe supported the school, spoke firmly to his son, and evoked his sincere promise to try harder. "I don't care what you do in life," he said, "but whatever you do, be the best person in the world when you do it. Even if you're going to be a ditchdigger, be the best ditchdigger in the world." John F. Kennedy had no intention of being a ditchdigger, but towards the end his work improved at Choate. Not at Princeton, where he went next, but at Harvard would his academic life begin to approach his potential.

Rosemary's problems had not diminished, and for a time Rose sent her to a special school in Providence. Her condition became more pronounced as she grew older, and as the Kennedys drew more and more publicity and attention, she was carefully kept out of the limelight. She appears in pictures taken during the period and was introduced to the steady stream of prominent men and women who came into the Kennedy household. But all her appearances were carefully timed and planned, and the secret was guarded. Once Rose wrote to Choate requesting permission for Jack to take her to a tea dance. "The reason I am making this seemingly absurd request," she said, "is because the young lady who is inviting him is his sister, and she has an inferiority complex. I know it would help her if he went with her. She is fifteen years old and is trying to adjust herself."

Ted got caught in the increasingly peripetetic quality of the Kennedys' life, and before he went to college, he had gone to some ten schools in England, New England, and Palm Beach, including

Cranwell, Fessenden, Gibbs (in London), Graham-Eche's (in Palm Beach) and his favourite, Milton—which was, he says, the first school he really enjoyed. But even for Ted, there was a consistency in his education, for Rose continued the patterns she had started in Brookline. "I remember going to Plymouth Rock on Sunday," says Ted, "and having to read, before we went out, about the Pilgrims. Each Sunday when we lived in New York, we used to visit different monuments or different places of historical interest." When they were in the Boston area, perhaps on a visit to the lively and popular Grandfather Fitzgerald, they were taken to the Old North Church, the Old State House, and out to Lexington and Concord by Rose, and she saw to it that they read popular histories and novels dealing with the Revolutionary period before they went and then talked about what they had seen when they returned. Rose still avoided small talk, had no patience with trivia; she still talked to the children about "something that would teach them, or would be of value to them. If Cuba was in the news, we talked about where Cuba was, and why it was so important to us; or if the Queen was visiting the United States, why there was a Queen...."

When the older boys were ready, they were encouraged to travel in Europe and to study with famous men abroad. Joe, Jr., before he went to Harvard, spent an exciting year studying with Harold Laski at the London School of Economics. Laski, a Jew and a Socialist, might seem an odd choice for the Kennedys. Rose had preferred Oxford or Cambridge, but her husband, already keyed to the winds of the New Deal, and deeply respectful of the vigour of Laski's mind, insisted. Joe, says Rose, "always encouraged them to make up their own minds" and wanted the children exposed to different viewpoints. Young Joe also travelled to Russia that year, and Jack and then Rose went in subsequent years. But his travels were never random; Rose encouraged him to see St. Peter's, the Colosseum, St. Paul's, the Catacombs, and the Roman Forum when he went to Rome and detailed her plans.

But there were also times when Rose seemed "not at home", when she was preoccupied with her inner life. A friend of Jack's who came to the house frequently remembers that Rose would forget she had seen him before; each time the children, rather cruelly, would introduce him by a different name—and then snicker when Rose failed to catch on. If it was a French name, he remembers that she would launch blindly into French. In later years Bobby, who had been to Europe on an extended trip, once bounded into the house at Hyannis Port with great ebullience—expecting a hearty welcome. Rose walked right past him as he raced up the stairs and asked simply: "Bobby, have you seen Jack?"

In 1936, Eugenio Cardinal Pacelli, who later became Pope Pius XII, stayed with the Kennedys in Bronxville after a visit with Roosevelt at Hyde Park. Most of the children became uncommonly shy and quiet in his presence, but little Ted, then four, sat on his knee and played with his cross. The cardinal later gave Ted his first holy communion, a great honour, and Rose has commented that "with all those spiritual advantages, Ted might have become a priest or even a bishop, but he met a beautiful blonde one evening and that was the end of it".

Meanwhile, Joe Kennedy was beginning to ressurect his family's and Rose's intimate involvement with politics. Was he thinking of his son Joe's childhood vow to become the first Catholic President? Was he seeking, for himself, a new kind of power and influence, now that his fortune was many times assured? Or was he convinced that Franklin Delano Roosevelt had a recipe that might change an economy whose hard times beggared his wildest fears—and frightened even a man with his security?

When Roosevelt first took office, Joe, who had helped substantially in his campaign, expected the reward of a high government position; it was not immediately forthcoming. Kennedy made known his desire to be Secretary of the Treasury, but Roosevelt instead appointed Henry Morgenthau—a man whom Kennedy disliked. Not until 1934, after two long years of waiting, did his support of the New Deal bear palpable fruit: Roosevelt appointed him chairman of the newly established Securities and Exchange Commission. The "lone wolf" banker was to be, ironically, "the cop on Wall Street's corner". And he made a superb cop. The SEC has always been considered one of the most important and lasting achievements of the Roosevelt administration.

After FDR's landslide victory in 1936 against Alf Landon, which Kennedy helped produce with his carefully timed book *I'm for Roosevelt*, Joe was appointed chairman of the United States Maritime Commission. It was an excruciating job, under the greatest pressure, and he emerged as an adroit arbiter in the complex wars between the profit-hungry steamship companies and the tough unions. He could speak from the shoulder, and the union members knew that he was interested in the horrible conditions of seamen and longshoremen, but also that he was capable of ordering striking seamen on an American vessel in South America thrown into chains. He could also settle $73,000,000 in claims for 1 per cent, or $730,000. He called the job "the toughest I have ever handled in my life, without any reservations whatsoever".

Rose, married to such a dynamic man, relied more and more on her own resources. Often she was alone, and she built a full life for herself while watching with great care the development of her children. She travelled a great deal during her years in Riverdale and Bronxville, often alone, sometimes with one of the children. In 1934 she went to England. "Tea at Embassy today," she cabled back home. "Lunch with Winston Churchill tomorrow. Kathleen starts school Monday in Paris." And she travelled with only Kick to Russia in 1936—a rather daring thing to do at the time. Her letters back were filled with instructive detail, about how different Moscow was from New York or Paris; how people went to the opera in old working clothes; how the secret police followed her friend Ambassador William Bullitt whenever he went out. "Everyone wears berets on their heads instead of hats," she wrote, "and everyone has to take their coats off when they go into a museum, so they will not take something...." She had a keen eye that missed little. And she always signed off with warm affection: "Love you all lots. Rose and Kicks" or "I shall be very glad to arrive home with all you eight little darlings. Much love and many kisses to you all."

Joe's posts with the New Deal had put him in direct contact with all the leading figures in the Roosevelt administration, and when he spoke of them at the dinner table, history truly became alive for the children. Money and business had never been discussed in the Kennedy home, but politics—that was different. It was exciting and caught the imagination; political talk became a virtual fever in the house. Joe, says Rose, "always encouraged them to be independent-minded, to compete, and also to stand up to him". They did stand up to him—sometimes with a vengeance. Joe, Jr., used to argue with his father a good deal about the "merits and demerits" of the New Deal, about capitalism versus socialism.

Hadn't he been trained by Harold Laski? Jack was impressed with his older brother and spoke to his mother about it all one day. "You know, Mother, Joe seems to understand the situation better than Dad." Rose spoke to her husband and told him Jack's opinion.

"I don't care what the boys think about me," Joe said, "because I can always get along all right. As long as they stick together, that's the important thing."

Rose loved the political discussions. Wasn't it the subject she knew best? And wasn't it, now that Joe Kennedy had assured by his wealth that his children need never enter business, an ideal vocation for them? The "other side of the coin"—responsibility? Jack was studying government at Harvard, and Joe Jr.'s vow to become President was now more than idle talk; more and more it was becoming an *idée fixe*.

In 1937, Robert Worth Bingham, then Ambassador to the Court of St. James's, returned from England—apparently a dying man. Though Joe Kennedy still coveted the post of Secretary of the Treasury and though Roosevelt knew it, the President was satisfied with Morgenthau and fearful of Joe's independent mind. He may also have been worried that the astute and ambitious administrator might himself choose to become the first Catholic President of the United States; he had done everything else he set out to do. When Bingham submitted his resignation and shortly thereafter died, Roosevelt began to look for a new ambassador to the Court of St. James's. To represent America in far-off Anglican England, he finally chose an Irish Catholic with nine children and a beautiful and charming wife.

Chapter Eight

Wife of the Ambassador

*Obviously, we had a superior
entry to nearly everything.*
—ROSE KENNEDY

The Kennedys took England like a whirlwind. They were fresh,
frank, Irish-American—and there were plenty of them.

Only seven came in the first instalment—"so as not to complicate
the housing problem", said Joe—but that was enough. England was
delighted with the bold Joe Kennedy and his lively and individual
"little ambassadors". Joe's hole in one on the Stoke Poges golf
course, his love of rugby and gallops on Rotten Row, his feet-on-the-
desk interviews with Fleet Street, his radiant energy and political
openness and refusal to wear traditional court dress—all won him
quick and enthusiastic admirers. He was popular with the press,
the public, and high English society—and he was hailed as "the
father of his country". And the children—with their thousand
questions and insatiable curiosity and disarming naturalness—were
the talk of London. They made an extremely handsome family, and
in 1938 a jittery England was particularly receptive to handsome
American families.

But it was Rose who most enchanted the English, who won their
hearts. "As slim and as young-appearing as a sixteen-year-old,"
they found her; strikingly youthful, "as vivacious as a screen-star, as
wise as a dowager"; thoughtful, endowed with impeccable grace.
They noted that it was almost impossible to tell who the forty-seven-
year-old mother was in the frequent photographs that appeared of
the large family; soon they even said she had "the prettiest and best-
dressed feet in Ascot". So youthful and so efficient, the mother of
nine and yet as trim and chic as a debutante! Nine? Impossible.
She indeed, as Roosevelt's son-in-law observed before she left for
England, made one "believe in the stork".

Joe had come alone in late February, and in early March, delayed because of Rose's appendectomy in January, the rest of the first instalment arrived at the American Embassy at 14 Prince's Gate like a bright new breed from a brave new world. They completely shattered the formality of the staid old building, with its imposing private drive in front, its massive double doors, its huge round entrance foyer known as Round Hall. They came with their fourteen huge trunks and innumerable suitcases, with their cooks and books and phonographs and governesses, with their Kennedy ebullience—and they wakened a house formerly inhabited, with solemnity and studied English reserve, by a childless Ambassador and Mrs. Robert Worth Bingham.

All that first day, Teddy, fascinated by the electric lift, kept inviting his sisters and Bobby to go up and down with him; he never tired of the lift and often ran the servants up and down, playing Department Store. The children called one another over and over on the interhouse phones connecting every room; they walked in Hyde Park with their nurse, Luella Hennessey, saw the swans in the Serpentine, marvelled at the guardsmen in brilliant red, and had to be restrained from picking the white crocuses. It was all a new and exciting world for them, and everyone who saw them delighted in their directness and vigour and curiosity. "Brought a lot of books from home," Bobby, then twelve, told the *Daily Express* reporter. "Mostly they're about airplanes. I'm going to learn to fly as soon as possible."

Rose looked thoughtfully at the crimson carpet edged with green, the chandelier in Round Hall, and the immense floor-to-ceiling mirror. She had been to the American Embassy before, for tea in 1934. She went into the Ambassador's study and remembered the full-length portrait of George Washington by Gilbert Stuart over the fireplace; she would place a photograph of the eleven Kennedys next to it, and on the Ambassador's desk a photograph of FDR, inscribed "To Rose Kennedy, from her friend Franklin D. Roosevelt." She liked the bright red geraniums, the blue forget-me-nots, the white daisies in the front of the house, and the private garden in back—which would be used for ballplaying by the children. The palatial Embassy building has thirty-six rooms, but many had designated uses; she told a reporter that first day that her houses in America had more space. The house needed redecorating, and she would have this done by May. It was fortunate having Hyde Park and Rotten Row across the street; the children, especially the boys, would enjoy nearby Albert Hall with its frequent athletic events. Kick and Eunice would be coming out within the next two years, and they would look resplendent on the broad staircase.

In the next few weeks she set to work, got out her card index of the children, arranged the distribution of her twenty-three servants and three chauffeurs, saw to it that her new home was running smoothly, and settled into her routine of going to early mass and walking several miles each day or playing a game of golf; her routine went with her, wherever she went. There were plans to be made, there would be presentations at court, and she and Joe were invited to spend a weekend in early April at Windsor Castle, as guests of King George and Queen Elizabeth. On March 18, Rose and Joe were received by the Queen in her sitting room on the second floor of Buckingham Palace, and the two mothers chatted about their children for thirty-five minutes. Rose wore a dark-blue two-piece suit and a small hat trimmed with flowers; the Queen wore an afternoon gown. The Queen asked about the Kennedy children and hoped she would see them soon; she was particularly interested in whether Rose still got up to see the children off in the morning. But it was the Windsor Castle weekend that thrilled Rose's imagination; she could hardly wait for April.

Joe and Jack remained in the United States, where both were studying at Harvard. Jack's work was steadily improving in quality, and Joe was beginning to mix an excellent academic career with forays into the vital political life of Europe; before the year was out, he was to take a post as assistant to Ambassador William Bullitt in Paris, and after the Munich Pact was signed in September, he slipped in and then out of Czechoslovakia and then to half a dozen other important European cities; he witnessed the fall of Madrid under the onslaught of Generalísimo Franco, and his letter from Valencia appeared in *The Atlantic*. Joe said of his firstborn's bold adventuring: "His mother will die when she hears he is in Madrid."

Rosemary was to finish her semester at Marymount Convent in Tarrytown, New York, and then come to England. Rose worried how her eldest daughter would manage in London, where she could not be watched with as much care; her condition had deteriorated, but Joe was still determined to keep her with the family and even to present her to the court. The public deception continued. A reporter who interviewed the family in England was led to write: "She is the quieter of the older girls, and although she has an interest in social welfare work, she is said to harbour a secret longing to go on the stage."

Eunice soon transferred from the Sacred Heart Convent in Noroton, Connecticut, and went off to the Sacred Heart Convent in Roehampton with Pat and Jean, where they met young ladies from the royal houses of Bavaria and Luxembourg. Bobby and Ted stayed in London and, dressed by Rose in grey flannel shorts or trousers, maroon jackets, and little British schoolboy caps, went to Gibbs, a local day school. They were avid ballplayers, Teddy collected stamps, and in the rabid family checkers and backgammon tournaments, Bobby was the most consistent winner. Rose avoided the tournaments, as she had any involvement with the sailing in Hyannis Port.

Rose had very practical ideas about the clothes the children should wear. She favoured navy blue suits and sweaters for general wear because they were acceptable anywhere and went with almost any accessories. Brown shoes were her consistent choice, and she bought the children only one hat for a season; the children usually went bareheaded, except when they went to church or to official engagements. The girls Rose dressed in sweaters and skirts, and especially preferred plaids, in gay colours; for herself, she favoured a soft grey and blue plaid in a trim dressmaker suit.

Kick was a radiant eighteen. She had been to a French convent, went with her mother to luncheons and teas and openings, and often served as hostess at her mother's frequent parties and teas at the Embassy; she got stockings by the dozen from the United States in the diplomatic pouch and was besieged by titled escorts. It was, for them all, the high-water mark in their social life. Ted asked if "Your Excellency" was his father's new name, and Joe was well aware that Presidents John Quincy Adams and James Monroe had held his post and that it had also been held by other such distinguished Americans as John Jay, Charles Francis Adams, and James Russell Lowell. The Kennedys indeed had superior entry to nearly everything. "If we went to the races," said Rose, "we

watched from the owners' boxes. We all had tea with the Queen."
They had their pick of the most select social invitations and were
themselves hosts at the Embassy to royalty and high English society,
and to the American players at the Wimbledon Tennis Tourna-
ment and the crews from Harvard and Yale, and to scores of
others. Rose was appointed honorary president of the American
Women's Club of London and entered immediately into the highly
engaging English social life at Cliveden and at the Astor mansion
on St. James's Square.

If Rose broke tradition, two months after arriving, by announcing
beforehand the names of women to be presented to the court, London was stirred—but she was more than forgiven. In fact, she and
Joe refused to follow the tradition of presenting touring American
women to the court and selected only from families actually resident
in England. Their restricted list ended by uncovering a profitable
traffic in such presentations: fees up to $5,000 had been charged by
certain members of the British nobility for arranging such presentations, and when the court now learned what had been going on,
certain important families were told that their presence was no
longer required at royal functions. At the glittering official presentation to the court, Rose was dazzling. She wore an exquisite
Molyneux gown, embroidered with silver and gold paillettes and
court train of silver lamé bordered with sequin bands; she carried
a white ostrich fan and wore a diamond and ruby tiara. (Twenty-
three years later, without alteration, she wore the same gown at a
spectacular and joyous Inaugural Ball.)

"Well, Rose, this is a helluva long way from East Boston, isn't
it?" Joe said as they dressed for dinner with the King and Queen
at Windsor Castle. They had come for the weekend of April 9,
and so vivid an impression did the whole event make on her that
Rose could describe it in precise detail sixteen years later in an
article written for Manhattanville College; nearly thirty years later,
when she gave slide presentations that included scenes from Windsor Castle, her excitement had not dulled.

On Saturday, a maid and valet were sent ahead with the luggage,
and the Kennedys followed, timing their arrival for precisely seven
o'clock. Rose says: "When I saw Windsor's round tower rising
above the trees, the standard flying about it as a sign that the royal
family was in residence—I will admit to a major thrill." Years

before, as a high school girl, she had first visited the castle with dozens of other American tourists. "And now I was going there again, but this time as a guest of the King and Queen!"

Their suite of rooms in Lancaster Tower was magnificent—with a sitting room upholstered all in red damask, a boudoir all in gold and white damask, with white wallpaper and a gold and white washstand. There were two bedrooms, the larger one with "an overpowering bed", also covered with red damask. The royal footman had assured them that it was not unusual for visitors to use the Windsor Castle notepaper, so Rose wrote letters to the children; she always wrote them from interesting places, using the special letterheads, and she encouraged the children to save such memorabilia.

"Dressing is a very active exercise," said Rose, "and even when one's clothes are all laid out ready, there is a deal of inevitable running about. Your washbasin may be a long way from your dressing table, and your shoe cupboard far removed from the neighbourhood of your stockings." She and Joe were precisely on time the first night at Windsor Castle, but she was almost late for lunch the next day because she had to search so long for a fresh pair of stockings among "the vast system of drawers".

At exactly eight twenty the footmen escorted the Kennedys to the Green Reception Room. It was indeed a helluva long way from East Boston—even from Bronxville. Rose was dazzled by the ladies, dressed in beautiful gowns embroidered with silver and gold, their diamond tiaras and heirloom jewellery gleaming, their long white gloves quietly elegant. The men wore traditional Windsor dinner dress, black suits with red collars. Rose had been to countless élite social functions, with the highest figures in American business, social, and political life, but beneath all her security and social ease, her confidence and poise, there was a part of her that remained Boston Irish Catholic, and she was awed by British royalty.

At precisely eight thirty the King and Queen entered the reception room. The Queen, Rose recalled, was wearing "a rose pink gown with opalescent trimming, after the style of Winterhalter, a double necklace and tiara of diamonds—and over all this loveliness, from left to right, the blue ribbon of the Order of the Garter". Rose curtsied to them both while Joe bowed deeply, and a little later the King and Queen led all the distinguished guests in to dinner. Rose

sat on the King's right, and Mrs. Neville Chamberlain, wife of the
Prime Minister, sat on his left (the Kennedys and the Chamber-
lains later became extremely close). While "exquisite subdued
music" was played, the King asked Rose about her nine children,
which, Rose later admitted, "always offered a safe, cheering, and
nonpolitical topic". There was an endless procession of courses, and
then there was a bit of good-natured teasing as the guests noticed
the high flowering currant decorations in the centre of the table:
this made it difficult for the King to see the Queen across the table,
which was necessary for them to give the proper signal to rise when
the dinner was over.

Finally, the King and Queen rose, in unison, and then led the
company from the dining room. In the Green Reception Room the
nine children again figured prominently in royal conversation, when
Rose spoke for fifteen minutes with the Queen—herself a ninth
child. Rose found it difficult to keep addressing the Queen as
"Ma'am", lapsed a few times, apologized, and then was told not to
bother further about it. "I found in her a real person," says Rose,
"a mother and every inch a Queen in presence."

The next day, Palm Sunday, Rose and Joe went to early mass
in town after breakfasting in her sitting room. When they returned
they watched the changing of the guard, and later walked through
the great 1,000-year-old oaks of the Great Park of Windsor. As
they came to an expansive stretch of a golf course that offered a
lovely view of the castle in the distance, they ran into Princess
Elizabeth "unsuccessfully hiding behind the shrubs. She was in a
pink coat and hatless, and smiled at us as we passed by". It was
one of "the most delightful weekends" they had ever spent.

Rose visited Windsor Castle again the next year at about the
same time, when the beleaguered Neville Chamberlain now looked
"worn and tired and older", and she would meet frequently with
royalty from all over Europe at Buckingham Palace. Several times
the Queen visited or dined at the Embassy, and the two women
had lively conversations about child rearing. Rose added to her
dinners the special brand of Kennedy informality, even when
royalty was present. She describes the important dinner given for
the King and Queen shortly before their historic visit to America
in mid-1939: "We wanted to give an atmosphere of informality

to the gathering. The menu broke with tradition by being printed in English rather than French."

Margaret Ambrose, Rose's longtime cook, prepared a distinctly American dinner for the King and Queen and the thirty-four guests that night—who included such notables as Lord and Lady Astor, Lord Halifax, the Duke and Duchess of Devonshire, and the Duke and Duchess of Beaufort. The meal consisted of mushroom soup, Baltimore shad roe, mousse of Virginia ham with Georgia peaches, roast young chickens, peas, potatoes, asparagus with Hollandaise sauce, and American coffee. The most remarkable dish for the King and Queen, though, was the strawberry shortcake dessert; their majesties had never eaten it before—and they loved it. Lady Astor did, too, and wrote Rose for the recipe, and then the newspapers printed the exotic new dish and gave it so much publicity that a number of London's leading restaurants placed it on their menu. (At another dinner, "shad" failed to make quite so startling an impression. Rose had ordered shad from America for the formal dinner, but it failed to arrive. Desperate, since the menus had already been printed, Rose and Margaret put their heads together. Finally, they decided on a substitute, and after the meal one duchess observed: "Your American shad is very good. It is much like our sole, isn't it?" It was *very much* like English sole.)

At the end of the long room in the Embassy the night the King and Queen came to dinner, Rose arranged a small table for her six youngest children; she always wanted the children, of whatever age, to participate in such auspicious occasions, to meet the people who *were* history. But being part of "history" was not always fun. It carried certain compromising demands. "The children were always told that they must remember their father was the Ambassador," says Rose. "One day Teddy came to me and asked permission to punch Cecil or Algie or a boy with some name like that on the nose. I asked 'Why?' Teddy replied, 'Well, he's been hitting me every day and you tell me I can't get into fights because Dad is the Ambassador." It was a humiliating situation. There was some extended discussion about the matter, and then "Teddy was given permission to punch Cecil or whatever his name was".

The family travelled whenever they could, and one reporter said that the "Great Kennedy Treks" were almost "like getting a circus out of winter quarters and into Madison Square Garden. It could be pandemonium, but Mrs. Kennedy handles it with dispatch". Rose recently recalled a visit to Ambassador Bullitt in Paris and was asked whether "all nine of you" had stayed there together.

"Well," she answered, "people didn't seem to mind, and we didn't care where we slept."

Rose herself Channel-hopped to Paris to see fashion openings, of which she was becoming an increasingly shrewd connoisseur, and once took all the children except Jack, who was in the States at the time with his father, to St. Moritz for winter sports. It was a typically not uneventful vacation: Bobby sprained an ankle; Joe, Jr., came within two seconds of winning the world's bobsled record, was seen frequently with skater Megan Terry, and wrenched his wrist seriously.

Rose had great fun introducing her father and mother to her new friends when they came over for a visit in 1938—and Honey Fitz was, of course, a great favourite. There is no record of whether he sang "Sweet Adeline" for English royalty, but unbeknownst to Rose, he did find time to send formal engraved invitations to all his cronies in Boston, asking them to dine with him at the Embassy. It was only when Mayor Frederick Mansfield of Boston cabled his sincere regrets that it all came out.

Though she loved the social life, Rose also had deep cultural interests to satisfy in London. She went to concerts frequently and loved Beethoven and Brahms, *Tristan and Isolde*, and the dramatic conducting of Toscanini. A part of her always remained independent and solitary, bent on continual self-improvement and private pleasure: she would go to art galleries alone, as she did to lectures when friends reneged, and she often slipped into a concert unnoticed and alone.

But a part of her remained, always, intently devoted to her children. Whenever she spoke of her experience in London, she included some statement to the effect that the children had got "a great deal out of it". She personally thanked Roosevelt at the end of her first year for having made possible so many exciting experiences for herself and the children. Kick, in particular, thrived in London. Her coming out was held in 1938, and her life became splendidly full. She had more than beauty and grace: she had her mother's vivaciousness—with more freedom—and her brothers' daring. Once she said: "I wish Daddy would let me have sherry when I go to parties. These English houses are so cold, I need something to warm me up."

"I'm sorry," said Joe, recalling the promise he had extracted from all his children that they not drink or smoke until they were twenty-one. "I'm afraid you'll have to drink lemonade and freeze."

Kick had always been Rose's favourite, and in 1936 the two had travelled alone to Russia, and often they would go to the fashion openings in Paris together. Close liaisons were reported between the beautiful young Kennedy girl and the young Earl of MacDuff, the Marquess of Granby, and finally the Marquess of Hartington —heir to the Devonshire title and estate. More and more, at balls, horse races, and throughout London, the lovely brunette was seen with the dashing Billy Cavendish, the Marquess of Hartington. Rumours of their engagement were everywhere—but were always denied. He was, of course, an Anglican—and Rose had her reservations.

Rose was of immense help to her husband, both socially and, when he'd listen, politically. She was an exceptional hostess, a superb social companion; social and political blunders were an impossibility for her—and she knew exactly when to talk about children rather than the issues. It is difficult to tell precisely how well she understood the incredibly complex political problems of the time; she tended not to speak on the issues; she knew what *not* to say. But surely she had one of the best-trained minds in the family: she had been an honours student, while her husband—though indisputably brilliant in business—had been only academically average in college; she had organized clubs devoted to current events and international affairs, and she had quit clubs when they served merely pale and tedious small talk with their tea. She never once displayed the public temper tantrums her husband could indulge in (once, when Joe, Jr., failed to get into the Yale game and thus win his varsity football letter at Harvard, he stormed on to the field and publicly berated and screamed at the coach). Rose was incapable of such a lapse; her self-discipline was too great; she had long ago learned never to let down her guard.

Like her husband, she probably gave Chamberlain more credit and sympathy than he deserved—possibly owing to a sincere personal friendship with the man and his wife, and because Rose rarely makes critical remarks about anyone. But she had an acute eye and ear, and often Joe would try out his speeches on her first. He read her his notorious Trafalgar Day speech beforehand, and she told him *not* to claim that democracies and dictatorships were compatible. But even here her reservations were less focused on the issue than on the propriety and appropriateness of his words. She told him: "You will have to produce concrete suggestions to bring home your point, and you know perfectly well that you will find yourself discussing issues which a diplomat should not raise." He did not listen to her sound advice. To his peril.

Rose has always viewed her attendance at the coronation of Pope Pius XII as one of the crowning moments of her life. She had met the new leader of the Roman Catholic Church in 1936, when he visited her home in Bronxville as Cardinal Pacelli. Joe, Jr., was in Madrid in March, 1939, but the rest of the family made the momentous trip to Rome when Roosevelt appointed Joe Kennedy the official United States representative. Rose was returning from Egypt, where she had been on one of her frequent trips, and went directly to Rome by herself. Then most of the children arrived with their nurse and governess, and Joe and Jack followed soon afterwards.

It was a magnificent day, filled with spectacular pageantry that soared in her imagination, and on the following day the new Pope first received Joe and then, after a short private meeting, summoned Rose. She was deeply moved as she left the antechamber and was ushered into the private room and presented to the Pope who would later name her Papal Countess, an honour he bestowed only once, only to Rose, during his entire reign. After speaking with Rose, the Pope summoned the children and presented them with rosary beads. For Rose it was all an unforgettable experience, a supreme honour that she could not have dreamed of receiving when she was a student at the Sacred Heart convents.

As the second year wore on, if Rose indisputably kept her popularity, Joe was beginning to receive raised eyebrows. The hounds of hell were baying in Germany, and the world waited on the pleasure of a little demon with a moustache. Just how far Hitler would go, how much he truly intended to grab were matters of conjecture. Pacify him, said some; stand up and risk war, said others. His power was immense, but would his generals stand by him if the Allies resisted his intimidations and threats? Would he back down—or was the bow already too deeply drawn? His air force, said such shrewd observers as Charles Lindbergh, had the power to level the great cities of Europe.

Politics, particularly diplomacy, was not the same as business; administrative skills were invaluable, but they were not all an ambassador had to carry in his diplomatic pouch. Brash and sometimes outspoken, fearless and without the refined skill or customary caution needed by an ambassador—particularly in a nervous England—by hints and by innuendos Joe Kennedy was suggesting close partiality for his friend Chamberlain's principles of appeasement—and he was proclaiming, a bit too loudly, especially for an England in desperate need of friends, America's position of isolationism. All that spring of 1939, while Winston Churchill pleaded for his country to recognize the dimensions of the impending disaster, the process of appeasing Hitler continued. The *Anschluss* occurred in early March; by the end of September the fatal sacrifice of Czechoslovokia by Chamberlain at Munich had taken place. Fight for the Czechs? asked Kennedy. Who were they?

Only three weeks after the Munich Pact was signed, Kennedy delivered his Trafalgar Day speech. Of it, even Arthur Krock, Joe's collaborator on *I'm for Roosevelt*, said: "Confusion and controversy necessarily flowed from that passage in Ambassador Kennedy's Trafalgar Day speech in London wherein he discussed his 'theory' that democracies and dictatorships should cease emphasizing their differences." The Ambassador had failed to listen to his wiser wife —and he was now even a longer way from East Boston than he had been when he and Rose, dressing for a royal dinner at Windsor Castle, had marvelled at how far they had come.

Soon insinuations of anti-Semitism and then defeatism began to follow Joe Kennedy. And before he had finished his two years and nine months as Ambassador, he was to lose the faith of the British people who had so loved him and his family when he first came and was to bury the Kennedy name under controversy and criticism and even humiliation from which it would not emerge until his sons came of age. Ironically, though this was to be the darkest period in his life, Joseph P. Kennedy was thereafter known as the Ambassador, and Rose, until she became "the President's mother", was referred to as "the wife of the Ambassador to the Court of St. James's". It was not a privilege accorded all former ambassadors.

In July, 1939, Eunice, dressed in a crinoline dress of ivory tulle and satin, had become the third Kennedy daughter to be officially presented to the court in the White and Gold Ballroom in Buckingham Palace. Then, barely a month later, everything changed. Rose, Joe, Jr., and Jack heard the announcement together. "Everything that I have worked for," her friend Neville Chamberlain announced to the British people, "everything that I have hoped for, everything that I have believed in during my public life has crashed in ruins." His voice was choked with emotion. It was the morning of September 3, two days after Germany invaded Poland.

Within an hour, Rose and her two oldest boys were speeding to the House of Commons. War had been declared, and already there was panic in the streets. Suddenly the air-raid sirens began to roar, and the three of them leaped out of the car and quickly followed signs pointing to the nearest shelter. There they huddled, gas masks on, silent and anxious, wondering whether Hitler was quite so efficient as to bomb so soon after war had been declared. A half hour later they left their shelter and headed off again towards the Chancellery; only when the all clear sounded did they realize they had been safe in the cellar of the dressmaking shop of Edward Molyneux.

On September 18, 1939, a grim and weary Rose Kennedy returned to the United States aboard the *Washington* with Kathleen, Eunice, and Bobby; it was so crammed with 1,800 passengers that cots had to be set up in the swimming pool, in the lounges, and on the covered decks. From New York, Rose flew directly to Boston, to celebrate her parents' golden wedding anniversary. The shrill whine of air-raid sirens still echoed in her ears; she still saw the bewildered children, with their shouldered bundles, being evacuated; she thought of the troops being quickly mobilized, of friends she had left in London, of the dreaded blackouts and the gas masks she'd had to carry. She was drained. Britain is too weak to be our ally, her husband would say, but Rose Kennedy remembered the faces and the spirit of a grim and determined people preparing for a long and desperate war—a people who were ever hopeful of American aid both her husband and eldest son opposed.

In Boston there was a reception for her parents. Honey Fitz was just as lively at seventy-four, and Josie almost as straight and quiet and proud as always. For a moment Rose may have forgotten what she had seen and heard—what she knew. At the Ritz Carlton reception, the "greatest living tenor" did not have to be asked to sing a certain favourite song, and Rose sat down readily at the piano and accompanied him. For a moment, the sounds of war and of war's alarms and the failures of politicians were hushed, and she may have remembered an earlier, simpler time when a beaming and indefatigable campaigner sang and stumped for a "Bigger, busier, better Boston", and she was his hostess and favourite booster, Rose Fitzgerald.

Chapter Nine

The War Years

When Spring shall wake the earth,
And quicken the scarred fields to the new birth,
Our grief shall grow. For what can Spring renew
More fiercely for us than the need of you?
—MAURICE BARING

"My darling—I am wondering when I shall see you and what is happening! It is all so heartbreaking," Rose wrote to her husband in England, soon after she and the children were back in the reopened mansion on Pondfield Road in Bronxville. "I just hope and pray daily that you are taking care of yourself and are not too terribly lonely. When the children and I start to think and talk about our experiences [in England] we realize what a superlatively inspiring position it was. I just wish I might be along with you. As I say—all I can do is to pray very hard that I shall see you soon. All my love always."

Rose did not complain. She never complained. Joe was indeed lonely in England, and daily threatened by the increasing German air strikes and bombardments; he had narrowly missed death several times. And Rose was both frightened for him and lonely, as she had often been before, but she maintained her outward calm, her pluck and industriousness; she was again the glue that held the family together. One of Joe's primary motives in seeking to avoid participation in the war was a deep-seated fear for his sons' lives; he did not think he could bear the eventuality of a lost son. While he continued to advocate isolationism, Rose continued to educate the children. Her houses in Bronxville, Palm Beach, and Hyannis Port were run with their usual regularity and purpose, and even with Joe gone the Kennedy vigour and electricity and discussions flourished. Rose encouraged them. She required the children to study the globe-shaking events that were taking place, and the older ones frequently debated whether the United States should give aid to England. "Ted is keen to know all the war strategy," she wrote to Joe, "and loves to find the places on the map. Jack ... gave a succinct argument as to why he thought America should help England with materials for the war." The children had met all the leading figures in British politics; the names in the news were real people to them.

The year 1940 began with a brief "Kennedy for President" boom in Massachusetts, but Joe announced in March (on a return visit to the United States for a health checkup) that his political life would come to an end when he wound up his duties as Ambassador. He meant it. The torch, flickering as it was, would be passed to a new Kennedy. In his place at the 1940 Chicago National Democratic Convention, his oldest son was to begin, with decision and sureness, to make his move towards national prominence, towards a long-stated goal of becoming the first Catholic President of the United States.

Rose saw that the realities of war and of the political figures and decisions that led to wars were becoming the primary concern of her second son. Jack spent most of the winter and spring at Harvard writing a senior thesis called *Appeasement at Munich: The Inevitable Result of the Slowness of the British Democracy to Change from a Disarmament Policy*. For it he received high honours, and his father was so pleased that he suggested it be published commercially. It was rushed into print, and when it appeared, with the more manageable title suggested by Arthur Krock, *Why England Slept*, and an introduction by Henry Luce, it sold 40,000 copies, was a Book-of-the-Month Club selection, and made the best-seller list; England was even more interested, and there its sales reached nearly a quarter of a million. The thesis also brought Jack a *cum laude* degree from Harvard. Joe could not attend, but sent a cablegram: TWO THINGS I ALWAYS KNEW ABOUT YOU ONE THAT YOU ARE SMART TWO THAT YOU ARE A SWELL GUY LOVE DAD. Jack had come a long way from his floundering days at Choate. As Rose— with Kick, Rosemary, Joe, Jr., Eunice, and a proud Honey Fitz beside her—watched him graduate, she saw her long years of steadiness and encouragement and discipline had borne fruit.

Though Rose did not know it, the summer of 1940 was the last all the Kennedys would ever be together again. Joe, in London, remarked lightly that the loss of sleep from all the bombings was not so unusual for a father of nine children, but he would much have preferred to be kept up by his little "ex-ambassadors"; there was a desperation in his attitude, an increasing sense that England was doomed and that the Nazi machine could not be stopped. Rose and the children closely followed the news of the war throughout July and August. Every day she rose early to hear the six o'clock news and then came in to tell the children about it and to discuss the events. She had a bulletin board on which she posted the day's headlines, and all the children were expected to read it and then be ready to discuss the issues. Rose's sister, Agnes, had died in 1937, and then, two years later, her brother-in-law had died, too; Rose did not hesitate to take the Gargan children into her family, and though they were away at school during the year, during the summer they stayed at Hyannis Port. "In the mornings we had to listen to the radio broadcasts," says Joe Gargan, "and read the newspapers. And during lunch she would give us a real cross-examination on what we had read, particularly on the news and what effect the news is going to have. This was a priority activity." Rose also gave all the younger children regular reading assignments and then queried them on what they had read; if they did not complete one of her assignments on time, she would not hesitate to deprive them of entertainment. "And always, all the time," says Ted, "we kept our diaries"; all the children were encouraged by Rose to "write what we did during the day, the ideas we had".

But if Rose kept them disciplined and alert that summer, she also watched their irrepressible enthusiasm with delight. So many of her children had her father's energy and excitement; they were interested in everything. A visitor to Hyannis Port that summer was fascinated by the family. "Jack was autographing copies of *Why England Slept*," he said, "while Grandfather Fitzgerald was reading to him a political story from a newspaper. Young Joe was telling them something that happened to him in Russia. Mrs. Kennedy was talking on the phone to Cardinal Spellman. A tall and very attractive girl in a sweat shirt and dungarees turned out to be Pat, who was describing how a German Messerschmitt plane had crashed near her father's house in London. Bobby was trying to get everybody to play charades. The next thing I knew all of us were choosing up sides for touch football and Kathleen was calling the plays in the huddle for the team that I was on."

Kick was not always calling the plays. Rose watched with a cautious eye as her vivacious daughter intensified her training to become a Red Cross worker. There was a special urgency in her efforts, and Mary Jo Clasby remembers spending half that summer wrapped up in Kick's splints and bandages. Kick frequently spoke about returning to London, but Rose would not hear of it.

Teddy was Honey Fitz's paper boy. Fitz, now a peppery seventy-seven, would read his usual eight or nine newspapers a day, make his interminable clippings, and continued to delight all the Kennedy children with his stories. Ted remembers a tale Grandfather Fitzgerald used to tell about his great-grandmother Rosanna, back in the old North End. She would cook flapjacks and he would say, "Mother, Mother, look at Freddie" (a younger brother), and then he would grab the flapjack and put it under his coat. "He never finished the story," says Ted, "because he would get to laughing so hard. The tears would pour down his cheeks."

When Joe, Jr., went off to the Democratic convention that summer, pledged to James A. Farley, Rose realized that a new political era was starting for her family. She followed the convention intently and learned that there were moments, as young Joe felt the behind-the-scenes pressures, when he wanted to change to Roosevelt. Men like Arthur Krock were impressed with the integrity he showed in his first political effort. When the convention was over, he headed West, spent some time with William Randolph Hearst, Jr., had a short "schoolboy crush" on Hearst's ex-Follies' wife, Lorelle, and then went to stay with his roommate Tom Killefer in Hermosa Beach. The long, firm arm of Rose Kennedy reached him even there. "Now remember, Joe," she wrote constantly, "do pick up your room!"

That fall, Rose had the large house in Bronxville chiefly to herself. When Joe returned from England in October (bringing an air-raid siren that he intended to use at Hyannis Port to call the children in from their boats to dinner), he found his family scattered. Joe, Jr., was at Harvard Law, Jack at Stanford, and most of the younger children were at convents and prep schools throughout New England; Kick, who had continued to argue unsuccessfully for permission to return to England, had joined the staff of the Washington *Times-Herald*. Rose found her husband exhausted,

The War Years / 133

The War Years / 133

embittered at what he took to be administration duplicity, and not at all anxious to support Roosevelt in the coming election. But he agreed, finally, to give a speech on FDR's behalf and to participate mildly in the Presidential campaign, admitting later that his wife's advice "carried the greatest weight". Rose, always an acute political tactician, urged him to remember how generous the President had been, appointing him, a Roman Catholic, to the ambassadorship; she argued tenaciously that he act with respect, that he do nothing that would make himself appear ungrateful. Joe would have acted out of his passion, out of his despair at an increasing number of disputes between himself and the Chief Executive. Rose was far more capable of thinking of the effect, of the political leverage; she may also have been thinking well into the future, when her sons would enter politics. An affront to Roosevelt at this moment might have undermined Kennedy's position in the Democratic Party; it might have crushed Joe, Jr.'s chances of rising should Roosevelt win the election; it might have soured the electorate on Catholics in high places. Rose was no doubt aware of all these possibilities.

But she was not always there to advise him. Days after Roosevelt's reelection in November, Kennedy finally resigned his ambassadorship, and then, several days later, in a startling interview with Louis Lyons of the *Boston Globe*, Charles Edmondson, and Ralph Coglan, Kennedy spoke vexing words about England and the President's wife. Rose was in New York at the time; had she been with her husband at the Ritz Carlton, the damage might well have been less. "Democracy is finished in England," Joe said, and though praising Mrs. Roosevelt's helpfulness and sympathy, he added: "She bothered us more on our jobs in Washington to take care of the poor little nobodies who hadn't any influence than all the rest of the people down there together. She's always sending me a note to have some little Susie Glotz to tea at the Embassy." Even *in* context, the words were ill chosen. Joe Kennedy had sealed his political career.

Rose would not have permitted him to make such statements, not only for political reasons but because, as a close friend says, she never says anything bad about anyone and will not let friends or relatives do so in her presence. When Edward VIII was preparing to abdicate, there was gossip everywhere; several women, who had seen him with Wallis Simpson in Europe, began to whisper about him in Rose's presence. "I don't think you ought to talk about that," said Rose firmly. "That is scandal"—and the talk stopped. There had been no one to stop Joe Kennedy at the Ritz Carlton in Boston.

With a mixture of sadness and pride, Rose watched Joe, Jr., within a year, decide to forgo his senior year at law school and volunteer to serve as a Navy flier. "I still don't think we should go into the war," he said, "but I thought I ought to be doing something, and I'll do whatever they tell me to do." Jack, after an unsatisfactory semester at Stanford, toured South America and then sought to volunteer first for the Army and then for the Navy. He was rejected for both. But he was determined not to allow an old back injury to keep him from service; after his brother's departure, Jack spent the summer of 1941 lifting weights and following a daily unceasing regimen of diet and exercise worthy of his mother. PT boats appeared in Nantucket Sound for the first time that summer —and Jack saw them. Soon after his father's fifty-third birthday celebration in Hyannis Port in early September, Jack was accepted into the Navy. Rose Kennedy now had two sons in the armed forces—with America on the brink of war.

But Jack and Joe, Jr., were mature young men. She had encouraged their strengths and watched them grow mature; she had confidence in their ability to take care of themselves. A more anguished concern during the tense months preceding America's entrance into the war was her daughter Rosemary. Her eldest daughter's condition had finally reached the crisis point.

Rose had never been able to talk about Rosemary, even to her closest friends; to this day it is a difficult process, and her words are always elusive. As late as the 1950's the reports about Rosemary that the family released were to this effect: "At St. Coletta, a Catholic school near Milwaukee, Rosemary, the quietest of the Kennedys, cares for and teaches exceptional children." Throughout the years both Rose and Joe had tried to keep her within the family unit—and to hide from others the fact that there was a serious problem. Rosemary *looked* normal and was in fact one of the prettiest of the five Kennedy girls. Though she had trouble reading, she had an uncanny ability to repeat or imitate. Local people in Brookline had been able to see nothing unusual as she passed or entered their stores on routine affairs, for Rosemary was well trained. When she was read to, even when she was quite young, she could repeat the words exactly, but she had difficulty constructing her own sentences and talking for any length of time. You could "talk to Rosemary", an acquaintance says, but you could "never really have a conversation with her".

The most obvious symptom in the early years had been her lack of coordination: she'd try to play tennis, but it just didn't work; she wanted to sail, like the other children, but could not be allowed out alone; she did a little swimming and played some golf and caught a football, but could perform none of these activities well. Joe, Jr., in particular, was always especially kind to her, trying to lob her a football or tennis ball, but Rosemary felt increasingly frustrated as she watched the younger children grow skilful in sports, become quick-witted and socially popular. What they did with ease, she could not do even with repeated and painful effort.

A prominent Boston doctor told Rose, when Rosemary was a child, that he detected damage on one side of her brain, possibly from forceps at delivery or from having been dropped when she was an infant; the other side was perfect. Mental retardation wasn't talked about in those days, and when it was, there was always the implication of fault and guilt on the parents' part; Rose is still anxious to tell listeners in her public appearances for the cause of mental retardation that she had six other healthy children after Rosemary. When the doctors finally suggested that Rosemary be put in an institution, Joe said: "What can they do for her that her family can't do better?" Rose and Joe both wanted her to share in the family activities; they did not want her to miss the fun or the excitement or the opportunities. She was prepared and then presented to the court in England, and she was kept within the family circle; she appears in innumerable family pictures, her appearance perfectly in keeping with the ten other handsome Kennedys. But if Rose was stoic and tight-lipped about her daughter, the pain was great—and she also had certain very real fears.

Her daughter's increasing frustration at her inadequacies led to severe temper tantrums. In London, while Rose constantly feared for her safety away from home, another problem had developed. Kick and Eunice were by then living exciting social lives, dating titled young Englishmen and attending a spate of parties and balls and teas and other social events. Rosemary began to want the company of young men too, and Rose became terribly troubled that a clever opportunist would turn her head. She was, of course, genuinely attractive, and she was showing an increasing anxiety for social liaisons. Rose knew that the Kennedy millions could be a great temptation.

Rosemary thus became over the years the first great tragedy in Rose Kennedy's life. As her tantrums became more serious and pronounced, it became clear that Rose could not continue her efforts to integrate her with the rest of the family; she *was* different and would not, suddenly or even slowly, become normal. She was regressing. Her memory began to fail. Her concentration was poor. Rose saw that it was genuinely dangerous to keep her at home, for she began to throw things, act irrationally, and jeopardize herself and others with her hysteria. And Rose continued to fear the appearance of an opportunist. It finally reached a head in the fall of 1941, and they all knew that a decisive move now had to be made. Rosemary required a place where she would be free of the Kennedy competition, the frenetic pace; she needed a place where she would be safe and secure. Joe was visibly heartbroken; it nearly killed him to send her away. Rose was deeply affected, too, but she said little to even her closest friends. At last Rosemary was sent to St. Coletta's School in Jefferson, Wisconsin, and there she has lived ever since in a private house with her own chauffeur and car. Rose and Eunice visit her regularly. There is a rumour that Joe had her in a car at Jack's inauguration, near enough for her to see her younger brother become the first Catholic President of the United States.

There is a remarkable solidity and consistency in Rose Kennedy's life; her closest friends speak constantly of how little she has changed, to this day, from the days when she was a young Boston belle. She had learned from her father a presence that would give her a private ease in all public arenas; her constant pursuit of excellence, her unfailing discipline had given her the firmness and ability to meet the most demanding challenges of motherhood; she had met Presidents and royalty all her life, and there would never be a social situation that could "unglue" her. She had—patiently, thoughtfully, and with constant attention and devotion—brought up a large and varied family, a family with remarkable vigour and drive. She had maintained her Catholic faith and lived the vows with which she had become a Child of Mary. It was now twenty-six years since she had married, against her father's wishes, a lanky red-haired young man with a world of ambition and had settled into that modest first house on Beals Street in Brookline. Though she was now one of the wealthiest women in America and though she had been to the fashion centres of the world and spent weekends with the Queen, her deepest concern remained her children.

The older ones were moving away, into new worlds—worlds that could be dangerous and that would prove whether all she had done had really prepared them. At fifty-one she remained the "solid base" for the family—never anxious, never visibly upset, never complaining. The family especially needed her solid good sense and unfailing balance as 1942 began, for the war was now no longer Europe's war or England's war, but also, very much so, America's—and Rose had two sons ready to see combat.

Rose was a frequent worker for war relief benefits and helped enlist important movie stars like Tallulah Bankhead to work with her, pouring tea at war relief gatherings. Her daughters rolled bandages, and even old Honey Fitz sang "Sweet Adeline" for the troops at the local USO in Hyannis Port, while *Mrs. Miniver* and *This Above All* played at the local theatres. (Fitz made a fleeting try—at eighty—for a political comeback by taking the stump against Joseph E. Casey in the Senatorial primary of 1942 but lost.)

The summer of 1943 Rose was again at Hyannis Port. It was quieter now, and she frequently walked the lonely strip of beach by herself and looked out over the choppy waters of Nantucket Sound; she listened more and more intently to the war news. Jack—who had worked his way, with his father's help, from an officer's desk job to command of a PT boat—was operating in the Pacific. Kick had left her job in Washington and finally got back to England to work with the American Red Cross and be with Billy Cavendish. Joe, Jr., had been an outstanding naval cadet and then flew un-inspiring Caribbean patrols; his desire was to serve in combat, based in England, and he would go there in September (bringing six dozen eggs from the Cape for Kick).

On August 6, Rose was listening carefully to the war news on the radio when she suddenly heard a simple announcement that

Lieutenant John F. Kennedy had been saved. Saved? From what? Joe had heard the news, too, on his car radio as he drove to Osterville; he became so excited that he drove the car off the road and into a field. The previous four days had been hell for him. On August 2 he had heard that Jack was missing in action, but he had not been able to tell the family; he did not even tell Rose, who later was to shield him. Perhaps "missing" would not—as it usually did in those tense years—mean "dead". What Joe did not know, of course, was that his son, after PT-109 had been rammed by a Japanese destroyer in Blackett Strait in the Solomon Islands, had fought furiously to save himself and ten older members of his crew. It had been an heroic effort, testing all his courage and stamina and ingenuity, but Jack had held his men together for four brutal days on the sea and then on a Japanese-controlled island and had finally brought them to safety. The shy young man who had loved *Billy Whiskers* and then *Ivanhoe* and then sailing and writing books had come out of a terrifying experience battered but no less than a hero.

In London, another drama was shaping up for Rose. Kick had decided to marry Billy Cavendish. Her letters home troubled Rose deeply. It was one of the few known times in her life that Rose Kennedy was visibly upset. Never in any sense had she indicated the slightest prejudice towards another race or religion; nor would she. But, as she has said: "We always required the children to maintain their integrity. We are Catholics, of course, and many of the families in Boston were not of our faith. But I tried to impress the children with the importance of observing the commandments of God and of the church." The church was always Rose's rock, and it was a matter of the greatest significance to her that her children retained their primary allegiance to it—and married within their religion.

Billy Cavendish was Protestant.

Kathleen, who had so many of her mother's qualities and her father's independent strengths, was more capable than either of them could ever be of putting deep personal affection beyond any other consideration; neither political nor economic reasons could have dissuaded her. Neither, finally, did the church. Joe, Jr., was in London at the time, and he could see and understand. "Never did anyone have such a pillar of strength," said Kick, "as I had in

Joe in those difficult days before my marriage. From the beginning, he gave me wise and helpful advice. When he felt that I had made up my mind, he stood by me always." Her father, who had always stressed individual judgment, could not, but if he did not stand in her way, neither would he give her away. Neither the Church of England nor the Church of Rome could bend to the other or to the young lovers, nor would the families. Rose was dead set against the marriage.

Kathleen Kennedy and William Cavendish, the Marquess of Hartington, were married on May 6, 1944, in a simple civil ceremony in the Chelsea Registry Office in London. Joe, Jr., stood in for his father and in a bleak wartime England gave Kick away. Rose and Joe did not fly over for the ceremony. Joe, in early April, had cabled his daughter: WITH YOUR FAITH IN GOD YOU CAN'T MAKE A MISTAKE. REMEMBER YOU ARE STILL AND ALWAYS WILL BE TOPS WITH ME. After the wedding, Rose sent no congratulations or messages of any kind. She could not have done so; she had not been told. It was one of the darkest moments in Rose Kennedy's life. While lying ill in a hospital bed, she was told the news by a friend who had heard it reported on the radio. She had very little to say to anyone and refused to speak with reporters—to whom she had always been receptive—about her daughter, the new Marchioness of Hartington. She asked a few of her closest friends to have nuns in convents pray "that everything would turn out all right".

Kick and Hartington had only slightly more than a month together before his Coldstream Guards were sent off for the invasion of Normandy. After he left, Kick returned home and was quietly welcomed back into the family by Rose at Hyannis Port. In mid-August, news reached them that Billy Cavendish had been killed by a sniper's bullet in Normandy. "I guess God has taken care of the problem in His own way," Kick was heard to say quietly, somewhat later, "hasn't He?"

Hartington's death came on the heels of another tragedy.

On August 2, 1944, all the Kennedys except Joe, Jr., were gathered at Hyannis Port; the Gargan children were with them in the house. Joe was summoned to the door, and the others continued talking while he was gone.

When he returned, Rose saw that his face was ashen. Two priests had come to tell him the news he dreaded most in the world to hear: his eldest son was dead. In a few words, Joe told Rose and the rest of the family. Though none of them would know the precise circumstances for many years, young Joe had been flying a PB4Y, loaded with thousands of pounds of high explosives; he was on a top-secret, highly dangerous mission, which he had elected to take rather than return home on the well-earned furlough he was entitled to. He had seemed to his friends, in the previous months, to have a fierce desire to excel, to prove himself in dangerous missions. He had known the risks and, following the Kennedy pattern, had taken them on, nearly to the day, the first anniversary of the day his younger brother Jack's PT boat had been struck. With tremendous force, his plane had exploded in mid-air. His body and that of his co-pilot were never recovered.

When Joe Kennedy finished his few terse words to his family, he went directly to his room and locked the door. He was never the same. It was left to Rose to console and hold together—as she had always done and always would do—the remaining Kennedys.

In later years, it was to his wife that Joe Kennedy always referred those who wanted to know about their eldest son, the young man who was determined to be nothing less than President. "She can talk of him," he would say, motioning to his wife. "I can't." And then Rose would provide the requested information, quietly, without emotion. He was a loner, she liked to say; like her, he preferred to travel alone.

Chapter Ten

The Campaigning Years

Public life is regarded as the crown of a career, and to young men it is the worthiest ambition. Politics is still the greatest and most honourable adventure.
JOHN BUCHAN

"I can feel Pappy's eyes on the back of my neck," Jack Kennedy told his good friend Paul Fay in early 1945; "when the war is over ... I'll be back here with Dad trying to parlay a lost PT boat and a bad back into a political advantage. I tell you, Dad is ready right now." So was Rose.

Though Fay and George "Barney" Ross, who both served with Jack in the Pacific, had "made book" as early as 1943 that someday he would be President, Jack was at first a reluctant candidate. His father, comparing the two oldest Kennedy boys, said, Joe "was altogether different from Jack, more dynamic, more sociable and easy-going. Jack, in those days back when he was getting out of college, was rather shy, withdrawn and quiet. His mother and I couldn't picture him as a politician." But Joe Kennedy insisted that "Joe was dead" and that it was, therefore, Jack's "responsibility to run for Congress. He didn't want to. He felt he didn't have the ability.... But I told him he had to".

Rose as well as Joe had always been exceptionally ambitious for her children; second place didn't count. Jack said he would have "kept being a writer", but as the war came to an end, he began to take on new goals. Perhaps they began as his parents' goals, but he had the ability and ultimately the vision to make them very much his own. Early in 1946, after a brief and undistinguished start as a reporter, he and his family decided that he should run for Congress representing the Eleventh District in Boston, where Honey Fitz had started his career as a three-term Congressman.

The war and his experiences on PT-109, his brother's death and his ascendancy within the family to "eldest son", his first-hand knowledge of politics from his grandfather, his father, his mother, and all the prominent public figures whom they had brought into his life—all these combined to urge him forward in the political arena. If he was reluctant at first, the genuine love of politics that lived particularly in his mother and her family soon became his. Mary Jo Clasby says of Rose: "I think she enjoyed politics from the time she was a child—really enjoyed it—found it fun and didn't find it a burden." Unlike his mother and his brother Joe, Jack had not loved it from childhood; but he discovered his talent soon and afterwards loved the "honourable adventure" of politics deeply. He found more than an ally and avid supporter in his mother: he found "a secret weapon".

I / 1946

She was the greatest pol we had in 1946....
—DAVE POWERS

When the tenacious old James M. Curley vacated his seat as Congressman for the Eleventh District, to become—still again—mayor of Boston, the Kennedys decided this was the ideal place for Jack to begin. The sprawling territory of the district included all or parts of East Boston, Charlestown, the North End, Cambridge, Somerville, the West End, and Brighton. It was a mixed and difficult Congressional district, but since it was predominantly Democratic, it was generally assumed that whoever won the primary fight would easily carry the election.

Though Jack was a stranger in the Eleventh District, Honey Fitz was well remembered, Jack and his brothers had gone to Harvard, his grandfather P. J. Kennedy had reigned in East Boston (where his father had been born), and his mother had been born in the North End. No one knew how much past history would count; everyone realized that his first task would be to make himself known. He had ten opponents in the primary fight, and he would have to come from absolute obscurity and inexperience to beat them all. Rose was enthusiastically behind her son from the start.

Joe Kennedy played a prominent role in the fledgling campaign of his son. From a telephone in his Ritz Carlton suite, behind the scenes, he plucked the strings of power. He knew everyone, and he called everyone; he opened doors and greased pathways. He did favours and had favours done for him—and for his son. He carefully invested a small fortune in Jack's campaign. But Jack surprised both himself and his father as he strode the streets of Cambridge and Charlestown and East Boston, growing more confident and relaxed each week, fielding questions, eliciting respect with his firm and frank manner, drawing admiration for his modest recounting of truly heroic war experiences.

But it was Rose, says Dave Powers, who was the only person then who really understood precinct politics—and that was always the greatest thing you could say about a Boston politician. She'd seen her father perform; she had seen him win. She had grown up with ward politics, and in 1946 she knew more people in the precincts than anyone else. She knew the value of charisma, of "pizazz"—for Honey Fitz had had that, if nothing else. She also knew how important it was never to forget a name, and her uncanny knowledge of the innumerable little details of campaigning in Boston, says Powers, made her extremely effective. She also brought other assets, not the least of which was her "double-barrelled name" Fitzgerald-Kennedy. Another asset, of course, was the fact that Rose was a Gold Star mother, and 1946 was a great year for the veteran. Powers remembers her speaking before all sorts of veterans' organizations; her reception at the Veterans of Foreign Wars Hall in Brighton was so positive that when she finished, Jack, who had come late, said: "They really love you in Boston, Mother."

Everything in Rose's life had prepared her to campaign for her sons—and campaign brilliantly. And to her very considerable skills, she brought a tenacious commitment to the future of these sons whom she had reared so carefully and thoughtfully to take their place in public life. She had helped, decisively, to create them. She knew them. She admired them. She would fight harder for their ascendance than for anything else she had ever fought for in her life. Even at eighty, she has been heard to say that she will live to see Ted President.

In 1946 she spoke chiefly at rallies, as opposed to the unique tea parties and social events she innovated and staged for the 1952

Senatorial campaign. "Sometimes," says Powers, "she'd appear just to hold the crowd—like she might take Brighton or some place like that while Jack was in Charlestown. Or some nights, when Jack couldn't get there or got held up, she'd take it by herself—and of course she was wonderful at it. She'd always give a great talk—not on politics, really—but she'd always tell them what they wanted to hear." She was always down to earth, and she always knew precisely to which group she was talking. The war was still very much on everyone's mind at the time, and she often spoke of her sons' experiences. Nothing could have been more effective. In the Eleventh District, "they loved a guy with guts", says Powers, and the story of Jack's courage and endurance in the PT-109 incident was often recounted. It moved everyone deeply—as Rose knew it would.

Honey Fitz, at eighty-three, did very little actual campaigning. Jack saw him practically every day because the Fitzgeralds still lived at the old Bellevue Hotel, where Jack had his campaign suite; but Fitz's friends were almost all over the hill by then, and some of Jack's closest advisers cautioned him against using his grandfather—with his checkered career—too heavily. Jack retained a tremendous amount of affection for the old man, but when Fitz advised, "I have a great friend over in the North End, Jack—now go and see him," the upshot was usually minimal. Paul Fay recounts a typical experience, when Fitz took Jack down to City Hall to introduce him to city workers. "No sooner had we reached City Hall," says Fay, "than Honey Fitz started shouting greetings to old friends. Soon his arms were waving, and the next thing you knew he was singing 'Sweet Adeline', and all the city workers in the huge room were singing it with him." When the festivities stopped, he started to head out the door with Jack. "Gramp," said Jack, "notwithstanding the impression to the contrary, it is your grandson who is running for office, not the beloved former mayor. Do you think we could try and get that message over before we leave?"

Jack himself was indefatigable. He could work all day and well into the night with his braced-up bad luck and then return the next day with the maturing and increasingly charismatic Kennedy smile. He even learned to do a lot of house parties, says Powers. "We'd have him scheduled for the Sullivans at seven, the Murphys at seven thirty, the O'Haras at eight, and there'd be five or six of those a night going from seven to ten. He did all those by himself, however; Rose wasn't there."

Not going to the house parties was probably another shrewd decision on Rose's part. It is part of the effectiveness of her method and effect that she always manages to create situations in which she can be both intimate and yet removed; the house party was too intimate, too informal for her style. She never descended from that slightly higher, slightly enchanted position she had achieved of near celebrity, near royalty, and she knew instinctively the dangers of overexposure. She functioned extremely well as a speaker and later even better as a hostess-speaker at affairs designed primarily for women. She knew where her strengths lay, and she would never do anything to undercut them.

For more than twenty years, the papers would continue to describe Rose, with almost monotonous regularity, as "a dark-haired elegant woman who has retained her youthful beauty". The dark hair she could control; the elegance and youthful beauty took hard regular work. She was aware of the impression she made, and the fact that her very appearance on the platform and then, briefly, on a reception line was in itself capable of drawing large crowds. Even when she campaigned for Bobby, at seventy-seven, an astounded old man exclaimed: "Look at those legs!" Her children knew her effect also; they sent her Mother's Day cards reading:

> Other mothers have this and that,
> But ours is one you can whistle at.

And in recognition of both her peripatetic qualities and her un-failing piety, both of which added to her public image:

> Grandma Moses sure can paint,
> But we prefer our travelling saint.

Beauty, poise, political savvy, purity, and devotion—they were difficult qualities to beat.

The crowning gesture of her "social" campaign in 1946 came at a massive tea party at the Hotel Commander in Cambridge.

Hand-addressed invitations were sent to every name in their files. Two thousand people appeared, breathless to see Rose Kennedy, her son, and the rest of the remarkable family; most of them were women. Such a reception gave the women a chance to hobnob with society, and it was an infinitely more effective political ploy than Honey Fitz's interminable rounds. It brought the voters to the candidate and to his family; it flattered them; it made them feel more important, more involved, more committed. When the women went home, they each told all their friends.

Jack Kennedy won 40 per cent of the vote in the field of ten and then easily went on to win the Congressional election. He won easily in 1948 and then again in 1950. He didn't even have to use his "secret weapon" again until he faced Henry Cabot Lodge, Jr.

II / 1952

It was those damned tea parties!
—Henry Cabot Lodge, Jr.

"When you've beaten him, you've beaten the best," Joe Kennedy told his son as they contemplated making a campaign against Henry Cabot Lodge. "Why try for something less?"

The 1952 Senatorial campaign in Massachusetts was primarily a political fight—the inevitable next step for Jack Kennedy. But the issues were slim, so it became in many ways an exceptional personal challenge—and also a challenge for the whole Kennedy clan. For years they had been marshalling their forces, making their plans for Jack's advancement. Lodge had been firmly entrenched since 1936 when Jack was still a student at Harvard, and he considered his own power so great that he boasted he would beat Kennedy by 300,000 votes. His father had handed Honey Fitz his last serious defeat, and the Lodges still represented the Yankee Brahmins that had goaded Joe. It was a severe political test for a young man and also a chance for the fiercely competitive family of Irish Catholics to band forces and fight, on open ground, a social rivalry that had existed for more than a century.

Rose wished her father was alive to witness the campaign. Although he would have been too old to help, he would have revelled in the old rivalry renewed. But on October 2, 1950, the colourful old Honey Fitz had died in his suite at the Bellevue Hotel. Josie was at his bedside, along with his sons Tom and John, Jr.; Rose was in Paris at the time and flew back immediately—which she did not do when her mother died. Fitz's will specified that Josie and his two sons receive portions of his estate and that, "for reasons best known to myself, I leave no part of my estate to any other relatives of mine." The absence of Rose's name was not a slur: she needed no part of his money, and he well knew it. He gave her the higher respect of naming his firstborn executrix of his estate.

The intervening years had brought other and unexpected sadness. On Thursday, May 13, 1948, Kick was flying from London to Cannes in a small chartered plane. Joe was in Paris, and he had made plans to meet his daughter on the Riviera for a short vacation together after some years of separation. The family was, as usual, widely scattered. Bobby was in Italy at the time, and Rose in Hot Springs, Arkansas.

The night was filled with rain and heavy fog, and the plane suddenly crashed into a mountain peak in southern France, instantly killing the two crew members, Kick's companion, Earl Fitzwilliam, and Kick herself. Her body was brought down from the cliffs in a simple peasant's cart, identified by Joe, and then flown to England. Rose flew to Derbyshire for the sad funeral of her spirited twenty-eight-year-old daughter, who had defied her heritage and married a Protestant. Kick was buried next to her husband in the Hartington family cemetery.

Tony Coluccio, an old Harvard friend of Jack's, had begun to lay the groundwork for the 1952 campaign as early as 1950, travelling throughout the state, enlisting the support of prominent citizens, gathering lists of future supporters. Later Larry O'Brien and Ken O'Donnell developed this base into a full-fledged network of state subcommittees. Behind the scenes (as usual) Joe Kennedy developed an impressive and well-oiled machine that arranged for regular popularity polls, new public relations ideas, and general strategy. Television was beginning to revolutionize politics, and Joe knew how to enlist its potent aid to bring attention to his son. He brought all his shrewd executive talents to the task of providing a razor-sharp "team" that handled the innumerable details of a

complicated campaign with previously unheard-of care and per-
fection. Bobby Kennedy, twenty-six and just out of law school,
was brought in for his first important campaign; he was installed
as manager and proved a tough, cocky, and even "ruthless" field
general. When the campaign was over, the word "ruthless" stuck,
but Jack insisted: "You can't make an omelette without breaking
the egg. I don't pay any attention to the beefs. Every politician in
Massachusetts was mad at Bobby after 1952, but we had the best
organization in history." And in Bobby's 1968 campaign, Rose
countered the charge many times, for it was indeed a misnomer;
Bobby, she said, was the most softhearted of her children.

The campaign was ideal for Rose Kennedy. There was some
trouble on both sides, drumming up an adequate issue—so the
campaign really became one of popularity and promotion, at which
she excelled. There were striking similarities between the two
candidates, both wealthy and well-educated sons of famous fathers.
But Jack, despite severe pains from his bad back, never let up; he
became an increasingly attractive candidate, independent in judgment (even from his father), thoughtful, quick-witted, and
genuinely hardworking. Lodge, feeling too confident that he would
win by 300,000 votes, campaigned for Eisenhower out of the state.
He stayed away too long.

A striking difference between the opponents was the ubiquity of
the Kennedy family—and their enormous popularity. Lodge had no
such support. The Kennedy girls were young and beautiful and
absolutely devoted to their brother. Eunice had developed into a
vigorous public speaker in her own right and a popular champion
of such social causes as better conditions for women's reformatories;
she was highly effective before large or small women's groups. And
with the addition of Bobby and Ted (then a Harvard undergradu-
ate), Kennedys seemed to be everywhere—ringing doorbells, speaking at women's clubs, talking on street corners. Every vote counted,
and they worked tirelessly, and in person, to cinch each one. But
the most dazzling and successful member of the family team was
Rose. Dave Powers says: "She was the greatest campaigner of
them all."

Jack had discovered that women voters outnumbered the men in
Massachusetts—a useful piece of information. They had usually
been neglected, but he and his advisers decided a direct appeal to

women might produce palpable results. Jack asked Polly Fitzgerald, the wife of Honey Fitz's youngest brother Edward, to hold a Sunday tea in Worcester. She was active in many women's groups and currently reigned as president of Rose's Ace of Clubs; eventually she became the principal organizer of the famous teas. Mrs. Fitzgerald was troubled by the prospect at first, but Jack said: "My mother will be there." The event was a sensation. Several thousand people came, and they were wildly enthusiastic when Rose stood up and introduced her son. Worcester inaugurated a new era in politics.

The strategists quickly convened, and everyone wondered whether the same thing could be done again the next week and the week after. They recalled the stupendous success of the reception at the Hotel Commander in 1946. They found that it could be repeated. Mrs. Fitzgerald recently explained how the teas were engineered: "We'd call people all over the state," she says, "who were outstanding in their community—usually it was a lawyer. It was difficult at that time to get a woman to work for you, because housewives and other ladies, well, they just didn't do this kind of thing; it was just very unusual for women to participate in politics at that time. The man we'd get from each community would form a committee of fifty women who were prominent for one reason or another, and we'd ask each of the fifty women to get in touch with ten people to see if they would come to the tea and then ask each of those ten people if they could think of ten more; in the end, you'd have five thousand people. We'd just start with the fifty and ask them to talk to everyone they saw at the hairdresser or the gas station or the bridge table to come, and that's the way it all worked and the way we were able to build up our card index files. Also, we engendered excitement and got people involved so that they'd bring their own tablecloths and silverware and that kind of thing. We'd send out all these invitations, although we never called them that; we called them 'announcements' because we wanted to get it across that everyone was invited who wanted to come."

"Reception in honour of Mrs. Joseph P. Kennedy, Sr., and her son, Congressman John F. Kennedy", the announcements would read. They would have the place and date—and in a lower corner, "Guests Invited". "Mrs. Kennedy was the big drawing card," says

Mrs. Fitzgerald, "there's just no doubt about it. It was still hard
to get people to come in the beginning, and the reason they came
at first was to meet Rose Kennedy."

There were thirty-three teas in 1952, and Rose was at most of
them. She worked on her appearances the way she had always
worked on everything from her Ace of Clubs to her children's
reading: with impeccable care and exact planning. She did her
homework. Before she'd speak to a group, she'd ask all kinds of
questions about the women she was going to address, and even
though she often gave the same speech at each different place, she
would adjust it slightly to satisfy the new needs; she also changed
her clothes—sometimes in her limousine—from a simple skirt and
blouse to expensive and elegant evening gowns, according to the
group she was meeting: it was a device she had learned from
Honey Fitz. Often she toured with John E. Powers, who was directing the campaign in the Boston area, and he says, "Rose wowed
them everywhere." Joe Kennedy, replying to Powers' request to
use Rose more actively in the campaign, had said: "But she's a
grandmother!" Powers insisted, stressing that she was "also a
Gold Star mother, the mother of a Congressman and a war hero,
the beautiful wife of Ambassador Joseph P. Kennedy and the
daughter of John F. Fitzgerald—which means that she's hot stuff
in Boston. I need her and I've got to have her." He had made a
shrewd judgment.

"For six weeks," says Powers, "every night about six I'd pick
her up and we'd go to meetings. Maybe the first place would be an
abandoned North End garage, and she'd put on a babushka and
talk to the women about children. And the next stop might be
West Roxbury, so in the car she'd change her shoes and maybe
put on a mink jacket."

After Lodge enlisted his beautiful sister-in-law, the former Fran-
cesca Bragiotti, to speak before Italian voters, Rose could counter
by beginning a speech in Italian to a group of Italians in the North
End. She knew which women wanted to hear about her children,
and she could trot out her famous index card file, explain it, and
tell over and over how her children had been rocked to sleep by
political lullabies. Wasn't she the daughter of Honey Fitz? Hadn't
she been in politics since the age of five? Others were more interested in clothes, and after some politicking for Jack, she'd say:

"Now let me tell you about the new dresses I saw in Paris last month."

The Kennedys were so glamorous and so exciting that it became a status symbol to support them. The children twice appeared on a television show called *Coffee with the Kennedys,* and everywhere they went they were greeted with awe. Rose could see that television was playing an important role in the campaign. She scrupulously watched Lodge and her son on television. Once she noticed that Lodge wore a tie with a design on it, and that this made a good impression on the screen, so she dropped Jack one of her little notes, mentioning how well his opponent's tie looked and was pleased to see that in Jack's next television appearance he had exchanged his plain tie for one with a design.

In her frequent appearances, Rose was always meticulously dressed, and Mrs. Fitzgerald says that this was far from an insignificant aspect of her effect: "It's flattering to an audience that someone cares enough about them to look that well." Especially if that person is Rose Kennedy. And she was also inspiring. Everyone knew that her eldest son had died in the war and that her daughter had died four years earlier, in a plane crash. She had had deep tragedy in her life, yet life had not vanquished her. The women were moved by the facts of her life, and after they stood on the long reception lines and shook hands with her and her daughters and Jack, they remembered it all their lives. She was a different kind of woman; they all were intrigued by her interest in politics and flattered by her presence; it made them feel important to have heard her—and they came back and talked to their neighbours. She had involved them, by carefully selected glimpses, in the marvellous behind-the-scenes world of her family, and when she asked them to vote for her son, they listened, and then they voted.

Even Jack could see the importance of appealing directly to the women. When he spoke before women's groups, he often began by telling the ladies that there were more women than men in Massachusetts. "Ladies," he'd say, "I need you." And then he'd tell them about the race between his grandfather and Henry Cabot Lodge, Sr., and complain that the election had been lost because women did not yet have the right to vote. He was no doubt correct.

What began as a general appeal, through newspaper ads and

invitations, to the women of the state, became in the end an organized effort by the whole family to win the women's vote. Eventually, in this campaign and in the Presidential campaign, PTA's, newswomen, clubwomen, and many other already established groups would be appealed to, to sponsor the teas and coffees. In such cases, there would be an already established circle of women, and the spark of Rose Kennedy would fire them to work as units on behalf of her son.

As the campaign moved into the last weeks, one of Rose's friends suggested that she ask people such as cabdrivers who they thought was doing best. On the way to Jack's Beacon Hill apartment by cab one night, she decided to give the plan a try.

"I think that young fellow Kennedy is going to win," the driver replied to Rose's question. She was delighted. But then the driver remembered the address he had been given, looked at Rose in the rearview mirror, and said: "You aren't by any chance related to him, are you?"

"Yes," said Rose. "I'm his mother."

"Boy, am I glad to meet you!" said the driver. "Your son owes me one dollar and sixty-five cents."

"I'll never do that again," Rose said later.

While Eisenhower was sweeping the country—and the state of Massachusetts—Jack pulled a dramatic upset: he beat Lodge by more than 70,000 votes. It had not been a "bought" election; like the early Honey Fitz, the whole family had simply "worked harder than anyone else". On the day they all received news of the decisive victory, Rose said: "At last the Fitzgeralds have evened the score with the Lodges."

III / 1960

What no one would ever face up to was the simple fact that the Kennedys just worked harder than anyone else. It was never money—although money helped; it was simple hard work.
—JOHN GALVIN

In 1956, when Jack Kennedy visited his mother and father at the family's rented villa at Cap d'Antibes after coming within a hairsbreadth of winning the Democratic nomination for the Vice Presidency, Joe told him not to be discouraged. Jack smiled and said that he was far from discouraged. In fact, his popular support seemed so great that he had just about decided to run for the Presidency in 1960. Rose says: "It was Jack's idea and nobody else's."

In the years that followed, Rose watched her son develop into an articulate public spokesman who faced the issues squarely; she saw him develop a quiet and winning wit and that rare quality called "style". Those around and behind him, for all the enthusiasm and excitement they could whip up and sustain, for all the brilliance of their strategies, could never again usurp his importance on centre stage. He had excellent "salesmen", but they had something to sell: he was not "sizzle" but very much "steak". Rose was there, and Rose was important in 1960, but those who charted the making of a new President said remarkably little about her. Though there were many others to help the family now, and in the forefront a young man who now knew precisely where he was going and how to get there, Rose Kennedy's help was no doubt greater than has yet been imagined.

There were some 120 teas given in the Presidential election of 1960, in most sections of the country. Polly Fitzgerald was their overseer, and Rose their principal attraction, often appearing with a woman more closely associated with the area—Marnie Devine in Michigan and (after the convention) Lady Bird Johnson in the South. *Look* magazine featured all the Kennedy women in its October, 1960, issue, proclaiming: "They are bright, energetic, and determined. The American political scene has never seen anything like them."

In 1953, Jack, then "the nation's most eligible bachelor", had married the exquisite and elusive Jacqueline Bouvier; the wedding, officiated by the family's close friend Richard Cardinal Cushing at St. Mary's Roman Catholic Church in Newport, was attended by 1,200 people and was considered a major social event. Now, in 1960, Jackie was part of the team, though she was pregnant with her second child and proved a reluctant campaigner—as, indeed, she sometimes proved a reluctant participant in the usual activities of the Kennedy clan. Eunice, who married Sargent Shriver in May, 1953, remained the most electric and persuasive, and she was joined by Pat, who had married actor Peter Lawford in 1954; Jean, wife of campaign strategist Steve Smith; Ethel, Bobby's athletic and vigorous—and fertile—wife; and Joan, twenty-four, who had recently married Ted and who proved an attractive and valuable campaigner. They all campaigned long and hard.

Eunice, Pat, and Jean had helped Rose stage the tea parties in 1952 and were all experienced boosters; with a country rather than a state to conquer, they were sent where they would be most effective. In the primaries, they all descended upon the target state like a whirlwind, and in the pivotal Wisconsin test against Hubert Humphrey they were a decisive factor.

Rose began the year with a two-day swing through New Hampshire in February; the New Hampshire primary was of course the kickoff of the long campaign, and she preceded Jack into the state, as an advance guard, by several days. She appeared at four to five gatherings a day, each time delivering a similar speech that included comments on Jack's youth, his dislike of war, his early training and success. Between receptions, like her father, she would lie down in the back of the car and take a catnap; on the way to Exeter, for a dinner and reception, she reached into her handbag and brought out a chicken sandwich; and at the Exeter Inn she explained that she liked to be called neither modish nor chic. "Dignified is what I like. I don't like to be overdressed, but to be dressed well enough so that people are interested." She was impeccable in her effects.

She spent eight strenuous days in Wisconsin, getting out each day at eight thirty for a round of speeches before college groups, women's clubs, and before television cameras. A strong undercurrent of religious controversy had begun to surface, and Rose met it head on, boldly holding a luncheon meeting with three prominent local Protestant ministers who had taken a strong religious stand against Jack Kennedy's election.

In West Virginia the Kennedy women were kept out of sight, and the New York *Times* speculated that they were considered "too attractive, too well-dressed, and too rich to parade before the people of this economically depressed state, with its thousands of unemployed coal miners". There was also less organized social activity in Wisconsin, and this increasingly became the area in which Rose could function best. West Virginia was a man's job, and so Bobby and Ted rolled up their shirt sleeves and took to the mines.

Rose once told in some detail the degree to which the Kennedys made politics fully a family affair, with each person contributing special skills. They had recognized in the Lodge campaign how important it was to appeal directly to ethnic and minority groups, so in 1960 the special abilities of all family members were carefully scrutinized. Jackie, because she spoke French and Italian so well, spoke before these groups. Eunice, who had once been received by Queen Frederika, was chosen for a Greek group. Pat, who was with her husband Peter Lawford for the filming of *Exodus* in Israel, spoke to Jewish community clubs, and Bobby—who had once gone to Poland—was assigned to galvanize the Polish vote along with Jack's brother-in-law, Prince Radziwill. The connections ran rather slim at times. They even sought a small Lebanese vote on the strength of a short visit Eunice had once taken to Beirut—and she carried some Lebanese silks to the platform for effect. Rose herself was elected to speak before some first-generation Germans in the Wisconsin primaries—since she knew some German from her travels and her convent years—but at the last moment local aides advised her that Wisconsin Germans did not like to be reminded of their origins.

Jack's wins in the primaries were decisive, and as the Kennedy operation moved en masse out to Los Angeles in July for the National Democratic Convention, there was a distinct aura of confidence about them all. Several days before the convention, Rose announced: "I'll go wherever they want me to go and do whatever they want me to do during the campaign." No one seemed to doubt that Jack would win the nomination.

Rose was now seventy and had shown virtually no sign of diminishing energy or effectiveness. Her public flaws remained minimal; she had maintained all her beauty and all her youthfulness, and if in her mid-forties she had made people believe in the stork, at seventy—and later, at eighty—she surely gave credence to the presence of some hidden fountain of youth. How does she do it? women wanted to know. Is she *really* as attractive and youthful as the papers say? Such surface questions were easily answered, but questions of a more probing or intimate nature usually remained speculation, for Rose on the platform and in every public interview is so rehearsed in her role, so sure of the precise impression she makes, that, as one reporter noted with exasperation, "penetration is effectively impossible". To every question one reporter asked her, he could sense her first pose an inner question before she answered: "Will the way I answer this question help or hurt Jack's campaign?" She never let down her guard.

While Bobby Kennedy and Larry O'Brien were engineering in Los Angeles what Joe later called "the best organization job I've ever seen in politics"—with walkie-talkies at the convention, a twelve-car Kennedy motor pool, fifty lovely Kennedy girls, and a daily Kennedy tabloid—Jack holed up in the Mauritania Apartments. Rose worked on the outside, right to the last minute. The day before the convention balloting, she gave a wave of a white kid-gloved hand to a press group, flashed her best press smile, and admitted to being seventy (though it was then ten days before her birthday) since "it wouldn't look too good for Jack if I were too young". She handled the press conference with "the agility of a pro"—giving her dress size, minimizing her son's youth ("he's old in wisdom gained from many years of travel"), proclaiming yet again that he had been raised on "political lullabies", advancing the cause of youth in the White House (since they have "a great deal of vigour, enthusiasm, and idealism, which we need now"). Asked bluntly if Joe was not "masterminding the campaign", she smiled and said: "Of course my husband has helped, as we all have." And asked about her husband's wealth, she drew out her old quip: "When I first read the papers that he had one hundred million dollars I went to him and asked: 'Why didn't you tell me you had that much money?'" His reply, she reported, was: "I didn't know myself." She was never stumped; there was never a question, however blunt and even intimidating, that she could not turn to a political advantage through careful twisting or with a "smidgeon of blarney".

Religion? "I don't know about it nationally or as an issue, but I think it's wonderful for children."

Political ambition? "If you're in politics, I suppose you always work to get to the top."

Joe's *real* part in the campaign? Her statement was a model of political quarter truth: "He never campaigns publicly. He works quietly and unobtrusively. He stays at home taking care of our business interests and our philanthropies."

Her son *was* young, but he had "met Winston Churchill and Anthony Eden and others who were making history before the Second World War".

Jack would keep us out of war because "his oldest brother had died in the war, so Jack knows the sorrow, the grief, the tears, and the heart-breaking grief and loneliness that comes when a mother has lost her eldest son."

If the answers became too familiar, if they were a bit too shrewdly slanted to contain, ever, the whole truth, they were surely brilliant politically. And always there was the possibility, when Rose spoke, of some new detail being thrown out and added to the mythos of that near-royal family the Kennedys—and more news about the Kennedys was always welcome. At times the fight itself took on the semblance of a family campaign, with a multiple Presidency as the goal; Rose frequently spoke of how "we defeated Henry Cabot Lodge" and of "our fight against Senator Humphrey in Wisconsin".

John F. Kennedy was acclaimed the candidate of the Democratic Party on the first vote; he won by within five votes of his headquarters' predicted total. It was a staggering display of teamwork and clockwork timing.

Rose and Joe took off for a six weeks' vacation at their rented villa at Cap d'Antibes, between Cannes and Nice. They swam at chic Eden Roc, a mile or so away, since their own villa on Boulevard du Cap was cut off from the sea by neighbouring property, and they played golf regularly at nearby Biot golf course. A reporter sought her out even there, and after an extensive interview she prodded him to ask a question that had not yet been asked.

"Well, young man," she said as he rose to leave, "you haven't asked me the one question all the other reporters have asked during the campaign."

"Oh," said the startled reporter, "and what is that?"

"You haven't asked me how it feels to be the mother of a man who is running for President."

The question was quickly reiterated, and Rose answered obliquely: "That, young man, is the right of every American mother."

As she prepared to return for the last two months of campaigning in the fall, she mentioned several times that she would go after "the grandmothers' vote". She was an expert. She now had sixteen grandchildren.

In September and October, Rose maintained a full schedule of tea parties and coffee hours. There was only one goof, in South Carolina, and that proved harmless. Polly Fitzgerald thought it would be a good idea to hold an integrated tea for Rose at the governor's mansion. A local Democrat sharply informed her that "the easiest way to swing South Carolina Republican is to have an integrated tea at the governor's mansion". Polly insisted that Rose would not appear at a segregated tea and also wanted the event to take place. She was finally persuaded to drop the whole event, and that's what was done, quietly.

Jack picked up impressive support after the celebrated television debates with Nixon. He was cool and poised and made an excellent impression on the screen. Nixon looked haggard and drawn; he was hesitant and obviously nervous. After the first debate—the worst for Nixon—Rose said: "I felt so sorry for Nixon's mother tonight."

As for the possibility of her son becoming President, she had no doubts. In a revealing statement that genuinely reflected the kind of absolute faith she always had in Joe Kennedy, Rose said: "My husband, Joseph, is sure Jack will make it. He's said so for more than six months. I'm an old-fashioned wife. I believe what he believes; he is right so often." And then, reflecting that total belief in the hard work her father had always stressed, she said: "If you're in politics, I suppose you always work to get to the top. If you're serious about it and work very hard, you naturally have some idea that you'll someday succeed. I've been in politics since I was five years old, and my son Jack has been in it for ten years. The belief that he'll succeed has been growing gradually. I'm used to the idea now."

As the campaign drew into the last days of October, there was evidence that Rose was tiring, but like the experienced politician she was, she knew how to pace herself, to conserve her energy for those moments that counted. On a final three-day trip to Michigan, before heading on to Chicago during the first few days in November, the reporters began to find her sharp and cool. "That's a political question," she'd snap, "and I don't answer those." When klieg lights were thrust on her, she announced: "I can't have this." And when she was pressed, between speaking engagements, she'd say, "I have no more time," and "The things I have to say, you will hear at the gathering."

She frequently closeted herself and took breakfast and lunch alone, despite constant invitations from local women, and when she was plane-hopping between Michigan cities, dressed in a simple tweed suit, as soon as she was in her seat she'd put on eyeshades and promptly fall asleep. In private situations she showed no urgency about the impression she made; she could retreat to her own world with ease—and needed such moments of peace. But when she faced the crowds of 400, 800, 2,000 she was fresh and quick-witted and moving. Appealing to the grandmother vote, she used the phrase "If Jack is elected, I hope baby-sitting in the White House will be one of my duties" seventeen times during the Michigan swing. She was capable of shaking hands for two straight hours in the heavily Catholic Bay City, which had turned out en masse to see and greet her. She could rest in private—and after the election.

American voters went to the polls on Tuesday, November 8, and by midmorning of the next day—after watching an early Kennedy lead dwindle dramatically—it was clear that the United States had elected its first Catholic President. The margin of victory was scarcely decisive, but it was enough. John F. Kennedy received 303 electoral votes to 219 for Richard M. Nixon. Kennedy carried only twenty-three states to Nixon's twenty-six, and in the popular count, Kennedy won by a mere 112,881 votes, or one-tenth of one per cent of the total vote cast.

That morning all the Kennedys got into four automobiles and drove a mile and a half to the Hyannis Port Armory, where the network television cameras were waiting. On the platform, to the right of her victorious son, sat Rose Kennedy, her back straight, her chin high, her whole appearance quietly triumphant and proud. Honey Fitz would have loved it; he would have known precisely what to sing. The President-elect sang nothing but in solemn mood pledged all his energy to advancing "the long-range interests of the United States and the cause of freedom around the world." The election had been frighteningly close, and the world problems he would soon face were awesome. But the torch had been passed.

When the family gathered for a formal session of photographing in the main house, Joe grumpily objected when Rose was seated in a huge wing chair. "That's an awkward pose," he said. "There are plenty of chairs in the house." Another chair was fetched, but then Rose found fault. She was next to Jackie, who was wearing a scarlet dress; she herself wore cerise. Rose said: "Our dresses clash horribly for colour photography." William Walton, Jack's friend and also an artist, thought otherwise, and the picture was finally taken with Rose and the new First Lady sitting in separate chairs, a few feet apart. Rose already looked like a Queen Mother of Camelot.

Chapter Eleven

The Queen Mother of Camelot

... a golden age of poetry and power
of which this noonday's the beginning hour.
—ROBERT FROST

No one who was there that Friday will ever forget it. It was one of those glittering days that never fade or chip in memory like the souvenir ashtrays and gold-glo dinner plates featuring garish portraits of the new First Family that were already being hawked that morning by every newsstand in Washington. Thousands upon thousands had converged on the city with all the abandon and unruly hope of a triumphant army, their revelry rocking the town day and night as they spilled their drinks over miles of hotel carpeting; they remained unsubdued even by the raging blizzard that had strangled the streets the night before, and they had made their way that night through eight inches of snow to hear Ethel Merman sing "Everything's Coming Up Roses".

At high noon they gathered in front of the newly expanded East Front of the Capitol, wrapped in blankets and masked with odd improvised scarves and coverings, cheeks semifrozen by the biting cold and eyes blinded by the blazing sunlight. They were basking in the spoils of victory. The torch was being passed, and it was a new generation of leadership; the word was going forth from that time and place, and the word was "Kennedy"—a name that was to dominate the whole decade of the sixties. January 20, 1961, was the birth of Camelot.

Rose Kennedy, as usual, was up early that morning. The day broke bright and sharply cold, and in Georgetown she walked with some difficulty through the heavy snow, past the abandoned cars, towards Holy Trinity Church, where Father Anderson Bakewell, SJ, was scheduled to hold a special mass to ask God's blessing for the inauguration. When she saw the policemen around the building, she thought with pleasure that Jack must have come. There had been a party the night before in the cavernous basement of Paul Young's Restaurant on Connecticut Avenue, hosted by the elder Kennedys, and since it had started several hours after midnight, no one had returned home until the early-morning hours.

Jack was not in the church when Rose entered. But he came shortly thereafter, alone, and sat in an end seat. The church was about four-fifths filled. He kneeled on his prayer bench during the offertory and consecration, but did not take communion because he had recently had breakfast. The bright sun was fully up now, and its diffused light through the stained-glass windows spread over the worshippers. The President-elect squinted now and then, deep in thought; newsmen hovered near the radiators in the back of the little church. "I didn't sit with him," said Rose, "because I was bundled up with a lot of funny-looking scarves and things, but I was delighted to think that he had gone." She had not urged him to go, though only because he had been so busy with the rush of his momentous new responsibilities. "But the fact that he did go on his own," she remembers, "and did think it important to start his new administration out with mass in the morning gave me a wonderfully happy feeling."

Just before one o'clock, at the southeast corner of the inaugural stand, Rose sat with her husband. Joe, wearing a top hat, had a broad, irrepressible smile; Rose, in dark glasses and a mink coat, concentrated on every word as, speaking without a coat from the East Front, her son John F. Kennedy invoked the nations of the world to "begin anew—remembering on both sides that civility is not a sign of weakness, and sincerity is always subject to proof.... Together let us explore the stars, conquer the deserts, eradicate disease, tap the ocean depths and encourage the arts and commerce." Years later, she would say how "fortunate" she felt as she watched her son being inaugurated on "that cold, cold day". A reporter who watched her said that her "looks defied clichés on mothers of Presidents."

The stiff, sharp wind blew, and the wiring went bad, and the sun obstructed the words on a poet's page, but Richard Cardinal Cushing kept on with his invocation and Robert Frost struggled with and then finished his poem. "The Gift Outright". And then there was a gala post-inaugural luncheon, and then a joyous parade with

32,000 marchers and eighty-six bands and a float carrying a model of Jack's PT-109. The crowds numbered nearly a million. Most of them forgot the cold. You could see the glow on their faces.

Despite hideous traffic jams, the five main inaugural balls that evening were jammed. The largest was at the National Guard Armory, festooned in blue and white satin, where some 12,000 ecstatic guests cheered, drank champagne and Pepsi-Cola, ate fruit-cake, and danced on the crowded floor to the music of Count Basie and Meyer Davis emanating from a giant carousel with a yellow umbrellalike cover that wheeled around so that each, in turn, could play. Joe Kennedy could not suppress an ear-to-ear smile all night long, and Rose was ravishing in her elbow-length white gloves and her white chiffon Molyneux gown, embroidered with silver sequins, the gown she had worn twenty-three years earlier, when she was officially presented at the Court of St. James's. She and Jackie flanked the President in his balcony box overlooking the massive and jubilant ball before they all slipped out and went to another of the inaugural balls. Joe, radiantly smiling, solicitously helped Rose climb over the chairs on their way out.

Rose did not return to the White House until mid-April, when she came for a few days' visit that included a luncheon with Premier Constantinos Karamanlis of Greece and a gay, informal party —the first large one of the new administration—for some 1,000 Congressmen and their wives the following night. She was no stranger to the White House after that and came periodically for short visits. In November she attended the historic concert by Pablo Casals in the East Room, which began a new cultural era in the White House. Casals had played for Teddy Roosevelt fifty-seven years earlier but had not returned because of America's recognition of Franco Spain. Rose sat in the front row, listening intently while Casals played selections from Mendelssohn, Schumann, and Couperin on his 250-year-old Goffriller violoncello. Among the 153 guests were Gian Carlo Menotti, Leonard Bernstein, Leopold Stokowski, and Eugene Ormandy. They all called the performance superb—and the administration that had made it possible, rare and enlightened.

When Rose stayed at the White House, she occupied the famous Lincoln Room on the second floor and slept in the nine-foot-long Lincoln bed, made of fine rosewood. Though she later stated that "the bedrooms are a little cosier at Windsor Castle where the rooms are connected", she enjoyed the room, with its portrait of Lincoln and the elaborately carved Victorian table in front of the fireplace, on which was propped up a matted copy of the Gettysburg Address, one of five copies actually written by Lincoln. On the small desk, which Lincoln used when he went to the Soldiers' Home near Washington (to escape the heat and crowds), Rose wrote frequent notes to her children and grandchildren on White House stationery. One of Andrew Jackson's magnolia trees was directly outside the window, and the room was flooded with sunlight during the day. Once the President was showing a group of distinguished visitors around the second floor and wanted to take them into the Lincoln Room. He opened the door—and then shut it quickly: Rose was taking one of her frequent catnaps.

"In eleven weeks," Jack Kennedy said, "I went from Senator to President and in that short space of time I inherited Laos, Cuba, Berlin, the nuclear threat, and all the rest. It was a terrific adjustment to make."

Rose had no adjustment to make whatsoever. Her role as Queen Mother of Camelot was entirely natural for her. She loved it. Nearly three decades had elapsed since a President's mother, Sara Delano Roosevelt, served as her son's official hostess; Rose first served as hostess for the visit of President Julio Arosemena of Ecuador and his family when Jackie chose to remain in Hyannis Port with the children. Comments about a possible Kennedy dynasty were already prevalent, and the subject came up in toasts at the White House luncheon. Arosemena's father had also been President of Ecuador, but Mrs. Arosemena confided to Rose that her ten-year-old son, Carlos Julio, Jr., had made up his mind to be a soldier. The Ecuadorian First Lady explained that her son didn't want to be President because he had heard "so many cracks about a family dynasty". As she would many times defend the presence of all her sons in politics, Rose replied with feeling and some exasperation: "I think it's wonderful if people want to serve their country; I think it's a great thing." She mentioned her admiration for the Adams family and said: "They were wonderful—something to be proud of.... I don't understand why people don't approve of it. I think boys should be encouraged to go into public service.

I think it's a thing to be praised." Later, a reporter saw Rose standing in the eighth-floor penthouse garden at a State Department reception. "Slim as a girl, in a white satin sheath embroidered in a pattern of shimmering beads, she was youthfully enthusiastic as lightning slashed the sky above the Washington Monument."

Rose was vacationing on the Riviera when the President and Jackie went on their enormously successful European tour in June, 1961. She met them in Paris, and was nearly Jackie's peer at the receptions with De Gaulle. Nearly, but this time not quite. For it was Jackie's triumph. Even Jack could say that he was the man who had accompanied Jacqueline Kennedy to Paris and that he loved it. Rose was escorted by General and Mrs. Lauris Norstad to the elegant dinner and ballet at the Palace of Versailles. The fountains had been turned on and lighted, and a soft rain diffused the light so that everything had that soft and hazy feeling of fantasy. But it was no fantasy. For a woman like Rose, who underneath was always so solid and foresighted, it was a very real pinnacle that had been achieved through real work.

Rose was especially interested in meeting Mrs. Khrushchev and travelled to Vienna for Jack's historic meeting with the Russian Premier. Rose enjoyed Mrs. Khrushchev's company immensely. "She impressed me because she spoke English so well," said Rose. "She shows a lot of initiative and fulfils her position very well." Mrs. Khrushchev also had a "wonderful smile. She was just like a neighbour you'd call in to help out if you were in an emergency."

Now and then Rose tampered in the affairs of her son, the President. She started collecting books and would then get them autographed by the prominent authors. "I had the memoirs of De Gaulle," she says. "I had Mr. Hoover's book on the Great Depression. I had Mr. Eisenhower's memoirs, and different ones —Sean O'Casey's plays—autographed by the different authors." Then she wanted to get one by Mr. Khrushchev—but he hadn't as yet written a book. Instead, she sent a photograph of Khrushchev and her son in Vienna to the Premier—who autographed and returned it. Then she gave it to Jack and asked him to sign it also, so that she could give it to his brothers and sisters for Christmas.

"Dear Mother," Jack wrote back. "If you are going to contact the heads of state, will you please contact me first or the State Department because it may lead to international complications."

Rose replied: "Dear Jack: Thank you very much for your note, and I'm glad you wrote to me because I was going to contact Castro."

And in relating that anecdote, Rose ended: "So then I didn't."

Once she also mentioned to him that in the two-tone camel's hair coat he liked to wear "he'd look much better if he held his hands behind his back like the British did". The President weighed the matter seriously, as he had her suggestion in the Lodge campaign that he wear a striped tie on television, and in the next photograph of him, Rose was satisfied to see her son with his hands behind his back.

On December 19, 1961, a little more than a year after his son had been elected, Joe Kennedy was about to tee off on the back nine of the Palm Beach Country Club golf course when he felt somewhat uneasy. It was an exquisite day, but somehow he didn't feel his usual vigorous self. "I really don't feel well today," he told Ann Gargan, "but it must be the cold I've had."

He chose to walk rather than ride an electric golf cart, but on the sixteenth hole he felt weary and tired and had to sit down. Ann sensed that something serious might be wrong and took him off the course and drove him the short distance to his North Ocean Boulevard home. Inside, Rose grew concerned, but he insisted that she not call a doctor. He told his granddaughter Caroline that he was going upstairs to rest, walked up—and then collapsed. He had suffered a severe stroke.

From that moment, Joe Kennedy was a man fighting death. His speech was lost and then partially recovered and then became impossible again; he was able to walk for a while with a cane but spent most of his time confined to bed and wheelchair. He fought hard for rehabilitation, aided by Ann Gargan, who devoted herself completely to her uncle; but there were intermittent setbacks, and his condition continued to deteriorate, slowly and painfully over the next seven years. Wherever she went after that, Rose always had Joe on her mind. "You know Mr. Kennedy has been ill," she'd say. Friends noted that she seemed always to be in some conflict about his "terrible inadequacy". She deeply sensed his inner frustration after having lived so dynamic a life, and several people have mentioned that at times she almost seemed as if she wanted him to die. After Bobby's assassination, a saleswoman at Bergdorf-

Goodman's reports that Rose, who was in shopping for a mourning dress, suddenly looked up in despair and said: "Oh, why did it have to be Bobby? Why couldn't it have been Joe?"

Rose had always been a loner, but she felt more and more isolated after Joe's stroke. Still, she continued to travel whenever she could. She especially loved Paris—and still does. She usually went for the fashion collections in February and July and liked to slip into the city unnoticed and go directly to the Hôtel Ritz at 15 Place Vendôme. There she always took the same room, No. 94, on the *quatrième étage* (the equivalent of an American fifth floor). Her room is not one of the Ritz's elegant salon-suites, decorated in Empire style with stucco murals of the Napoleonic-Egyptian period or with gilt sphinxes on the fireplace and furniture. It is a modest single room with bath, and costs, modestly, only a little more than $30 a day.

Each time she entered the white door to the room, with its polished brass hardware, Rose saw the old wooden wood bin and the brass umbrella rack near the entrance. She liked the simple room, almost a "nun's room" it has been called, decorated, appropriately, in rose-red. It has rose carpeting, with a deeper red-leaf pattern woven into it and a rose satin bedspread on the slightly oversized bed; a soft chair between the closets and the fireplace is upholstered with rose fabric. There are two little night tables, a dressing table, and a simple desk. The most attractive feature of the little room is its walk-on balcony, which looks down upon an appealing interior garden and courtyard. The room is at the back of the huge hotel; it is exceptionally quiet, and her privacy is assured.

When she went to Paris, Rose wanted only to be seen on formal occasions. She was the mother of the American President now, and she wanted her privacy. She preferred to go about in the streets unnoticed, unrecognized in dark glasses, low-heeled shoes, and a green or black celluloid visor. The Ritz—particularly her small "rose room"—was Rose's private oasis and retreat from her vigorously social life and from the ubiquitous press. The hotel is ideal. For all its grandeur, the Ritz seeks to be truly homelike. Television is unknown, the radio forbidden. The Ritz does not even have a telephone for floor service; each room has, on a bedside table, a small battery of buttons marked "chambermaid", "valet", "waiter", and "service privé"—for those with private servants quartered elsewhere in the huge building. Every room also has a built-in clock, since César Ritz (its founder and a Swiss), like Rose, had an obsession about time. Bills are still handwritten, for the machine-printed statement is regarded as too impersonal.

Rose loved Paris. She was there when the President's son died shortly after birth and when her mother died; neither time did she return to America, though she had returned when her father died. In the mornings she always rose early, often boiled her own coffee or tea on her little Meta (a French hot plate), perhaps ate a banana or orange she had bought on the street, and then attended seven o'clock mass regularly at the Église Catholique Polonaise on the Rue St.-Honoré or the Église St. Roch. At least three times a week, between eleven and twelve, she took French lessons with Mlle. Paule Lafeuille, a remarkable woman, slim and with reddish-brown close-cropped hair, who taught such prominent figures as Ambassadors Douglas Dillon, Amory Houghton and Charles Bohlen, General James Gavin, and many others. Her charge was amazingly low: $3 per hour.

One Sunday morning at ten o'clock Rose asked her teacher if she could come to the Ritz to give a lesson. "I know it is Sunday," she said, "and I don't want to interfere with your personal life. Are you back from church?"

"Mrs. Kennedy," said Mlle. Lafeuille, who had not been to church in many, many years, "it's a long time since I came back from church." She went to the Ritz at once.

Though Mlle. Lafeuille says that when Rose first came to her in the early 1960's, she "spoke French fluently with a strong American accent", Rose may still have been smarting from a reporter's judgment, shortly before the election, that her French was "not so fractured as it sounded fried in bacon grease". She needed *"petits perfectionnements"*, Mlle. Lafeuille recalls, and remembers her first sight of Rose in the little "nun's room, surrounded with French newspapers and magazines—trying to fight the language". Together they read *Le Monde* and *Le Figaro*, and Rose displayed her vital interest in politics and humanity, reading in French and then asking questions about what she did not understand. Mlle. Lafeuille found her not at all like most Americans, who feigned interest in French affairs, but deeply concerned. Together they once went to

Versailles, the night the private apartments were to be illuminated as they had been in the time of Louis XIV, by candlelight, and Rose was avidly curious the whole time—noticing everything, constantly asking questions of her guide, displaying a vibrant enthusiasm for the historic palace.

She has remained a perpetual student. She is, says her teacher, "a woman of extreme elegance who *gardait son jeunesse*"—literally, "kept her youth", as opposed to those older people who merely *try* to look young. "Evidently," she says, Rose "is the root of those marvellous young men who all look so much much like her. . . . She gave me the impression that she would never die, that she had everything in front of her. That she would study a foreign language at her age makes her forever seem like a young girl."

But if she was a student in Paris, she was also an impeccable connoisseur of fine clothes, with an unfailing interest in the newest fashions. She visited the leading salons regularly and is noted for being energetic, decisive, and extremely well organized. One of her *vendeuses* says, *"Elle est très difficile"*, another that *"Elle est toujours pressée"*. She is difficult during fittings and keeps a hawk's eye on every step of the proceedings to make sure that all is perfect. She comes for private morning appointments, rather than the three o'clock showings, speaks French in these houses of *haute couture*, prefers bright colours (particularly rose), makes sure her choice is always *"assez discreet"*, understands dressmaking, and is something of a fabric expert in her own right. Everywhere the *vendeuses* marvel at her vivacity, youthfulness, and remarkable figure.

Even when Jackie, under protest from American couturiers (and her husband) abandoned Givenchy for Oleg Cassini in New York, Rose continued to shop vigorously in Paris at least twice a year. Since the thirties, when she was pronounced "the best-dressed woman in public life" in a poll of style designers (Ginger Rogers was, at the same time, honoured for "best exemplifying the dress dictates of the typical American girl"), Rose has been one of the leading figures in the demanding fashion world. She is still constantly mentioned in *Women's Wear Daily,* and she regularly appears on the Best Dressed list—which usually sports at least a few other Kennedy women, either in-law or flesh. Such accolades don't come by chance.

Whether she wears a large strawberry-coloured straw hat or a

St. Laurent gown, a white felt slouch hat and red-and-white check suit, or a jewelled pink Givenchy evening gown, Rose has that same quality her father had: a defined sense of rightness and style. Givenchy (her favourite for night clothes) and Nina Ricci (her preference for day wear) head her list, but Goma, St. Laurent, Lavin-Castillo, Dior, Balenciaga, Grès, Griffe, and even the less fashionable Rouff are patronized when she is in Paris. She wears clothes from them all—and wears them to advantage. Even when, on her seventy-seventh birthday some years later, she wore a print dress to match that of her sixteen-year-old granddaughter Kathleen (Bobby's daughter, who has the same birthday) and mod white mesh stockings and buckle shoes, she met and won the moment.

Rose's elegant friend Helene Arpels was her most frequent companion in Paris, and her advice was always highly valued when making a selection. On Mrs. Arpels' suggestion, black-and-white sketches were sometimes sent to Rose, who occasionally ordered from these. Some of the houses keep a dummy of her, as they do for such fashion leaders as Elizabeth Taylor and Sophia Loren, and are thereby able to fit her from a pattern she has selected. At times, Rose has bought two or three of the same dresses and then left them in different places.

When Genevieve Antoine-Darriax was *directrice des ventes* at Nina Ricci, she took care of Rose personally and often sent sketches of new patterns to America with letters written in English. Always the teacher as well as the student (if not quite as "thredbare" as Chaucer's Clerk of Oxenford), Rose replied in French, with the original letter enclosed and corrected. "She would explain certain idiomatic phaseology," says Mme. Antoine-Darriaux, "the proper turn of a sentence; she would correct my spelling and grammar mistakes. She would go to a great deal of trouble—and then always asked me to do the same thing with her letters, written in French. But of course I never did."

Of all this concern over her looks, Marie Greene says: "It's obvious that Rose has always paid an enormous amount of attention to her appearance, but then, that's just the way some women are, don't you think? It just matters to them more. It just doesn't matter all that much to me, and this has always driven Rosie crazy. She was always at me about your bag matching your shoes, the way to wear pearls, and once even sent me four lipsticks with directions like 'this one should be worn with blue serge' and things like that." Marie promptly got the entire scheme all mixed up and finally had to tell Rose: "For God's sake, don't do things like this to me—I can't keep track of what goes with blue serge and all the rest." And Marie remembers another time, when Rose sent her a jet bag, all handmade, for combs and brushes and the like. One day when they were driving in the Boston area, Rose suddenly spotted the jet bag on the floor of the car and "was, to say the least, somewhat floored herself—if you'll excuse the pun. *'Marie,'* she said, obviously aghast, 'do you realize that I paid a hundred and thirty-five dollars for that bag?' I did, and loved it, but tried to explain that I was involved in so many things that I always ended up changing my bags in the car. That's not the kind of thing Rose can understand."

A New York makeup specialist who saw Rose a few times when she was filming a television short offers a few close-up observations on Rose's striking youthfulness and bearing: "She has one of those typical Anglo-Saxon angular faces where there is little fat under the skin.... Her bone structure is the main thing, however; it's the same thing that Garbo and Hepburn and Lana Turner have." He noted that at her age she of course had had her hair dyed and didn't think it should have been done so black: "There should be a softer look, because dyes are indiscriminate, you know, and you don't get a pure black. What's remarkable is her vigorous growth of hair; there's nothing sparse—it's very virile." But he was even more impressed, as so many others were during and after Jack's administration—both professional fashion people and friends and audiences—with her bearing: "She stands very straight, and she moves with great sureness; her whole personality is in line with her beauty. Everybody today seems to slouch, but there's something, somehow, *regal* about Rose Kennedy." Eugenia Sheppard, the fashion columnist, insists that the important qualities Rose possesses, her freshness and youth, "can't be something that's brought about by makeup men or artificial methods. Her eyes are always fresh and shining, and she even looked fabulous at lunch!"

A Paris hairdresser remembers Rose coming one day in August. She came by foot, wearing a black dress, black sports shoes, and black scarf.

"I am Mrs. Kennedy," she said as she entered.

"Yes, the mother of John and Bob," said the woman who greets incoming patrons. "You are very much loved in France."

"Yes, I know, *ma petite*," Rose said, patting her arm.

She had her hair set and then afterwards, under the dryer, put a black band over her eyes and played with her rosary beads. As she was preparing to leave, she said: "I wear my scarf because when I pass a church I go in to say a prayer, and all the churches in France are so cold."

Though she enjoyed privateness in Paris, Rose was no recluse; she appeared regularly, and often unexpectedly, at most of the important artistic and social events of the season. Wearing a white-and-blue organza Givenchy ball gown and chandelier earrings, she sat in the front row at Bryon Janis' Thoiry concert; she regularly attended receptions given by Ambassador Shriver and her daughter Eunice, either at their home on Avenue d'Iena or in the Embassy residence garden at Rue Faubourg St.-Honoré. She glittered at the Paris Ball in her silver-blue brocade.

Honey Fitz called her his "rambling Rose"; she has always liked to travel widely. She went to the French sector in Berlin in 1963 and was horrified at the "tragic and heartbreaking" situation of split families created by the Berlin wall. Often she vacationed with her close and energetic friend Mary Lasker, and especially enjoyed staying at the lavish Villa La Fiorentina at St.-Jean-Cap-Ferrat, between Monaco and Nice—so fine an Azurian property that it could command a $14,000-a-month rental before it was sold to advertising's Mary Welles. She appeared at Copenhagen for Ambassador William McCormick Blair's wedding and visited the jewelled villas of posh Mount Bürgenstock, overlooking Lake Lucerne in Switzerland. Wherever she went—to the Riviera or to Ireland—she attended early mass every morning and maintained a tight regimen of walking about two miles a day and watching her diet with exceptional care. She still does.

Rose's social life in America was no less glittering than in Europe. At Palm Beach she attended the opening of the Poinciana Plaza in a long dress of cerise crepe, with flared skirt and draped panel, and danced all evening at the Polo Ball at the Celebrity Room of the Poinciana Playhouse. With her close friends Helene Arpels, Mary Lasker, and the Duchess of Windsor, she led a vigorous social life when in New York, attending the opening of the new Van Cleef & Arpels shop, the Candlelight Ball for Manhattanville alumnae at the Trianon Ballroom of the New York Hilton, and the April in Paris Ball. At times she seemed to be everywhere—and always smiling, always impeccably and fashionably dressed.

Truman Capote says, "It's true, you know she does turn up at everything. I think she loves to dress up, be seen and all that. She's very socially minded, and I think she's had a good deal of the social climber in her. The social scene, whatever that is, *does* matter to her." Capote has found her "very talkative, very outgoing, extremely gregarious". One night after a dinner party at Jean Smith's, when they all left rather late at night, Rose asked him if he would see her home. "I said, 'Of course,' and then, of course, we couldn't get a cab. She immediately said, 'Let's walk,' and that's just exactly what we did: we walked like about thirty blocks to the Plaza Hotel, and she talked, as I recall it, the entire way—going on about things like how Central Park didn't frighten her at night and how she wasn't afraid of anything and every other subject you can think of."

Capote also remembers a party at the John Hay Whitneys. He was sitting next to her on a sofa when Mayor John V. Lindsay suddenly arrived. He remembers her saying, "Who is *he*?" She was immediately impressed. "She is a very, very sharp-eyed woman. When she was told who he was, her instant response was, 'Well, Bobby'd better start worrying.'" Though Capote observes that Rose always looks "like she's just had nine vitamin B_{12} shots", he admits that she is "not the sort of woman I'd like to spend a long ocean voyage with. . . . What she is really is a *public perfect person*".

Many of Rose's social activities were connected with charity and women's groups, for which she also lectured and gave talks. In May, 1963, she gave a series of slide presentations and lectures in Massachusetts, seven in that many days and three in one day. These were for charity and Catholic women's groups and were billed as "An Evening with Rose Kennedy". They were filled with family reminiscences about the children, the family's years in England, the meeting of such dignitaries as De Gaulle and Queen Elizabeth. The three dozen slides showed close-ups of the places and personalities and even the menus at dinners she attended; as she read the menu items in French, a number of men were seen walking out for a short smoke. Elegantly dressed in a black crepe sheath dress, with pearls and elbow-length black gloves, she advised the women to discourage drinking by their children. "Please, please tell them that to be sophisticated, to show that you've been places, you don't have to drink," she said. "The girl that does will lose her figure, her face, and her looks." She urged everyone to travel to Europe—though at one of the presentations a reporter noted that only half looked as if they could travel to New Haven—and even gave them such intimate travel advice as not to overload their suitcases with heavy clothing. "A couple of pairs of snuggies," she advised, "and a couple of sweaters will do." She finished her presentations with an abrupt "That is it" and then sat on the arm of an easy chair while more than a thousand people queued up to shake—as one woman put it—"the hand that rocked the cradle of the President of the United States".

Being the mother of the President, she was also able to be much more effective on behalf of her abiding crusade: mental retardation. In October, 1963, the President signed a bill authorizing a $329,000,000 programme to deal with mental retardation, through the construction of community health centres and through research and treatment. At the time Rose was proud to note that the Joseph P. Kennedy, Jr., Foundation had donated more than $16,400,000 since 1946 to hospitals, institutions, day-care centres, and research projects. There were then eighteen centres around the country, and a great portion of Rose's time was devoted to securing public support for the work. She wanted the mentally retarded to lead simple and productive lives, making things and doing jobs that were often frowned upon by normal people but which gave them pleasure and a sense of productivity. Rose's frequent appearances on behalf of Flame of Hope perfumes are a constant reminder to her and to others of the condition that afflicts her oldest daughter, and which led, in the fall of 1941, to her final separation from the mainstream of the ebullient Kennedy life.

For all her personal wealth and all her obvious spending, Rose has the reputation of being "tight with money". She thought nothing of paying for a nephew's tuition at prep school and college —but never thought to give him spending money. Once during World War II she ordered raspberry jam from the Wakefields, who ran the Toll House Restaurant at which Rose and Joe had stopped for years. Sugar rationing had become severe, and Ruth Wakefield simply did not have enough coupons to secure the proper sugar for the jam. Someone suggested that frozen raspberries be used instead of fresh, since that way sugar would not be needed, and that's what was done. "Well, did I get a letter!" says Ruth Wakefield, who then tried to explain to Rose that she had been extremely anxious to please the Kennedys and that now, under the circumstances, she wouldn't expect any payment. Which proved to be the case. "We didn't get a penny."

Rose's tightness has even prompted local gossip in posh Palm Beach to the effect that her servants are not paid the going rate and that she doesn't buy new furniture. One wit claims that the Kennedy house is "the place on County Road where the Salvation Army truck *delivers*". Rose asked for an itemized account of a $38 bill run up by her grandchildren one summer at Hyannis Port at the local candy store, and she once, while visiting the White House, told Mary Gallagher (Jackie's secretary) that a masseuse from Elizabeth Arden would cost $17, which was too much. Mrs. Gallagher finally secured one for $7.50—and that was fine.

Close observers deny rumours to the effect that there was friction between Jackie and Rose. They are in many ways radically different people, from different eras and with different temperaments. It had been obvious from the beginning that Jackie had little love of campaigning and less for political discussions; she literally hated politics at first, though later, when the campaigning was over, it provided her with the stage on which to shine as gracious hostess, accomplished public lady, linguist, and charmer. Perhaps it was her very reticence and brooding beauty, that mysterious and elusive quality, which eventually made her such a sought-out figure for columnists and cultists. Rose was, of course, the ultimate political woman.

Though they were always cordial to each other, friends say they lacked a "clubbiness" and rarely sat down for long chats about such subjects as the children. Jackie once said, in an often-quoted comment, that Rose was too selfish and thought only of herself; Rose has made no public criticism of her daughter-in-law. Everything for Rose has a purpose. Jackie was always more poetic. After Jack's near-fatal back operation in 1954, Jackie had presented him with a leather-bound book of all his speeches in the Senate, the foreword was a long epic poem describing the Kennedy family in

Ireland, their coming to the United States, and finally the culmination in Jack Kennedy; she had written it herself.

Rose puritanically meets social obligations; Jackie was frequently late—and sometimes did not come at all. Jackie was known to closet herself in her room sometimes when she visited the elder Kennedys and even refuse to meet visitors. Once in Palm Beach, Rose asked Mrs. Gallagher: "Do you know if Jackie is getting out of bed today?" Mrs. Gallagher was not sure and was told: "Well, you might remind her that we're having some important guests for lunch. It would be nice if she would join us." Jackie was recuperating from the birth of John at the time and conducted most of her affairs from the bedroom, where she also frequently took her meals. When told of the request, Jackie mimicked her mother-in-law's words and voice—and then never appeared.

Interestingly, Jackie got along extremely well with Joe Kennedy. The two talked together for hours, frequently went out in the *Marlin* together at Hyannis Port or Palm Beach, and teased each other with abandon. She once used his favourite expression in a parody—"The Bear Who Had Moxie"—and he was delighted. One observer reports that you could hate Joe Kennedy but you could also love him, because of his frankness and spontaneity; Rose was cordial and gracious and intelligent, but between her and Jackie no such spontaneity was observed during those years.

In March, 1962, Rose underwent an operation for a pelvic hernia. Dr. Roy Heffernan, a Boston specialist, said that "on a lady her age" the operation was "moderately serious but not especially dangerous". On the morning of the operation, however, Rose shopped and "attended to business", visited her ninety-four-year-old mother, Josie, ate steak for lunch with her brother Tom, in Dorchester, and then checked into St. Elizabeth's. The operation went smoothly, and she was recovered and able to campaign for Ted in his Senate race within a short period of time.

Ted's campaign and ultimate victory produced some of the first truly sour criticism of the Kennedy family in the liberal media. With Bobby Attorney General and Ted running strong for the Senate, they were beginning to take on the distinct picture of a dynasty. Rose spoke up loudly on Ted's behalf—anticipating and pooh-poohing the question of his youth with mild irony and her dry New England wit: "I agree with those of you who are opposed to my son, or at least I can understand. Jack was 'too young', as I recall. So was Bobby 'too young'. But they're doing pretty well, aren't they? Matter of fact, I wanted Teddy to go into the church. But the trouble was that he wanted to start out as a bishop."

Joe, though he now saw few people and spoke with extreme difficulty, was strongly behind Ted. "Now it's Ted's turn," he had said to Jack not long after the Presidential election and before his stroke. "Whatever he wants, I'm going to see that he gets it."

"This wasn't a sudden decision," said Rose. "It was all thought about and discussed, like the Presidency. Ted's father said he should run for the Senate, that he was up to it, and we must encourage him."

There was a lot of family deciding going on behind the scenes, and when Ted beat Eddie McCormack in the September primary fight, James Reston of the New York *Times* wrote a sharp critique. "Teddy's victorious headlines here," he said, "are resented because he is demanding too much too soon on the basis of too little.... What is particularly surprising about all this is that the Kennedys do not see this line of criticism at all, and in fact deeply resent it. They have invoked the new pragmatism, but cannot see that, where the family was concerned, they applied the old nepotism." Rose resented such talk about political dynasties and kept speaking about the Adamses.

Ted got his Senate seat, and Rose made a special trip to Washington to see her youngest son sworn in. Characteristically, she appeared two days early and showed up unannounced at the State Department Auditorium just before the beginning of the Royal Shakespeare Company's performance of *The Hollow Crown*. She was not recognized at first as she strode into the foyer alone, wearing a maroon velvet cloak over a pink, brilliantly encrusted evening gown. A flustered usher escorted her to a single vacant seat next to Stewart Udall's wife. She explained that she had come to Washington early to see the performance and also the opening of the National Gallery, at which the "Mona Lisa" was being unveiled.

Rose continued to serve as hostess for official White House receptions. In October, 1963, she presided at the state dinner party the President gave for Emperor Haile Selassie and was a "show-stealing stand-in" for Jackie, then on a two-week trip to Greece. Dressed in a brilliant green satin gown, glimmering with gold and crystal beading, she fascinated the "King of Kings", and she in turn took an immediate liking to the diminutive emperor with his salt-and-pepper beard and proud temperament, who was presumably a direct descendant of King Solomon and the Queen of Sheba. They both were delighted when members of the Joffrey Ballet, dressed in purple spats and red-spangled flapper dresses, danced a maverick ballet for the assembled dignitaries. It was a new era for the White House, a Camelot of song and dance and art. Later, when asked whether she would campaign for Jack the next year, she said: "No, I'm retiring. I found out tonight that I was one year older than Haile Selassie."

In mid-November, 1963, Rose was at Hyannis Port with Joe and Ann Gargan and a few members of the staff. In the mornings she went to early mass at St. Francis Xavier and then worked on her voluminous correspondence; later she played golf on the tough Hyannisport course, napped, and spent a few hours with her ailing husband. Joe's condition had deteriorated; he was partially para-lysed now and unable to speak. His fierce will tried but could not break the weakness that held him. Ann Gargan, who had devoted her life to her uncle since that day in Palm Beach two years earlier, was proving a wise and thoughtful companion. She gave Joe en-couragement and stimulation and love. "Ann has also taken a lot of the emotional strain off me in times of crisis," says Rose.

It was almost three years now since that cold day when Robert Frost spoke of a new and golden age "of which this noonday's the beginning hour". She had time to think of those years during the quiet days on the Cape before the traditional family Thanksgiving. Rose would later say of Jack: "He exulted in the power he had to do good, to effect changes, to contact the important people of the world, to see if he couldn't arrange peace and a better way of life for people. He loved that—working in that atmosphere and in that milieu, and it was what he had sort of looked forward to all his life." Perhaps he had *not* actually looked forward to it all his life, but she knew that now it was for him a Camelot.

Chapter Twelve

Four Days in November

*I don't think there's any point being Irish
if you don't know that the world is going
to break your heart eventually. I guess we
thought we had a little more time....*
—DANIEL PATRICK MOYNIHAN
November 23, 1963

November 22, 1963, was one of those deceptively warm and golden-
yellow days that often come to the Cape in late autumn like a gentle
intermission between the hyperactive frenzy of the summer months
and the grey winds and bitter isolation of winter. The sky was a
deep blue, and patches of clouds drifted slowly overhead; the
temperature was in the mid-fifties. Hyannis Port was nearly deserted. The summer people had long since abandoned their huge
shingled houses, leaving them bleakly boarded up against the
savage storms to come, and the narrow, bumpy streets were finally
tranquil again, splattered haphazardly with damp and brilliant
fall leaves from the tall maples and elms and gratefully devoid of
the tourists who had turned each summer season into an ever-
worsening nightmare from that moment in July, 1960, when, 3,000
miles away, John F. Kennedy had received the Democratic nomination for the Presidency.

They came each year now like an annual human holocaust,
besieging the small community with honking horns and zoom
lenses, cluttering the landscape with blistered flash cubes and dried
peach pits, creating general havoc both on land and at sea out of
their desperate determination to catch a glimpse—however fleeting
—of the President or Jackie, their children, in-laws, cousins, any
Kennedy at all. In the first intoxicating weeks that followed the
1960 convention, it had all seemed like a continuing carnival, and
the Kennedys' neighbours had briefly basked in their sudden pro-

minence, the stream of celebrated visitors, and the novelty of constant crowds and television crews. They had joined in the revelling and even snapped pictures of the melee themselves, for souvenirs; one shot, which featured an exceptionally broad-beamed woman in Bermuda shorts from the rear, who was bent over and attempting to peer through the fence on Irving Avenue, had become Jackie's favourite photograph of the 1960 campaign.

The novelty, however, had long since worn off, for both the Kennedys and their neighbours. The streets were clogged all summer long now, with traffic that no security force seemed capable of controlling (natives, who were required to attach a special sticker to their windshields simply to gain entrance to their own village, frequently found alien cars and picnicking strangers camped in their driveways), and the waters of Nantucket Sound, the setting of so many past days of freedom and full sails for the Kennedys, had become as congested as the Long Island Expressway on a summer Sunday evening. A small armada churned relentlessly back and forth in front of the Kennedy compound: Secret Service launches, Coast Guard cutters, press boats, and a continuous convoy of sight-seeing power launches that disrupted races and regattas and shattered the salty offshore breeze with blaring bullhorn bulletins that brought the passengers swarming to the rails with binoculars. On sighting a white-uniformed figure on the distant beach, one female passenger had become so excited that she literally started to step overboard, forgetting she was at sea, to try to get an autograph from the woman who, she was convinced, was Caroline's nurse.

The pandemonium had reached its peak during the summer of 1963, and the mounting protests and pressure from the townspeople had become intense enough to make it doubtful that the President and his family would be able to return the following year for their vacation in the place that he, along with the rest of his family, loved more than any other. But in Hyannis Port, as in every other community across America on that serene and sparkling Indian-summer afternoon, the last thought that ever occurred to anyone was that there would never be another Presidential summer for John F. Kennedy.

At the Big House at the end of Scudder Avenue, Rose was not thinking any farther than the week ahead. While she and Joe had always savoured the autumn silence on the Cape, always lingering late into the fall, long after the houses around them were shuttered and darkened, they eagerly looked forward to their children's visits. Teddy and Joan were expected the next afternoon; they were celebrating their fifth wedding anniversary that night with a gala party in their Georgetown house, then taking a planeload of guests to Cambridge aboard the *Caroline* for the Harvard-Yale game, and they planned to finish out the festivities at Hyannis Port. It was a familiar pattern; the year before Ted had brought twenty-five members of the visiting Bolshoi Ballet troupe to his Squaw Island home for a pre-Thanksgiving luncheon with his mother.

Three days later, Rose's other children and grandchildren would begin arriving for the Thanksgiving weekend the Kennedys traditionally celebrated at the Cape; the turkeys had already been ordered from the local market, and arrangements were already under way for a family hockey game at the Joseph P. Kennedy, Jr., Memorial Skating Rink that Rose and Joe had donated to the town six years earlier. On Wednesday, Air Force One would be arriving at Otis Air Force Base, and the Presidential helicopter would land soon after on the broad green pad in front of the Big House, as it had many times before, bringing to the Compound the First Family and all the entourage and accompanying paraphernalia of the travelling White House. Air Force One on Friday was half a continent away, in Texas.

As always, Rose had risen at six that morning and driven herself the two miles to St. Francis Xavier on South Street in Hyannis. She had lingered, as always, after seven o'clock mass for private meditation and then returned to the house for breakfast with her husband.

Ann Gargan had, as usual, joined Joe and Rose at the table. She had been living with her aunt and uncle for six years now, after being forced to abandon hope of becoming a nun when she developed multiple sclerosis just two months before she was due to take her vows; she had rarely left Joe's side during the two years since his stroke. That Friday, however, she planned to leave Hyannis Port for a short visit to her sister, Mary Jo Clasby, who was then living in Detroit.

Rose played nine holes of golf at the Hyannisport Club that morning, carrying her own clubs in a canvas bag; when she returned, she had lunch alone and then retired to her room for her customary afternoon nap. Ann and Joe watched the news on television in Joe's room, which showed film clips of the President's Houston speech the night before, his earlier appearance in Fort Worth that morning. She then kissed her uncle goodbye, assuring him she would be back in a few days. He dozed off quickly, and the house became hushed as Ann packed a few last things and changed into her travelling dress.

Dora, the Kennedys' longtime maid, heard it first over the kitchen radio and shrieked up the stairs at Ann Gargan, who was having her dress zipped up by Rita Dallas, the Ambassador's nurse. The sound irritated her no end. Dora knew, after all, that the elder Kennedys were napping. There could be no reasonable cause for such a racket. Shrieking like that, which was sure to wake them, was totally inexcusable. Ann rushed quickly to the head of the stairs to hush her up. Before she could say anything, Dora shouted up the stairs: "Someone has taken a shot at the President!"

In shock and disbelief, Ann raced back to her room and turned the television on to a blaring volume level that brought Rose herself out of her bedroom. As irritated as Ann had first been, she asked her to turn down the set. Ann and Rita reached simultaneously for the knob, but they were too late: Rose had caught the gist of the bulletins that were now pouring in like unsteady machine-gun bursts. Horrified, trembling, she sat down, fearing the worst. Minutes later, the phone rang; it was Bobby, calling from Virginia.

When she hung up, Rose's face was suddenly haggard and ashen. "I can't stand it," she said. "I've got to keep moving."

She returned to her room, and Ann and Rita could hear her walking back and forth, back and forth, from one wall to another. In a little while she returned to the room where Ann and Rita now prayed and wept inconsolably.

"We'll be all right," Rose said with her customary stoicism. And then, turning to Ann, she said: "I'll be outside."

"It was sheer horror for her," recalls Ann of that dread afternoon. "The only thing she could do was walk, and she walked for the rest of the afternoon." She headed across the lawn and down through the dune grass to the beach, and there on the windblown sand, she paced up and down. The beach was deserted, the afternoon air grew suddenly chill, and the small and solitary figure paced up and down, up and down the patch of beach beside the grey sea.

The three shots fired on a noonday street in Dallas not only shattered America but shook the world, engulfing the entire globe in a universal tidal wave of shock and unfathomable sorrow. In an age of instant communications, the news spread like a seismic tremor; within hours after the tragedy, an estimated 98 per cent of the world's population knew it had happened. One of the few who did not know was the man it would shatter most: Joseph P. Kennedy, who slept peacefully in his second-floor bedroom in Hyannis Port as whole cities and continents came to a virtual stop. When he awoke from his nap, Ann Gargan went in to tell him. "As you see," she began hesitantly, "I haven't left. There's been an accident—" And then she stopped abruptly. Rita Dallas had entered the room and was frantically pulling her elbow; Rose had just told her to tell Ann to wait until one of the boys arrived. "If anything happens to him," Rose had said, "I couldn't stand it."

"My car got banged up," Ann improvised lamely. "That was the accident. That's why I can't go. So I'm staying."

Later Ann recalled: "Uncle Joe had always had the theory that you should never announce bad news in the evening if nothing could be done about it, and Aunt Rose was following his advice."

Rose herself was becoming increasingly distraught; she was desperately worried about what the news would do to Joe; she was confused about whether she should pack immediately and fly to Washington. She was anxious to do *something*, to keep active, but she was uncertain where she should be and how she could do the most good.

At four fifteen a call came through from Air Force One, which was bearing her son's casket back to Washington. It was the new President, Lyndon Baines Johnson, and his wife, Lady Bird. Rose spoke to them and accepted their sympathy. "I wish to God there was something I could do," said Johnson. "I just wanted you to know that." He handed the phone to Lady Bird, and she said: "We feel like the heart has been cut out of us. Our love and our prayers are with you." It was real now. The unthinkable had truly happened.

Rose wanted to walk again. She couldn't stay still. Teddy and

Eunice had arrived by this time, along with Joe Gargan, Ann's older brother and Ted's close friend. A biting breeze was blowing now, and they all bundled up against the wind to stroll the beach again. Herring gulls hovered above the breaking waves, searching for clams and crabs washed up by the heavy seas as they walked in silence mostly, attempting to sort out their inner turmoil, attempting to find some path out of the swirling chaos of the afternoon.

Turning suddenly to her nephew, Rose, for no apparent reason, said: "Joey, you should read more."

"Yes, Aunt Rose," he responded like a dutiful schoolboy.

"Read Marlborough, Fox, and Burke," she continued. "Like Jack."

When in the deepening November darkness Rose finally returned to the house, the atmosphere was becoming more strained by the minute; everyone attempted to cope with the staggering shock while maintaining an outward façade of normality for the benefit of Ambassador Kennedy. But his suspicions were growing. Though he was unable to speak, he had never had any trouble communicating his thoughts, particularly when displeased, whether over a dessert or choice of a television channel. He would raise his eyebrows sharply and shake his finger in a very definite way, and, as Eunice later recalled, "there was just never any question as to what he was trying to say."

He was clearly displeased now. Ann kept fussing with the television set, where every network carried news of the assassination, and claimed that something had gone wrong with the set and that she was unable to get a channel. She played his favourite records, and then, Teddy, who had not been expected until the next day, walked into his bedroom. He had had to give a speech in Boston, he announced casually, and had decided to drop in to say hello.

At supper, Ted and Eunice got into a spirited argument—making a gallant effort to re-create the atmosphere of other days. But it was no good. The Ambassador sensed that it was all a charade. He knew that something horrendous had happened, and they all knew that he knew; but they continued, not knowing what else to do. Afterwards, in the bedroom, Teddy in desperation yanked the wires from the back of the television set, assuring his father that they would have it fixed in the morning.

Saturday morning was soggy and unbearably bleak, as if in reflection of the nation's mood. It was a morning without a sunrise; the black night simply became less black. Few people across the country had been able to sleep through the long and desolate night, and Rose had scarcely slept at all. She looked weary and drawn as she left the house to attend a high requiem mass for her son, escorted by two state troopers, who at times seemed almost to be supporting her bodily. Inside the church, Rose sat in the fourth pew, only a few feet from where her son Jack sat when he attended Sunday mass. She looked up once at the television camera that had been placed near the altar and ordered it taken out, but throughout the mass, television hand cameras could be heard cranking and grinding, cranking and grinding from a rear balcony. Rose's fellow communicants remember her sitting up straight, her head held high, her eyes fixed directly ahead. Ann Gargan joined her in her pew shortly after her arrival, and Ted and Eunice sat across the aisle; the others returned to the house at the end of the mass, but Rose remained for a second mass. On leaving, she informed the waiting newsmen that she was returning to the house to have breakfast with her husband. Then, almost as an afterthought, she added: "He has not yet been advised."

Joe was already at the table when she returned, his suspicions of the night before intensified by the fact that his morning paper was not by his plate. When he saw Rose coming up the steps in a black hat, her face concealed behind a black veil, he knew finally, without any doubt, that his family had suffered still another disaster. Afterwards, he went for his regular exercise period in the heated pool with Ann, but he became increasingly impatient; it was obvious that now he had to be told.

When he returned to his bedroom, Ted and Eunice joined him. Ted, in a halting voice, began with almost the same words Ann had used the previous afternoon. "There's been a bad accident," he said. "The President has been hurt very badly." The Ambassador looked up sharply. He scrutinized his son's face. He concentrated on every word. "As a matter of fact," Ted finished lamely, "he died."

Joe wept as inconsolably as he had for his eldest son nearly twenty years earlier and then asked for more details. As the flag outside the house was lowered to half-mast in the rain, Ann brought him the newspapers, and a repairman was summoned to fix the television wires Teddy had ripped out the previous evening. Then, like the rest of the numbed nation, they sat there solemn and transfixed, gazing at the flag-draped casket lying in state on a black catafalque in the East Room as hundreds upon hundreds of dignitaries and friends filed past to pay their last respects.

"Rose was the magnificent one," a close friend remembers. She was always unobtrusively available, ready with advice when it was needed, soothing the ravaged emotions of her family by her calm presence; she was also typically organized, managing even to think of such details as extra pairs of black stockings to take to Washington for her daughters to wear at the funeral. To renew her strength, she several times donned raincoat and scarf and went out into the heavy fog and drizzle to walk on the dunes in solitude.

Sunday morning the air was cold and brisk on the Cape as Rose once again attended seven and eight o'clock mass at St. Francis Xavier, this time sitting in the vestry and emerging only to receive communion with the other parishioners. Later, at eleven o'clock mass, the seat that President Kennedy had always occupied in the second pew (and which is now marked with a simple brass plaque reading "John Fitzgerald Kennedy 1917-1963") was left symbolically empty, and sobs were audible in the congregation. At four twenty-one that afternoon, Rose and Ted and Eunice boarded a Jetstar at Otis Air Force Base for Washington.

At one that afternoon, the flag-draped casket had been placed on a caisson in front of the North Portico of the White House and, pulled by six matched greys, had been borne in solemn procession to the Capitol. Three years earlier the President had made the same journey amid the gaiety and cheers of a triumphant inaugural, but now the crowd of 300,000 that lined Pennsylvania Avenue was as hushed as a huge cathedral; the only sound that could be heard was the mournful sound of muffled drums, beating like muted heartbeats that punctuated a nation's grief.

At the White House, Rose's son-in-law Sargent Shriver greeted her and took her up to the Lincoln bedroom, the room she had always loved best on past visits. Weary from the trip and the strain of the past forty-eight hours, her awesome composure suddenly broke, and without warning she collapsed in her son-in-law's arms. "It just seems so incredible," she sobbed. Shriver did his best to console her and expressed his genuine amazement that both she and Jackie were bearing up so well. And with that, Rose was herself again. "What do people expect you to do?" she said. "You can't just weep in a corner." She then summoned her daughters to give them the black stockings she had brought from Hyannis Port.

That evening, Rose went with other members of the family to the Great Rotunda of the Capitol. There, flanked by an honour guard, the casket had rested all afternoon, far below the great dome, surrounded by friezes and paintings celebrating important moments in the nation's history. A young widow and her daughter had knelt beside it that afternoon; Jacqueline had kissed the flag, and Caroline had quietly placed her hand on her father's casket. That evening Rose too knelt silently in prayer before the draped and imposing catafalque, the same one on which Abraham Lincoln had lain a century earlier. And later that night, thousands of men and women, an astounding 250,000, trooped mournfully past the bier as the President lay in state; by two in the morning the line stretched out into the darkness for three miles, and the line of cars coming into the city stretched all the way to Baltimore.

Monday morning in Washington was clear and crisp. The leading dignitaries of five continents—De Gaulle, Haile Selassie, chancellors, kings, queens, and prime ministers—had arrived to pay their homage. Slowly the sombre procession followed a restless, riderless black horse and a flag-draped casket drawn by six matched greys from the Capitol to St. Matthew's Cathedral. The drums, the muffled and steady rapping of the drums, were relentless.

Rose was too upset and even near collapse to walk in the procession. She remained secluded until the last moment, when everyone was seated, and then took her place in the first pew, in the seat reserved for her between Jacqueline and her grandchildren. She heard her longtime friend Richard Cardinal Cushing—who had officiated at Jack's wedding and delivered a benediction at his inauguration—say: "Oh, God, who alone art ever merciful in sparing of punishment, humbly we pray Thee on behalf of the soul of Thy servant, John Fitzgerald Kennedy...."

At Arlington, Rose stood silently while the last moments of the ritual, the final folding of the colours, was accomplished. Fifty jet planes roared over the silent assemblage on the hill in Arlington, and then Air Force One, starkly, flew over alone. Once only, Rose removed a handkerchief from her purse and quickly reached under her veil and wiped her eyes. A twenty-one-gun salute echoed from the hills. When Bobby, in the final gesture, tried to hand his mother the torch to light the eternal flame, he noticed that she was too deeply absorbed in prayer; she did not even see him, and he handed it to his younger brother instead. Finally, the eternal flame was lit, and the muffled and unceasing beat of the drums ended.

In one of the receptions upstairs at the White House after the funeral, Rose spoke for some moments with Haile Selassie, who had lost his own son some years earlier. "It's wrong for parents to bury their children," she said. "It should be the other way around." The emperor agreed. "It's a violation of nature." The phrases were familiar. One of Jack's favourite poems, recalls Ted Sorenson, was Alan Seeger's "I Have a Rendezvous with Death." The President was moved, says Sorenson, "by the fact that Seeger had been cut down in the brilliance of his youth. 'It is,' he once said at a war memorial, 'against the law of nature for parents to bury their children ... a son with all his life before him.'"

Shortly after the burial and the subsequent reception at the White House, Rose flew back to Otis Air Force Base. Now she showed the strain completely. As she stepped down from the plane, her face was deathly pale; her eyes were fixed on the ground; she clenched her hands, in black gloves, tightly together in front of her—as if in constant prayer. She said nothing, and the few reporters who had come to observe and perhaps to interview her could only avert their eyes and step back, their heads deeply bowed.

All that week, Rose went to St. Francis Xavier each morning and stayed for two masses. Each day she said and studied the fourteen stations of the cross, standing alone and rapt in prayer in the little hushed church, perhaps remembering her promise as a Child of Mary to obtain "from 'Our Lady of Sorrows' courage to suffer as she did, standing at the foot of the Cross." Once she drove to church herself; usually she walked away very quickly, her fingers clasping her rosary beads. She mentioned once that memories of her son flashed constantly in her mind.

By Thursday the remaining Kennedys had gathered for Thanksgiving dinner. Bobby and his family were not there, but most of the others were, along with most of their children. There was even a touch football game before dinner, and Eunice—who was pregnant—played with some of her old vigour. The children saw movies in the afternoon and were served their dinner early. Later the silent Ambassador took his customary place at the head of the table, Rose hers at the other end, and the family began their usual meal of turkey, stuffing, turnips, nuts, and all the rest. The family had once more closed its ranks. They would endure.

On Friday, Rose was driven 80 miles by Frank Saunders in a heavy November rainstorm to see her ninety-eight-year-old mother in Dorchester; Josie had been alive when President Lincoln was assassinated. Because of her extreme age, the old woman was told nothing of what had happened. Rose also visited briefly with Mrs. Edward Moore at the Ritz and then returned the same day to Hyannis Port. Plans were being made to move down to Palm Beach within the next week or so, and there were already plans for memorials to the late President.

Somehow, Rose found time to call Marie Greene. The house had been innundated with calls and letters and telegrams, and it was impossible to get through to anyone inside. Rose had known this and called to let her old friend know that she was all right. It was a gesture typical of Rose Kennedy.

Chapter Thirteen

More Lightning

... somehow the Kennedys draw the lightning.
—JAMES RESTON

"In all the years we've been married," Joe Kennedy once said, "I never heard her complain." The image of Rose Kennedy in the years following the President's death beggars belief. Not only did she never complain, but how, everyone asked in hushed voices, did she even survive? How did she bear it? How could she possibly keep going? And yet the degree of activity did not slacken; her crosses were never heavier than she could bear. She could say, quite simply, "God wanted Jack, or He would not have taken him." She did more than survive and keep going: she persevered and triumphed. "Willpower, just willpower," she has said, "doing what's necessary, keeps you going."

Whoever else was present at the innumerable memorial events and projects that followed the death of the President, Rose was always there and in the forefront—and, often enough, she was the only family representative active and present, going alone, carrying her own suitcase when she could.

In January, 1964, less than two months after the assassination, she was present at the Boston Symphony Orchestra's memorial concert at the Cathedral of the Holy Cross, performed during a solemn pontifical mass celebrated by Cardinal Cushing. The vaulted cathedral was filled to its capacity of 1,800 persons, and Erich Leinsdorf conducted Mozart's *Requiem in D Minor* brilliantly. He had chosen the piece because it, like the work of John F. Kennedy, was left unfinished by premature death.

In February, Rose attended, along with Bobby, Ted, and Eunice, a dinner for the Joseph P. Kennedy, Jr., Foundation for Mental Retardation at the Americana Hotel. President Johnson was there, and while he was never an intimate or special fan of the Kennedys,

Rose heard him say of the family: "They have been granted more than their share of greatness—but they have also been dealt more than their share of grief. The senseless, mindless murder of their martyred brother and son brought endless, timeless grief to every American family." He compared the Kennedys to the Adamses, the Lees, the Randolphs, the La Follettes, and the Roosevelts and ended by saying that "Our generation is proud and blessed to have known the Kennedys."

A month later, Rose attended a solemn ceremony in Paris, inaugurating the Avenue du President Kennedy. The avenue, formerly Quai de Passy, fronts the right bank of the Seine in a fashionable residential section. "Never perhaps has the death of a foreign chief of state so profoundly moved every Frenchman and every Parisian," said Jean Auburtin, president of the City Council. Ambassador Charles E. Bohlen was present, as well as André Malraux, and both flanked Rose as she stood dignified and straight through the half hour ceremony on the cold windy street.

From Ethiopia (where the library of the new Haile Selassie I University was designated the John F. Kennedy Memorial Library) to New York, streets, airports, libraries, and other buildings and places acquired the Kennedy name. There was a new Kennedy cultural centre planned for Washington, committees were established in more than forty states to raise funds for the John F. Kennedy Memorial Library in Cambridge, and Rose spoke movingly before a joint legislative committee in Boston during a hearing on the necessary legislation. "My son never thought in terms of a memorial for himself," she said in a choked voice, "but if he had planned one, he would have wanted to to be closely identified with Massachusetts." Rose and other members of the family travelled as far as North Carolina, Germany, and the Vatican to help raise funds for the $10,000,000 project that would be built on two acres of Harvard's Charles River-bank property.

Once again the legacy of the eldest son had passed, and Bobby was beginning to brood about his own career. Should he pursue public office or even retreat to the quieter world of teaching? And if so, which office? "It was a kind of crossroads for me and my family," he said early in 1964. "Should I make a fresh start on my own in a new career away from Washington?" None of the Kennedys had shown the slightest interest in business, and one of

Bobby's few commercial ventures, delivering newspapers when he was a boy, had ended in a fiasco: they had had to be delivered for him by the chauffeur. There was speculation that he would seek the Vice Presidential nomination and that he would simply drop out of public life when Johnson released him. But that spring he kept in the public eye and on St. Patrick's Day gave a moving speech in Scranton, Pennsylvania, at the Lackawanna County Friendly Sons of St. Patrick dinner. The degree to which Irish history in Boston had affected the whole course of Kennedy family politics was shown in his dramatic evocation of the early days of the Irish in Boston—the insults, the bigotry, the slurred references to "lace curtain Irish". It had been the driving force behind his grandfather Honey Fitz, behind his mother, and behind his father. At the end, he read the "Liberator", a ballad about the death of Owen Roe O'Neill, with its haunting quatrain:

> We're sheep without a shepherd,
> When the snow shuts out the sky—
> Oh, why did you leave us, Owen?
> Why did you die?

On June 19 it looked as if the Kennedys had suffered still another tragedy. Rose was in Hyannis Port, having breakfast with Ann Gargan, when she heard the news. Teddy, flying from Washington to West Springfield, Massachusetts, suffered a near-fatal plane crash in which one passenger was killed. One of his vertebrae was smashed, and two others were damaged; he broke two ribs and suffered a partial collapse of one lung. Worse, there was massive internal haemorrhaging. He was hospitalized for months and had to wear a painful Stryker back-brace frame; reports at first suggested that his back would never heal properly. Several days after the crash, while the precise extent of the damage was still not known, Rose attended the unveiling in Philadelphia before a crowd of 10,000 of a bronze memorial tablet commemorating the spot where the late President had once delivered a Fourth of July speech. She knew how to keep busy and how to meet her obligations.

Rose's largest effort during that first year was to begin, in November, a three-week European tour with the poignant John F. Kennedy

Memorial Library exhibit of her son's memorabilia. At Kennedy Airport in New York a black-garbed Rose admitted to reporters that being near the mementos would be difficult. But it was "necessary" to go, she insisted. "Everyone likes to see a member of the family," she explained, "and we are doing it because people have been so very generous in their tributes." Her favourite item, she explained, was not her son's rocking chair, but a letter he had written when he was nine, asking for an increase in his allowance since his expenses, now that he was a Boy Scout, were greater.

The exhibit began in Dublin and was visited by more than 40,000 people; from there it went on to Frankfurt and Berlin, and then she met it for its opening in Paris. At the Palais Chaillot, she spoke French as she showed visitors the various items, adding something personal about each. She paused longest at the Presidential desk and told how little John-John liked to play hide-and-seek under it. There was a plastic-encased coconut shell on which Jack had scratched a rescue message when he and the crew of PT-109 were marooned on one of the Solomon Islands. There were hundreds of photographs, drafts of the President's principal speeches (edited in his own hand), even scraps of paper and menus on which he had doodled or scribbled. More than 52,000 people attended the exhibit in Paris.

Returning to America periodically and then flying back for new openings, Rose was with Queen Ingrid of Denmark when the display opened in Copenhagen at the Town Hall; she was received by West German President Heinrich Lübke when it opened in Bonn; she was in Brussels, Athens, and finally, in February, opened the exhibit in London at the Royal Exchange before it was returned to Washington. It is now on permanent display at the Kennedy Memorial Library at Harvard.

When Bobby decided to run for the Senate in New York, Rose broke her vows not to campaign again; she even spent her fiftieth wedding anniversary in drab little Newburgh, stumping for her third son. Again her aid was more than public; she gave him private counsel throughout the campaign—though on one of her interminable notes of advice she appended the comment: "This may be the last time I'll write a letter like this, because I remember it's Socrates who used to give a lot of advice in Athens, was finally given hemlock to drink!"

Between campaigns and memorials, Rose continued to be interested in charity events. She attended the *Ballo in Maschera* in Venice, in September, 1967, which raised money for Venetian artisans stricken by the flood. The ball was a magnificent affair, held in the Palazzo Ca' Rezzonica, beneath stirring Tiepolos. Prince Rainier and Princess Grace were there, among 500 other celebrities, including Aristotle Onassis, Clare Boothe Luce, Gian Carlo Menotti, J. Paul Getty, Richard Burton and Elizabeth Taylor, and Douglas Fairbanks, Jr. At one point, photographers edged Rose into a corner and clamoured for photographs. "Now, don't take my picture until I get my clothes on, and don't dirty my dress," she pleaded as she adjusted her white feather boa and white heart-shaped plume. Sixty years after she had left West Concord, Massachusetts, Rose still loved to wear a plume; it was, perhaps, the symbol of the romantic social life she loved and which had always gone hand in hand with her private devotion, her shrewd sense of politics, her tight self-discipline.

The day after the ball an Italian photographer found himself sitting next to an elderly American lady on the flight from Venice to Paris. For a while they sat reading magazines and newspapers, and then lunch was served. He noticed, for no particular reason, that the woman did not eat all the food on her little tray.

"Are you American?" the photographer asked.

"Yes," the woman said.

"Do you like Venice?"

"Yes," she replied. "It's nice. I come here many times." And then, to the photographer's bewilderment, the woman started wrapping up a banana carefully. When she finished, she put it into her purse. "I'll eat it later," she said. "I like them very much."

"Where do you live in America?" the man asked.

"Boston." And then she put the pepper and salt and the sugar and several other portables into her purse along with the carefully wrapped banana.

"It's a nice city," said the photographer. "I've been there. Were you born there?"

The woman leaned over slightly and whispered: "I am Rose Kennedy."

In 1968, at seventy-seven, having sworn off campaigning still again, Rose entered the lists in Bobby's difficult primary fights for the Democratic nomination for the Presidency. Bobby, hesitating until the last minute, had decided to make his bid. "These are no ordinary times," he said, "and this is not an ordinary election." It was not. Hubert Humphrey represented the old establishment, and Eugene McCarthy was obviously running a noble and spirited —but doomed—campaign. The youth of America were restless; the minorities were nearly frantic in their search for a political champion; the Democrats, weary from all the bludgeoning the Johnson administration had taken, wanted a winner. And Dick Nixon had a new face and a new style. "Men are not made for safe havens," Bobby quoted from Aeschylus, and plunged into the campaign.

"They just needed all the help they could get," Rose said when she took the stump once again, with only a touch less of her old vigour. Campaigning for the "women's vote" in Indiana, Nebraska, Oregon, and California, a few changes could be seen in her method. Television was even more important than in the 1960 primaries, and she paid particular attention—in her television talks and kaffeeklatsches with Ethel—to what she wore. "I wouldn't think of wearing a print," she said, "because they don't photograph well. I also make a point to wear light hats because they are flattering with my dark hair."

When Bobby won in Indiana, there were sharp comments about the money the Kennedys had spent, and Rose made her famous blooper in a *Women's Wear Daily* interview. In all the years of campaigning, it was probably the only one she'd ever made. Asked for the millionth time about the Kennedy millions, she abandoned her usual response: "Please don't talk about money. Quite enough has been said on this subject." Instead she said: "It's our money and we're free to spend it any way we please. It's part of this campaign business. If you have money, you spend." She sounded, for a moment, like her husband. "The Rockefellers are like us. We both have lots of money to spend on our campaigns. It's something that's not regulated. Therefore, it's not unethical." Soon afterwards, in Oregon, she was shrewd enough to play light with her slip, saying: "I don't talk about high finances anymore—if I did, they'd send me home tonight."

Rose was in Nebraska for Mother's Day and stressed her son's youthfulness and enthusiasm. "When people say to me that they're wonderful children," she said, "I always say, 'They ought to be. They've been given every opportunity and advantage.'" Even the most jaded reporters were impressed.

"There she is," said one in Los Angeles, after watching Rose perform before blazing klieg lights and an army of hungry photographers and newsmen, "in her socko pink Dior dress grazing the tops of her knees, defending her son with a mother's intensity against the charge that he is ruthless, turning her own bloopers into a joke, lightly sketching in the background that gave rise to the Kennedy mystique." She had spoken often about Bobby's presumed ruthlessness and countered by either calling him "as gentle as Jack" or saying: "He was on the crime committee. There he was fighting criminals. They're tough and you have to know how to handle them. Later, when he was Attorney General, he was fighting gangsters. They're a tough bunch, too. In politics, you find that it's the uncomplimentary tag that sticks."

She stood straight as a poplar before hundreds of members of the American Contract Bridge League in Los Angeles and even dazzled that austere group. Observers were once again stunned by her youthful appearance. "She had her face lifted, of course," said one scrutinizing woman, whose friend retorted, "But you can't buy that sparkle in her eyes." (Actual estimates on how many times she *has* had her face lifted vary from seven to none; a leading makeup specialist, Eddie Senz, who prepared her for a television appearance recently, says: "I really don't know, and I can usually tell pretty well by the folds near the ear where the skin has been removed. I'm considered something of an expert in this business, and I just wouldn't want to be quoted one way or the other on that; I rather assumed that she must have had one, but there was no physical evidence that she had.")

Afterwards, she worked the lobby of the hotel, shaking hands, chatting, moving from one end to the other with her compelling Kennedy smile and studied openness. To the question "How does it feel, the prospect of being the mother of yet another President?" she replied: "It is wonderful to think that people have that much confidence in a member of your family. The possibility of it happening again—it's overwhelming. For one mother to have this experience *twice!*"

After eleven weeks of hectic, even frantic, campaigning, marred by narrow victories and the recent defeat in Oregon, Bobby Kennedy stood on the podium in the crowded Embassy Ballroom of the Ambassador Hotel in Los Angeles and smiled broadly as his supporters cheered. He had been campaigning night and day for weeks, and the strain had told. Friends had noted that he frequently brooded and that his comments were often fatalistic. He was physically exhausted. But he had won the California primary. "So on to Chicago," he said, raising his hand, "and let's win there." The crowd went ecstatic.

He headed out through a velvet curtain into a kitchen passageway for a meeting with reporters.

Rose had flown back to Hyannis Port to watch the results on television with Joe. They and Ann Gargan had watched the set until shortly after midnight. When it seemed certain that Bobby had won, Rose went to bed. Shortly before six o'clock, as usual, she got up to attend early mass. She had just washed her face and turned on the television in her bedroom to see the final results when Ann Gargan came in. She was told quietly what the screen now showed.

Ann had been called by the Associated Press somewhat after three that morning, but she had decided not to wake either Rose or Joe, in accordance with their longtime principle not to wake or trouble someone with bad news at night when there was nothing to be done.

Bobby was still alive, the television said. There was still a modicum of hope this time. Ted had been in San Francisco; he flew to the hospital and then called his mother: there seemed very little hope.

At six forty, Rose emerged in a blue spring coat and grey-blue scarf, and was driven by chauffeur Frank Saunders in the family's blue Imperial to St. Francis Xavier Church. Photographers were already waiting, but she entered unseen through a side entrance.

A mass was scheduled for the late Reverend Thomas McLean, and the Reverend Thomson, pastor of St. Francis Xavier, asked relatives if this could be postponed. But Rose insisted that the intended mass continue, and the Reverend Thomson, on his own initiative, conducted a concelebrated mass. Rose listened intently while several priests offered mass for the recovery of her son; she shed no tears and now and then merely lowered her head and raised her hand slowly to her forehead. Later she received holy communion and, when the church was emptied, made the fourteen stations of the cross.

The weather, which had been rainy for four days, grew bright and pleasant. At midmorning Rose came out of the house and began to walk back and forth on the broad driveway behind the house. She was wearing a light-pink coat, sunglasses, white socks, and Oxford sports shoes. Eight or ten photographers who had managed to scale the back fence, interrupted her as she had so often been, with clicking cameras. They were, admittedly, amazed. "There was Rose, walking around and around, bouncing a tennis ball, just like a little girl, really—missing it and kneeling down to get it," Ted Polumbaum, a seasoned Kennedy photographer, later recalled. "Just walking and bouncing, walking and bouncing."

Several of the reporters and photographers jumped right down on to the lawn, and she snapped at them: "You should be ashamed of yourselves. You should know better than that."

A little later she got into her navy-with-white-top Ford with a rear bumper sticker saying in red, white, and blue "Kennedy", and drove off quickly alone. She went to the Hyannisport Club golf course to play several holes of golf; starting on the fifteenth tee and carrying her own clubs, she played through the tough narrow fairways and wiry weeds, working off some of the tension that was building up. Neither bouncing the tennis ball nor playing golf was unusual for Rose; from childhood, movement and action had been antidote to despair.

Constant phone communications were kept up with Ted and other close members of the Kennedy circle on the Coast. The news was progressively grim. "Extremely critical as to life." She had thought briefly of flying to the Coast but decided to remain with Joe. Cardinal Cushing came that evening and said he had never met a woman with more courage. "She has more confidence in Almighty God than any priest or religious I ever met," he said.

The next morning, shortly after she rose at six o'clock, Ann Gargan told her that Bobby was dead. She had expected it. Again she went to mass, this time dressed in a white suit with a white mantilla, and heard the requiem mass conducted by Father Terrence F. Keenan. Sitting several pews behind the one where the late President used to sit, she seemed, at least outwardly, quite calm. Again she waited until the seventy-five or so communicants had left and then again made the fourteen stations of the cross. She told the Reverend Thomson that she did not want to become "over-emotional" and then left the church by a side exit, made her way through a battery of news and television photographers, and was driven back to Hyannis Port.

By Thursday the grief and strain were beginning to tell. Dressed again in a white suit with a white mantilla over her thick dark hair, her face was pale, and a distinct nervousness began to break through now and then. The news and television photographers were everywhere, and when the Imperial limousine arrived at the little church, the Reverend Thomson came out and led her through the kitchen and hallway of the rectory to her seat in the pews. Towards the end of the early mass, her head began to rock from side to side. She dropped her purse. Twice she asked an aide to speak with reporters near the front entrance, to ask them to lower their voices. She said that people could not concentrate on their prayers with such distractions. When the service was completed and she was finally alone inside the quiet church, she asked that the doors be closed. They were. She prayed alone for some time and then left the way she had come, her head bowed, her jaw set. Her face was extremely pale; her deep pain was now obvious.

Later that day she boarded a Northeast Airlines plane at Hyannis Airport for a flight to Boston and then went to New York alone. There she found time to stop into Bergdorf-Goodman's on Fifth Avenue to purchase a few simple mourning clothes. And then she went to St. Patrick's Cathedral. The light inside was dim, but several people noticed a slight, solitary figure in black, praying. When the coffin was brought forward, the woman joined the small procession of relatives—and they saw it was Rose.

At eight o'clock on Friday morning, dressed all in black, Rose was led into St. Patrick's Cathedral. As she walked towards her seat in the first pew, she saw her grandson Joe, Bobby's oldest boy, standing silently beside the mahogany coffin. All night, thousands upon thousands of mourners had trooped past the coffin; there had been an estimated 100,000.

Rose sat with an "almost beatific look" during the pontifical mass for her third son. She saw the bread and wine, the gold chalices, and other sacred vessels used in the communion carried to the high altar by eight of her grandchildren. Towards the end of the ceremony she saw Bobby's three oldest boys, wearing white surplices, serve as acolytes. She took her glasses off, put them on again, read from the prayer book, took them off again, and looked back up at the altar. Jackie, nearby, wept behind her black mantilla veil and once raised the fingers of her left hand to her lips to choke back a sob.

As Ted movingly eulogized his brother, Rose lowered her head slowly several times and closed her eyes now and then. As she looked out at her youngest child and sole surviving son, she appeared to several observers to be holding back tears. Her face wore a half-smile of worn resignation. But she did not cry.

Then the long and final journey began, by motorcade to Pennsylvania Station and then—through endless delays—in the funeral train to Washington. Ethel, pregnant with her eleventh child, was magnificently under control—as were all the Kennedys. Only Jackie had broken down when the casket was placed before the altar on Thursday night. Sitting in the car that held her son's coffin, Rose urged the children to wave and be seen by the hundreds of thousands who had waited so long. "Start to wave ... wave," she repeated. Joe walked back and forth among the cars, saying, "I'm Joe Kennedy. Thank you for coming." He shook hands with a firm grip and repeated the phrase: "Hello, I'm Joe Kennedy. Thanks for coming." Ethel went through the cars also, saying, "Nice to see you." Heads turned, and mouths fell open, and one woman said: "Good God, will you look at this!" Joe was a Kennedy and Ethel had long since become as ardent a member of the family as a religious convert.

At Arlington National Cemetery, not more than a few feet from the grave of the late President, Robert Kennedy was finally laid to rest. As Rose left the site, she stumbled alone for a moment, alone and unaided in the dark along the grassy hill. Then, surrounded by her grandchildren and clutching only a single white candle, she regained her poise and walked off to the waiting cars.

In August Rose planned to leave for Europe and invited Mary Jo and Dick Clasby, Barbara Fitzgerald Value, Pat Lawford, and other members of the family at the compound to dinner on the night before she left. When Barbara got there, the house was deathly still. Mary Jo told her, "Aunt Rose is sick."

"Is it serious?" she asked.

"Yes," answered Mary Jo, saying that she had sent her own children home. Barbara offered to leave herself and to take her children, but Rose had sent orders down: the food had been cooked, and they were to eat it. Earlier she had given everyone a sombre speech about Biafra, with the distinct message that they had to eat everything; nothing was to be wasted.

Everyone finally sat down at the big table, but with all the mystery about what was happening upstairs, a relative recalled that "it was like the Last Supper". Barbara's children didn't care for the swordfish; they didn't like the stewed tomatoes. They fussed and grew so cranky that she was beside herself. Finally, the children were excused and went off to see a movie at the golf club.

Then Pat Lawford came down and told the little group: "Mother says not to leave. She's coming down to dinner." So they all sat there and ate a bit more and in a few moments heard footsteps coming down the stairs. It was Rose. She had on a robe and a string of pearls and was carrying her bag. "I'm so sorry," she told them, "my watch stopped."

They watched solicitously as she ate her noodles and talked about the "most fascinating book" she'd just read about Onassis. She went on to tell them about a bracelet and jewels he'd given to her. Marie Greene had thought it was probably from some little shop in Athens that copies antiquities from the museum, but she had sent her chauffeur into Hyannis the next day and it had been appraised for about $1,500. "They say, Beware of Greeks bearing gifts," she told them.

The phone was ringing constantly, since the news had got out that she was not well, but since no one knew precisely what was wrong, the family's answers were vague but reassuring.

Earlier, watching the news upstairs with Joe and Ann Gargan, Rose had suddenly clutched her chest and said she was ill. Ann had taken her by the arm and brought her into her room, put her in bed, and then pulled a blanket over her. Her hands were ice cold. "You'd better get me my rosary, dear," said Rose. Ann had called the doctor. The next morning the doctor convinced her to go into the hospital for routine tests. Everyone was sitting around like a "bowl of jelly, trembling", through all this, but after mass she went to the hospital, took the tests, came back and took a rest, and then went to the hairdresser at noon. What was wrong? No one really knew, but for Rose none of it was finally enough to get her to postpone a trip to Paris. She packed, left for Boston at six o'clock, saw her brother Tom at Massachusetts General Hospital, brought him some flowers from her garden (because at that time of the year florist flowers weren't nearly as lovely as her own, she said), and at eight o'clock that evening calmly boarded a plane and flew to Paris.

One of the practical consequences of Bobby's death was the necessity of raising almost $3,500,000 to pay for the deficit in his campaign spending. That fall, Ted took charge of the dinners (usually $500 to $1,000 a plate), scheduled for Boston, New York, San Francisco, Los Angeles, and Washington. He tried to keep the events from becoming moribund, as easily they might, and frequently needled Rose. He called her a "shy and retiring person" as shown by her increasingly frequent appearances on national TV talk shows and on the cover of national magazines. He said, "My mother called me and said that she had read that Mr. Nixon was not planning to use the Oval Room, and then she added, 'Well, I think *someone* ought to use it.' So we're looking into that." He made a pointed reference to her Indiana blooper, when Rose had said that it was their money and they could spend it any way they chose. "We invited Mother here tonight," said Ted wryly, "to show her whose money we were spending."

The glittering array of Democratic leaders grew quiet when Rose herself prepared to speak. The ornate, high-chandeliered ballroom of the Sheraton Plaza was hushed. "Bobby, to me he was always Bobby. When I think of him, I think of children. His personal life was filled with children. I used to tell him, take Ethel and go away for a quiet vacation ... just the two of you. But they'd go, and the children would always be right behind them."

She completely captured the audiences, standing elegant and proud and dry-eyed as she spoke of the son who some said was her favourite. In a firm, strong voice, she spoke of his tousled, wind-blown hair. "How sad we are," she ended, "that we shall never see Bobby again. What joy he brought us. What an aching void he has left in our hearts." Rose said: "We admired him, we loved him, and we miss him tremendously. I know that I shall never see his like again "

Chapter Fourteen

Beyond Tragedy

I know not age nor weariness nor defeat.
—John Buchan

"Teddy," Rose told her only remaining son not long ago, "you can never afford to let down in a non-election year." It was advice she had always lived by. Rose Kennedy never let up.

As she moved into her mid- and late-seventies, Rose's round of activities continued at their unbelievable pace. She was present at literally hundreds of public events, from the dedication of new children's cottages in the Bronx (one of Bobby's projects) to the gala Rose Ball in St. Louis, at which Cliff Robertson was presented with an award for his contribution to the cause of mental retardation for his performance in *Charly*. When the Joseph P. Kennedy, Jr., Foundation presented awards for recognition of research, leadership, and service to the mentally retarded, Rose was usually there. She went on "highly scented" missions on behalf of her Flame of Hope perfumes, and once, with a 103-degree fever, she held a press conference at a supermarket in Hyannis in her white mink toque, told reporters she photographed better in white, and then shook hands with literally hundreds of eager shoppers.

She appeared at the Crippled Children's Guild in St. Catherine's, Ontario, and at a black-tie dinner in Toronto for the Canadian Association for Retarded Children. She was a luncheon guest of Sweden's King Gustaf at Drottningholm Castle near Stockholm, to dedicate a programme to aid retarded children in that country, and she hosted a benefit dinner at El Morocco for the Children's Recreation Foundation, Inc. (founded by Bobby for disadvantaged children). She went to a piano recital by John Pennick at the Academy of Music for the benefit of the Philadelphia Association for Retarded Children and even took up cudgels in the "war on measles" (which may cause encephalitis and then lead to mental retardation).

One of her less publicized concerns was the Special Education School for English-speaking Mentally Retarded in Paris, housed on the top floor of the American Cathedral. She had heard of the school in 1966 from Mrs. Charles Bohlen, the Ambassador's wife, and had then called from the Ritz herself to arrange a visit. She came by herself in a taxi (as, later, she left alone), and wore a navy blue dress, mink jacket, diamond pin nestled in the mink, long white gloves, and a white floppy hat. At first the children, who had been told of her visit, were shy, but she was warm to them, sat down and did cutouts with the younger children, took a cutout from one child and said she'd give it to John-John, and asked the older ones questions.

"Do you know the name Kennedy?" she asked several children.

No one answered, but a ten-year-old boy leaned over and kissed her on the cheek. She asked if they knew President Kennedy.

A slightly older boy said: "Someone shot him in the head."

Rose said: "Yes. He was very good."

The boy said: "The other one was very bad. They put him in prison."

"Yes," said Rose, "he was a bad man."

Later she went into a room with reporters (who were present at her request) and told them how the President had been the first to employ a handicapped worker in the White House and how there were now thousands of handicapped or mentally retarded people employed by the government.

Mrs. Philippe Newton, director of the school, had discussed her hope of integrating the Special Education School with the regular American School in the suburb of St. Cloud, and when Rose returned to the United States, she contacted Mrs. Marjorie Crick, director of Exceptional Children Education for the Palm Beach County Schools. Mrs. Crick wrote an extensive letter explaining how the Royal Palm School was related to the regular school, and in the fall of 1968 Mrs. Newton was finally able to associate her institution with the American School in Paris. It now functions in a unique way, which much pleases Rose, who constantly stressed the need to bring the mentally retarded into a closer and more natural relationship to the central core of society. It is connected but separate—with separate facilities and faculty, but with the possibility that individual pupils, according to their ability and need, may take special classes in say, art, gym, or some other subject in the regular school. It is the kind of school and life that would have made Rosemary's childhood far more pleasant.

In 1965, Rose presented a $1,450,000 cheque from the Joseph P. Kennedy, Jr., Foundation to Yeshiva University for the construction of a major new building on the grounds of the Bronx Municipal Hospital Centre. Several years later she lifted a spade to break the first ground of the nine-storey brown-brick building, which would provide extensive facilities for training and research. The greatest credit for the building, said Dr. Samuel Belkin, head of Yeshiva University, must go to "a great, courageous lady of vision". The building is called the Rose Fitzgerald Kennedy Centre for Research in Mental Retardation and Human Development.

The social world continues to matter deeply to "that beautiful elder glamour girl". Like her father, who would change clothes frequently to suit a day's appearances, and her sons, who constantly changed shirts, Rose is aware to the last earring what will be most effective. Though the invitation read "informal dress", she recently, during a visit to the French Riviera, went to a party aboard the USS *John F. Kennedy* in a full-length blue-print evening dress, a long matching stole, a spate of diamonds, two gold purses, and a perfect and recent coiffure. It may not have been the right outfit in which to manoeuvre in and out of gigs and up ship's ladders, but she managed it deftly—and upstaged Princess Grace and other international beauties.

If she seems always on the society pages—at an April in Paris Ball or an Art and Decoration exhibition—it is the more amazing that her private life remains so full. She continues her daily routine of attending early mass daily, often in dark clothes and oxford shoes, a kerchief over her head; more than once, driving to or from the little church in Hyannis Port, she will be mistaken for a household servant. In the late morning she works with her secretary for several hours on her mountains of personal and organization correspondence, plays a few holes of golf, takes lunch and then her ritual nap, and then goes swimming. In only slightly modified form, she takes the pattern with her when she travels, living in her own orbit. In Palm Beach, she plays several holes of golf every afternoon at precisely four o'clock, usually dressed in colourful pants suits and beginning on the back nine. She likes to walk along the water's edge alone, her hair tied up in a scarf, and attend St. Edward's Church in Palm Beach, kneeling alone at the back, saying a half hour of prayers for the dead, praying at each station of the cross, and then walking home briskly. In Palm Beach, while others send their chauffeurs, she often waits in line for tickets at the Palm Beach Playhouse.

In the winter she skates with her grandchildren at the Joseph P. Kennedy, Jr., Skating Rink in Hyannis—and several times has worn, without alteration, the same navy blue skating outfit she once wore at St. Moritz in 1938; remembering the accidents then, and the accidents since, and with that curious sense of selflessness she often displays towards her family, she once said to Ted: "If we slip, let me fall. We've got a history of too many bad backs in the family." At seventy-nine she went on a cruise aboard the Loel Guinness yacht and swam three times a day in 56-degree water. She still watches her food with a hawk's eye, even to the point of obsession with vitamins and minerals. When she came to her brother Tom's recent wake, as mentioned, she brought her own food— a roast beef sandwich, "so she'd get the right nutrients", recalls Tom's daughter, Barbara Fitzgerald Value, "or whatever for that day, and wouldn't have to get involved in all the hoosey-goosey being served".

Nor has her learning ceased. She continues to study French and German records and takes a special interest in television programmes dealing with capital punishment, drugs, and the ecumenical movement. She always has time to write those interminable notes to her daughters and daughters-in-law, advising them that "apples are a good purchase this year", reminding them of upcoming Catholic observances, exhorting them to exercise greater discipline over the children. She remains a shrewd disciplinarian and teacher of her grandchildren. "When their mothers are worried that my grandchildren will ruin their teeth eating popcorn and candy," she says, "I show the children a drawing of the President rescuing one of his shipmates after his boat was torpedoed in the war, by holding the lifebelt strap in his strong teeth. In a few minutes they are drinking their orange juice and milk and coming up to show me their white teeth."

She sent notes to Ted also, after television appearances, telling him his hair was too long, his sweater didn't fit (and when he came home with a beard after sailing off the New England coast, she got a razor and promptly had him shave it off). After Ted made a *faux pas* as president of an investigating committee in the Senate, she phoned and told him: "Teddy, you know Kennedys are never supposed to make decisions unless they have all the facts in command. You weren't sure of your facts, were you?"

Nor are her notes and concern restricted only to family. She once called Everett Dirksen to compliment him for going easy on Ted in a critique of her son's speech condemning an American action in Vietnam. As noted, she was almost as concerned for Nixon's mother after the Kennedy-Nixon debates on television as for her son's success. One observer remarked: "No one would have been completely surprised had she called Jimmy Hoffa at the end of Bobby's seven-year effort to send him to prison. She *thinks* about other people."

When her grandchildren and nieces and nephews are staying with her, or she with them, she shows a striking consciousness about their vitamins and minerals—"pushing the carrots and celery strips" whenever she can. When one niece was taking a special course in college and working especially hard, Rose saw that she was served a small piece of beef fillet—while the others at the table ate the regular meal—because, said Rose, she needed the protein.

There has been speculation that Rose disapproved of Jackie's marriage to Aristotle Onassis. But she had always been genuinely impressed by the shipping magnate and once said: "You know, Joe did so many things coast to coast, but this Onassis, he did things on a worldwide basis." Friends close to the family say that she was indeed impressed by Onassis' wealth and also saw that at his age he would not be a romantic rival to the memory of her son. Before the news broke publicly, Ted made a special trip to Hyannis Port to solicit his mother's blessing. "Mother," he said, "I'm going to take a cruise on Onassis' yacht. But I must tell you, I won't be alone. Jackie will be with me."

"Well," replied Rose, "what's so extraordinary about that?"

"Onassis is very much in love with Jackie."

There was a short silence, and then Rose said: "I've known Onassis for fifteen years. He's a fine man."

Cardinal Cushing, the gaunt, gruff family adviser, stood by Jackie completely. To those who criticized her, he said: "They are so far from the truth that nobody would believe me if I said what I know." He gave his blessing, in the face of Vatican criticism, and Rose said: "I think she will be very happy. It was a completely solitary life for her."

Though she did not attend the wedding, two of her daughters, Pat and Jean, did. Rose has since been a frequent visitor on the *Christina*, Onassis' yacht, and friends say that Rose and Jackie are closer now.

Early in July, 1969, Rose attended a gay Fourth of July celebration at the American Embassy in Paris. She would be seventy-nine in a few weeks and planned to return for a family celebration in Hyannis Port. She looked marvellous, wearing a pale turquoise-blue silk dress with small white figure patterns on it, carrying a white bag, wearing white shoes, and sporting a lovely gold bracelet. Mrs. Philippe Newton was there and thanked her for helping with her retarded children's school.

"Because I am the mother of a President," Rose said, "my name carries a great deal of weight. Therefore, I am able to accomplish what others cannot." She circulated freely and, as always, enjoyed meeting new people—one of whom was Jane Fonda (who, on the hottest day of the summer, was dressed in knee-length boots, a leather mini-mini skirt, copper-colour long-sleeve satin blouse, Indian-style purse with a leather fringe, and a scarf formed into a band around her short blonde hair). Rose mentioned several times that she had to return to America soon, to be with her husband, "who is ill".

On Saturday, July 19, three days before her seventy-ninth birthday, Rose was taking a dip in Joe's indoor pool at the Hyannis Port house; since her husband could rarely use it anymore, it was no longer kept hot for him. At three she planned to attend a book bazaar at St. Francis Xavier. She had promised to autograph books about her sons, as she had done in two previous years, and had even donated a number of books. They had sold out before she arrived, and at two o'clock a woman called to ask if she could bring more. Ann Gargan took the call and said she was sure her aunt would be glad to; Rose enjoyed helping the little white clapboard church and was pleased that the bazaars were always profitable.

But minutes later there was another call. It was Ted, and he suggested that she not attend the bazaar because newsmen would be sure to barrage her with questions. Within hours the more garish headlines read: TEDDY ESCAPES, BLONDE DROWNS.

Some facts were clear at once: Teddy, driving a young woman home from a party on Chappaquiddick Island, had run his car off Dyke Bridge in the middle of the night. Out of panic or shock, he had acted irrationally and only informed police of the event—in somewhat confused terms—a full eight hours after the accident. The girl, twenty-eight-year-old Mary Jo Kopechne, had been drowned.

It seemed, finally and irrevocably, like the end of the Kennedy myth. There were no more sons, and in the aftermath of the grotesque event, it seemed sure that Ted—who was once called "that chubby little boy with the terrific disposition"—had committed political suicide. Man had landed on the moon that week, but the mystery and shock of Chappaquiddick almost usurped the historic event with its ambiguities and impact.

Scores of friends and advisers scurried to and from the Compound in the coming days; reporters were kept strictly out. It became so crowded that sleeping space became scarce. Press security was extremely tight, as it always was for the Kennedys when they wanted it that way; for such an extraordinarily public family they had always had the ability to keep private all that they chose. But rumours and speculations about everything from Ted's relationship to Miss Kopechne to the reaction of his family were rampant.

The New York *Times* found "gaping holes" in Ted's public and artfully candid appeal to his electorate for advice, and the television talk reminded many of Richard Nixon's 1952 "Checkers Speech". After being closeted for a week with such longtime Kennedy brain-trust figures as Ted Sorenson, Dick Goodwin, and Robert McNamara—all hastily summoned—Teddy delivered a speech which gave every appearance of a shrewd political ploy designed at any cost to save his political life.

What was the truth? The whole event reeked of duplicity and fraud—and from a Kennedy, the family in which a nation had once invested its dreams and hopes, the event was the more shocking. Some called it "the classic rich kid's stunt"—running away from an accident—there were rumours that Ted had wanted Joe Gargan to "stand in" for him as the culprit; and columnists spoke of his "hustling heart strings" in his television speech. One rumour claimed that Rose had spoken firmly to Ted on several occasions and insisted he meet his public responsibilities.

Several friends had detected in Rose for some months a "burning desire" to see Ted in the White House. He had almost been a serious candidate in 1968, after Bobby's assassination, and there were many who thought not only that he had made a mistake in not actively seeking the nomination but that he would have beaten Nixon. In March, only a few months earlier, there had been reports that Rose had said, at a party at the home of Gloria and Loel Guinness in Palm Beach, that Ted had definitely decided to run for the Presidency in 1972.

Joe, Jr., Rosemary, Kathleen, Jack, Bobby, the long illness of her once-dynamic husband—and now the political future of Ted. If her heart, once again, was broken, she never showed it that long week or in the weeks that followed. She kept her head and chin high while the politicians brooded and plotted to save her only remaining son from almost sure political death. She gave her firm counsel and then walked among the flowers, asked what performances were being given at Tanglewood, saw that her grandchildren were kept busy and active (indoors, since the weather was poor all that week), and went regularly to spend time with Joe. No one saw her cry; no one saw her brood. She was always neatly dressed and coiffured; her voice carried its familiar husky authority. Though she did not attend mass the first part of the week, but had a priest come to her in the Compound, she and Ethel went together from Wednesday on.

"This is a good life," Rose told a reporter. "God does not send us a cross any heavier than we can bear." And even at such a crucial moment, she was still capable of injecting her usual levity by stressing that she was really only seventy-nine that week—not eighty, as some reports had her. She thought such a misrepresentation was "very unfair".

As was customary with all interviews she granted, Rose—even at this threatening moment in the history of her family—had the presence of mind to go over what she had said patiently. Her political caution was typically meticulous. She referred the correspondent to Euripides' tragedy *The Trojan Women* for a better understanding of the grief she knew the Kopechnes felt; she asked him to mention that her father, Honey Fitz, was a member of Congress when she was five years old; she wanted him to stress how "magnificent under tremendous strain" Teddy had been, attending so many fund-raising dinners to erase Bobby's campaign debts, meeting family and Senate demands, comforting individual family members over the years in their moments of illness and pain. She saw no need for Teddy to retreat from politics, and wondered if something might be added at the end of the article to the effect that Honey Fitz, Joseph P. Kennedy, and all her sons had always viewed politics as a "worthy ambition and an honourable profession". What is important, Rose stressed is, "how you accept, how you cope with what happens. How you cope is the important thing —not the events themselves".

It was singularly apt advice, for the nation was concerned both with the event and how her son had coped with it. But Rose remained steadfast: "I'm sure Ted can rise above all this."

Rose coped by retaining, in the midst of it all, her regular routine. Within a few days she was regularly attending seven o'clock mass at St. Francis Xavier Church and playing her few holes of golf by herself every day, carrying her slight collapsible bag with three clubs—a seven iron, a spoon, and a putter. She generally stayed out an hour or two. Always, her incredible discipline and incredible capacity for organization held her together. Though terribly upset by Teddy's problem, she went on as if nothing were amiss. Several weeks after the catastrophe, she called a niece at eight o'clock in the morning to ask when she was arriving with her children. Would they be at Hyannis Port in time to go out in one of the power launches? If so, she wanted to be able to tell the cook so that the proper sandwiches could be prepared. The niece, standing there in her pyjamas, not yet having packed a thing or given her children breakfast, was dumbstruck. "There's Aunt Rose," she says, "with all that's on her mind with this whole Teddy thing, thinking about *lunch*. That's the way she is and always has been—and you end up feeling like a disorganized mess just talking to her." In August Rose headed for Paris to see the new collections.

*   *   *

On November 18, after long years of struggle as an invalid, Joseph P. Kennedy died in his Hyannis Port home after suffering a severe stroke several days earlier. The clan had been summoned from all over the world—what was left of them. At his bedside when he died at 11.05 A.M. were Ted, his only surviving son, and his wife, Rose.

Several times that afternoon, Rose, a black scarf covering her head and ears, walked again along the desolate beach with Jean, Pat, Eunice, or Ted. Though she moved with deliberation, her head was erect and her shoulders were straight. Now and again she paused and looked thoughtfully out over the slate-grey November ocean, cold and foreboding. The family attended a special mass that evening offered by the Reverend John J. Cavanaugh at the little church in Hyannis.

Rose requested a white funeral mass, signifying joy, at which the priests wear white instead of the traditional purple or black vestments of mourning, and the white mass was duly celebrated on a rainy November 20 by Cardinal Cushing, the old friend and spiritual adviser who within a year was himself to die. Only the family and very close friends were present. John F. Kennedy, Jr., nine years old, stood rigidly and in a clear, loud voice recited the Twenty-third Psalm; other grandchildren served as altar boys or bearers of the gifts of the wine, the water, and the chalice to the altar. Morton Downey, the Irish tenor and close friend for more than forty-five years, sang César Franck's *Panis Angelicus*. Ted Kennedy offered deep thanks to Ann Gargan, for "her loyalty, devotion, and great love" to his father for so many years and then read a moving tribute to his father written by Bobby for *The Fruitful Bough* (a privately printed volume of memoirs and appreciations of Joe edited by Ted) and a prayer from his mother. Ted's voice faltered as he read his mother's words: "I thank thee, O my God, with all my heart for all thou has done for me. I thank thee, especially, for my husband, who with your help has made possible so many joys and such great happiness in my life." The epistle for the mass began: "Brethren: We have become a spectacle to the whole world, to angels as well as men."

As the family made the 80-mile drive to Brookline, the bleak weather of the morning changed and the skies cleared. Joe Kennedy was buried after a simple graveside service in the family plot at

Holyhood Cemetery, not far from the Beals Street house at which he and Rose had started their marriage fifty-five years earlier, and which he and Rose had bought, restored, and turned into a national monument. Ted escorted his mother to the grave, and six of Joe's twenty-eight grandchildren were honorary pallbearers. In his will, Joe left the bulk of his undistributed estate, estimated at between $200,000,000 and $400,000,000 to the Joseph P. Kennedy, Jr., Foundation for the mentally retarded.

Tillie Gavin, an old friend, had repeatedly insisted that Rose would go to pieces when Joe died, that his death would finally destroy her monumental self-control. It did not. "Why do you seek rest?" asked St. Thomas Aquinas. "You were created only to labour." Despair would have been a kind of rest, an indulgence Rose never permitted herself. There was still work for her to do, and she had learned too well not ever to let down her guard.

The lines in her face are deeper now. Her throaty voice is, now and then, not quite so strong. The flash and sparkle are still very much in her eyes, but there is a growing film over them. She continues her rounds of charity balls and Flame of Hope presentations and has only begun to limit her appearances to the more important events. She still holds her grandchildren to a course of excellence—quizzing them on their lessons, even at breakfast, whenever she visits them. She is also still the greatest promoter of the legendary Kennedy ebullience. "Whenever one of us returns from a trip," she says, "we are all eager to know, What is the place like? If someone new is in town ... we want to know, Have you met him? When we get together we want to know, What books have you read? What new plays have you seen?" Recently she affirmed: "It's fun to be a Kennedy. One of my grandchildren doesn't want to ever change her name—she always wants to be a Kennedy."

Now and again the inner tension breaks through. At a presentation of the film *Romeo and Juliet* at Mar-a-Lago, the legendary home of Marjorie Merriweather Post in Palm Beach, she fingered the ticket for her evening wrap over and over during the course of the evening. Finally it fell to pieces. But she was still capable of laughing lightly, fitting the pieces back together, and then presenting the ticket for her wrap.

Usually Rose is too active to be nervous. Wherever she is, she finds ways to keep appropriately busy. On Christmas Day in Paris, as the sixties ended, the spacious Old World rooms of Ambassador and Mrs. Sargent Shriver's official residence on Avenue d'Iena were elaborately festooned, and the tree was gigantic and glittering; the atmosphere, however, was as addled and disoriented as any household with five young children. Toys were indiscriminately strewn in all directions, remnants of foil wrappings and shredded ribbon still clung to the upholstery, children careered over the ornate carpeting and up and down the marble hallway in battery-powered mini-motor cars, shattering the decibel level and the nerves of every adult in their path. In the continuing confusion, no one took particular notice of the petite dark-haired figure in plain black slacks who padded in and out of the debris in her stocking feet, occasionally stooping to pick up a stray truck or talking doll, an odd bit of ribbon here or there. Her manner was that of a distant maiden aunt, grateful to be included in the holiday festivities and doing her best to be helpful.

In a nearby room, the Shriver family, en masse, were soon collected and then positioned for photographs. The little dark-haired woman made no effort to join them; she continued to tidy up the room with the gigantic Christmas tree. When she left to go upstairs, no one was even aware of it, but when she reappeared late in the afternoon, everyone was unabashedly astonished. Rose had made one of her remarkable transformations: there she was, coming down the straight main staircase, a kind of apparition, chic and regal in diamonds and a full-length black mink maxicoat and matching mink toque. The toque was tipped fashionably to one side.

Now that the seventies have begun, Rose's pace is not much diminished. She was born when the Wright Brothers were still building bicycles and has lived into an age when men, prompted by her son's vision, are flying to the moon. She has persevered. Whether at a *haute couture* house in Paris, where she will make sure every last stitch is right and every seam straight, or in her dogged pursuit of political pinnacles for her children and grandchildren, she does not flag or understand defeat. She perseveres in terms of her own education, painstakingly ploughing through the small type in *Le Monde* in her little "rose room" in the Ritz, continuing her lessons in French, staying actively abreast of a thousand current issues, a thousand people's needs. She never lets herself settle, says a close friend, "for anything less than getting everything possible out of every situation".

Tough. Pierre Salinger has said that if he had to sum her up by one word, that would be it. In the sixties, a reporter claimed that she had "a mind with the simple functional strength of a crowbar ... she's half Irish charm and all business". In her eighties, this is still true.

Peripatetic as always, she celebrated her eightieth birthday in Ethiopia, with her friend Emperor Haile Selassie, and dedicated the John F. Kennedy Memorial Library in Addis Ababa. But she returned in time to campaign for Ted, standing straight in those interminable receiving lines with her youngest son and oldest grandson, Joe, day after day until the election was assured. Seventy-five years after Honey Fitz became a Congressman and she got her first lesson in politics, Rose still remembers all she learned—and continues to learn more. "Don't take a close lens of me, please," she says to photographers. "Take me from a distance."

Sometimes, when one sees her, it is easy to forget all she has suffered. But no woman in modern times has more right to repeat, as she does, her voice rarely faltering, Hecuba's lament over her dead grandson in Euripides' *The Trojan Women*:

> O, men, secure when once good fortune comes—
> fools, fools, Fortune's ways—
> here now, there now. She springs
> away—back—and away, an idiot's dance.
> No one is ever always fortunate.

One wet cold morning a small solitary figure sat in the back of a limousine speeding through the deserted streets of Hyannis Port. The route was the same one she had taken for forty years. It was the one that her second son, Jack, had taken with his entire family in a triumphant motorcade on another November day to the Hyannis National Guard Armory, past the helicopter pad on the sloping lawn where touch football had become an institution, past the shingled cottages, most of which were deserted now. It was November again, and the time and the place were mixed in her memories with birthdays and Thanksgivings and violent deaths.

November on the Cape is often a time of mellow quiet and brisk, sparkling days—of blue and brilliant days that evaporate into sodden stretches of oppressive grey and savage hurricanes. It had been raining steadily for three days, and on a Tuesday morning late in the month a bleak and bone-chilling wind was blowing off the grey and chopping waters of Nantucket Sound. Huge maples had been stripped of their last yellow leaves, and the landscape had turned soggy and desolate. It was a morning when leaving the comforting warmth of a bed seemed unthinkable.

Petite and purposeful, a small dark figure had suddenly emerged from the big house on the end of Scudder Avenue and darted out into the forbidding and bleak November dawn. The steps were wet and slippery, it was only six forty-five, and Rose Kennedy had been suffering from a late-autumn cold; but she moved lithely and was dressed in the customary conglomerate of apparel she favours on the Cape—fitted and slightly dated black pants; soaring high heels reminiscent of movie stars of the forties; a fashionably belted coat with fur collar and cuffs from a recent collection.

The family chauffeur, dressed in army surplus foul-weather gear, was waiting for her—the only unusual aspect of the scene, because Rose usually drove herself to morning mass. She walked rapidly through the blinding downpour, slipped into the car, and was soon heading along the route she had taken for forty years.

Ten minutes later the blurry headlights of the car shone through the thick fog and illumined the little white clapboard church on South Street. A few cars were drawing up near the front entrance. A lone grey gull perched on the steeple, its head tucked down into its wings. The chauffeur got out of the car, opened a huge umbrella, and then Rose got out and hurried into the church. She entered alone. Inside, the lights were especially warm and comforting after the darkness outside. She sat in a familiar pew, close to those once occupied by her dead sons and listened intently as the familiar mass was celebrated. Later, when the mass was over, she lingered until all her fellow communicants had left. Then, slowly and alone, she began to move to each of the fourteen stations of the cross, each representing a moment in the Crucifixion sequence, from the condemnation of Jesus to death to His interment in the sepulchre. She studied, as she had done so many times before, each station carefully, repeating to herself:

> We adore Thee, O Christ, and praise Thee
> Because by Thy Holy Cross Thou hast redeemed the world!

The church was stone silent and empty except for the solitary figure of Rose Fitzgerald Kennedy.

Index